Essays that Changed Australia

Meanjin
1940 to today

Edited by
Esther Anatolitis

MELBOURNE UNIVERSITY PRESS

Meanjin was founded on Yagarabul land and today works on the sovereign lands of the Boonwurrung, Bunurong and Woi Wurrung (Wurundjeri) people of the Kulin Nations. Our colleagues and writers work on sovereign First Nations lands across the continent. We honour and respect Elders past and present: their culture and their custodianship, their wisdom and their provocations.

MELBOURNE UNIVERSITY PRESS
An imprint of Melbourne University Publishing Limited
Level 1, 715 Swanston Street, Carlton, Victoria 3053, Australia
mup-contact@unimelb.edu.au
www.mup.com.au

First published 2024
Reprinted 2024

Cover design by Stephen Banham
Typeset in 10/13pt Plantin Light by Cannon Typesetting
Printed in Malaysia by 1010 Printing Asia Limited

NATIONAL LIBRARY OF AUSTRALIA
A catalogue record for this book is available from the National Library of Australia

9780522880977 (paperback)
9780522880984 (ebook)

Contents

Introduction

What does it mean to change Australia?

Esther Anatolitis

THE INTENTION WAS there from the very beginning: powerful writing that would forge a nation.

Starting out in 1940 as a modest collection of eight poems, *Meanjin* rapidly adopted an ambitious scope that spanned the continent and addressed the world, presenting influential essays alongside new work in all literary forms. By refusing any hierarchy between forms—challenging us to read equal political weight into essays and poetry—*Meanjin* continues to capture the cultural moment as only a literary journal can.

This collection is the first ever anthology of *Meanjin* essays. Readers have enjoyed anthologies of *Meanjin* fiction and interviews, as well as anthologies that survey the journal across particular time periods—but this is the first time we've collected 'brief, well-considered articles and essays dealing with aspects of contemporary art, literature, philosophy, religion, ethics, modes of conduct, and the mentality that lies behind these cultural systems in Australia.'[1] Those are the words of founding editor Clem Christesen, embarking on this transformative project in a time of war with the explicit aim to bring a 'new Australia' into being: one that would distinguish itself from colonial culture, and be infused by First Nations culture, starting with the journal's

1. Christesen, CB (1943). 'The *Meanjin* "School"', *Meanjin* 2.2 March 1943

name, its covers and artwork style. That second aim would take *Meanjin* decades to approach meaningfully—in a nation forged over the sovereign lands of hundreds of First Nations—and remains an important focus of our learning.

That transformative work has now entered its ninth decade, and across that period, no literary project has matched *Meanjin*'s impact on Australian culture. **Chelsea Watego**'s 2021 'Always bet on Black (power)' roars with the fire of a manifesto. **David Yencken**'s 1988 'Creative City' initiated a global urban planning movement. **Jenny Hocking and Nell Reidy**'s 2016 essay on marngrook changed Australian football history. **Arthur Phillips**'s 1950 'The Cultural Cringe' has long since entered the vernacular. And we're just getting started.

Sovereignty and place. Cities, towns, suburbs, streets and homes. Power, class and culture. Writing as a political act. How to choose just twenty pieces? And how to engage with a *Meanjin* archive whose own cultural legacy has often been as problematic as it's been impactful? Let's begin.

Sovereignty and place

This anthology is bookended by two literary giants—two elders of First Nations writing.

Fitzroy Blak **Tony Birch** was still a student when he wrote '"Nothing has changed": The making and unmaking of Koori culture'. Today he is one of Australia's most critically acclaimed writers. This 1992 essay remains one of *Meanjin*'s most cited pieces, as well as one of the essays for which Birch is most renowned. It's a ground-breaking piece: the first major essay to confront the casual, structural and deliberate racism behind Australian place names, and the all-too-often superficial approaches to replace colonial names with Indigenous ones. Presenting ignorant, offensive and racist language from historical and contemporary records, Birch makes it very straightforward for us to understand exactly why these processes keep failing: 'This is a form of radical conservatism: the history is not unknown, but is repressed by building monuments to murderers.' Birch's essay was instrumental in moves to overcome false consultation and grow institutional respect for First Nations cultural sovereignty. Three decades later, it remains a clamorous example of how 'so much has changed' and 'nothing has changed' can both be true at the same time.

Yagarabul and Gabi Gabi Elder and linguist **Gaja Kerry Charlton**'s 'Makunschan, Meeanjan, Miganchan, Meanjan, Magandjin' offers a rigorous account of 'meanjin' as a historically distorted place name, presenting linguistic evidence for *Magandjin* as 'the original word for an area of what is now called Brisbane.' By drawing on cultural and family history as well as linguistics, Gaja Kerry reframes our understanding of how words, names and languages are transmitted over time. 'Popular use,' she writes, 'does not make it accurate. It is the right of First Nations peoples to address historical errors.' This 2023 essay is the first of the refocused Meanjin Papers that open each edition: works by First Nations Elders offering a story of place—and presented before the contents page, colophon and editorial—so that we always begin reading by listening to Elders. Gaja Kerry's piece had immediate and widespread impact, and received strong coverage in Indigenous and non-Indigenous media.

Respecting and honouring cultural sovereignty is important work for *Meanjin*—something these two essays that changed Australia expose critically. It was in Brisbane that Christesen founded the journal, and by his own account, he chose the name 'deliberately' because it 'was the aboriginal word for Brisbane'; 'it means "spike" and was the name for the finger of land extending from the city proper to the Botanic Gardens, University and Domain'; it has 'a symbolic meaning'; and the four footprints on the first edition's cover 'are the footprints of aboriginal cult-heroes'.[2] Mythologising First Nations culture in White terms, and featuring 'Aboriginal-style' cover art by non-Indigenous artists, came to characterise *Meanjin* across its first decades. It wasn't until 1977 that Aboriginal and Torres Strait Islander writers were first published in *Meanjin*—in a special 'Aboriginal Issue' edited

2. Christesen, CB (1943). 'The *Meanjin* "School"', *Meanjin* 2.2 March 1943

by Jim Davidson, *Meanjin*'s second editor. And it wasn't until 2023 that *Meanjin* dedicated an entire edition to work by First Nations writers and artists, guest-edited by Eugenia Flynn (Larrakia and Tiwi) and Bridget Caldwell-Bright (Jingili and Mudburra).

Meanjin's early decades were a time when well-meaning settlers had sought to develop a distinctly Australian culture that refused to accept a Eurocentric authority, turning instead to what was unique about Indigenous peoples and the Australian landscape. Unfortunately, too many of these attempts stopped short of actually engaging with and learning from First Peoples, preferring instead to appropriate Indigenous languages and culture into their own work. You'll see a group called the Jindyworobaks appear in a few of our pieces: the collective of non-Indigenous writers formed in Adelaide in the 1930s who borrowed a Woiwurrung word from hundreds of kilometres away to frame their literary movement as a 'joining together'. Writing in 1978, **Tim Rowse** calls the movement a 'parochial defensiveness' in his 'Heaven and a Hills Hoist', while back in 1950, **Arthur Phillips** praises their 'protest against the alien symbolisms' of Eurocentric writers in his legendary essay 'The Cultural Cringe'. Initially, *Meanjin* saw itself in opposition to the Jindyworobaks, prompting Christesen to invite the movement's founder, Rex Ingamells, to write a piece for the Summer 1941 edition themed around 'Nationality'. In his brief essay 'Australianism', Ingamells refers to likeminded literary groups such as 'Australia First', and concludes that '[t]he Australianism of the people must be their own synthesis of forces originating within and without the country… we must desert time and circumstance, find original value: which may only be really done in the imagination.'[3]

There is, of course, no context-free position from which culture originates, and no amount of imagination can replace learning from First Peoples. A generation or more of Australians encountered what they understood to be Indigenous culture from movements like the Jindyworobaks and Australia First,

3. Ingamells, Rex (1941). 'Australianism', *Meanjin* No. 6 Summer 1941

as well as from the pages of *Meanjin*. Given *Meanjin* always fostered a strong global readership, this problem compounded, casting a long shadow. When, as recently as 2018, *Meanjin*'s then editor Jonathan Green pulped an entire edition and issued an apology for 'obliterating the word Meanjin with the hashtag #MeToo', it was clear there was a lot more work to be done. 'It's a reminder of my privilege', Green wrote at the time, 'to not see what now seems so obvious.'[4] A powerful absent presence in this anthology is the excellent essay 'What happens when you tell someone else's story?' by Waanyi writer and two-time Stella Prize winner Alexis Wright, commissioned by Green and published in *Meanjin* 75.4 Summer 2016. Look out for a forthcoming anthology of Wright's work, where this essay will feature prominently.

For decades now, the First Nations voices published in *Meanjin* have been fierce and strong, as you'll see from pieces throughout this collection and across our archive. There's a lot more to be said about First Nations writing in *Meanjin*—so we're planning an entire anthology, guest-edited and critically framed by two leading Aboriginal and Torres Strait Islander writers. Your *Meanjin* collection won't be complete without it.

Cities, towns, suburbs, streets and homes

The most important change happens at home. The ways we set our tables, nurture our neighbourhoods and design our cities. The stories we tell, and the stories we don't tell. Which ball we kick on the weekend, how we kick it, who we cheer on and why.

Sport is Australia's most familiar cultural battleground—that, and the tiresome History Wars, which explain why so many Australians refuse to accept marngrook as the origin of Aussie Rules football. **Jenny Hocking and Nell Reidy**'s 2016 'Marngrook, Tom Wills and the continuing denial of Indigenous history' sets out all the evidence clearly for the first time,

4. Green, Jonathan (2018). 'A Note from the Editor of Meanjin', published online at www.meanjin.com.au/latest/note-from-meanjin-editor/

refuting the common counter-arguments that fixate on a lack of written evidence. After all, the authors argue, the High Court of Australia's ground-breaking 1992 Mabo judgment was able to 'acknowledge the significance of ethnographic and oral history to historical understanding of Indigenous communities,' and even 'admitted such material as "traditional evidence" of ownership.' This essay was the first to link marngrook evidence to the place where Tom Wills—the settler credited with inventing the game—grew up. While the authors describe Wills as someone who 'spoke the local Indigenous language and there is no doubt he formed close relationships with the Mukjarrawait people,' we now know of evidence revealing that Wills directly participated in massacres of Indigenous people.[5] The essay was published just one year after Adnyamathanha/Narungga man and 2014 Australian of the Year Adam Goodes performed a celebratory war dance that had been taught to him by young players in an AFL Indigenous All-stars workshop; the racist onslaught he faced led to his early retirement from the game.[6] All of this makes this essay even more essential reading on Australian cultural change.

David Yencken's 1988 'Creative City' is the first exposition of an 'experiential' approach to city-making, now a commonplace term in exhibition design, artistic direction and urban planning. Yencken argues passionately for a city that stimulates everyone's creativity—as a social justice goal. Cities of complex, overlapping systems have long ago become politically inaccessible to poor and disadvantaged people; to ensure everyone can 'perceive and understand' cities in equitable ways, '[w]e have to be creative

5. Wills is quoted at length describing these events in an 1895 *Chicago Tribune* article titled 'Old Days in Australia', discovered in 2021 by historian Gary Fearon. The article's claims are supported by Wills biographer Greg de Moore and journalist and Wills novelist Martin Flanagan. See www.abc.net.au/news/2021-09-19/experts-add-weight-to-discovery-tom-wills-indigenous-massacre/100469428
6. For a brief history, see the National Museum of Australia's resource on the AFL's apology to Adam Goodes at www.nma.gov.au/defining-moments/resources/afl-apology-adam-goodes

in every realm.' This means creating neighbourhoods and cultural experiences that directly redress 'racial discrimination or oppression, poverty, unemployment, isolation and alienation', and 'work with local people in local environments'—because 'architectural egotism is a sin'. This essay remains one of *Meanjin*'s most cited: its publication helped spark a global movement in urban planning that centred creativity for the first time, making it an essay that changed the world and not just Australia.

Global events have also made **Susan Parham**'s 1990 'The table in space: a planning perspective' even more relevant now, in the wake of another global pandemic, as we continue to rethink the design of our homes and neighbourhoods. 'As long as we maintain the hidden supposition that cooking is a chore and eating a pleasure,' she writes, 'every woman is a kind of servant.' Parham takes a welcome feminist approach to the ways Anglo-Australian culture eschews shared cooking, communal eating and outdoor dining. Contrasting Italian, Spanish and Greek approaches, as well as the exceptional shared experiences created for our streets by arts festivals, Susan looks at the design of kitchens, houses and neighbourhoods. To make sure we stop building on arable land and start opening a warmer hospitality to one another, 'good gastronomers', she writes, 'will have to become good urban designers too.'

'Heaven and a Hills Hoist', **Tim Rowse**'s 1978 classic, was the first essay to confront the critics of Australian suburbia, arguing against a homogenous, 'individualist and apolitical' understanding of the ways we live. From Marx, Nietzsche, and Vance and Nettie Palmer, to the Sentimental Bloke, Dame Edna and the iconic 'Life. Be in it.' campaign, Rowse characterises a diverse Australia where 'the world of work, industrial conflict, politics and collective action' is very much at home in the suburbs. The essay has had great influence, changing the way Australian culture is discussed by the academy and the media, and remains one of *Meanjin*'s most cited essays.

It's a very different Australia that the celebrated writer and life-long *Meanjin* friend **Vance Palmer** observes in his 'Battle': one with 'settlements [that] have always had a fugitive look … Very little to show the presence of a people with a common purpose or a rich sense of life.' Written for the March 1942 'Crisis' issue published in the thick of war, 'Battle' speaks to common fears of invasion and conquest—against which Palmer exhorts writers and artists to make us the 'Australia we are called upon to save.' In his eyes, Australia had 'no monuments to speak of, no dreams in stone, no Guernicas, no sacred places.' This essay that changed Australia was an electrifying call-to-action in its time, but speaks only to a colonial Australia—albeit one at the cusp of becoming 'even more aware of itself'.

Arthur Phillips speaks to this directly in his 1950 polemic 'The Cultural Cringe', where he implores us to stop grounding our cultural standards in imperialist, Eurocentric ideals, and commit instead to 'the gradual processes of national growth'. Unsurprisingly, this is our number-one most cited work—even if few Australians recognise it as an essay first published in *Meanjin*. Reading back, it strikes me that Phillips was too quick to suggest that 'ultimately paint is always paint, a piano everywhere a piano.' The Cringe applies equally to visual art and music as it does to literature; every artform is subject to a critical gaze that privileges a particular culture, challenging us to progress 'in the art of being unselfconsciously ourselves.' I'm also struck by the early concession in Phillips's essay that 'the assumption [of our inferiority] will often be correct' given we lack Europe's 'long-established or interestingly different cultural tradition' as a means of distinguishing ourselves in the eyes of the world. Of course, decades would pass before Australians would come to share a common understanding of First Nations culture shaping this continent since time immemorial. Today, 'we—unhappy Cringers' continue to use Phillips's provocative neologism as a household word as we continue to understand our place in the world.

Power, class and culture

Meanjin is where Australia's finest writers set out their fiercest ambitions. Every single one of the essays in this anthology addresses power, class and culture—because not doing so is simply impossible. There is no such thing as a politically neutral position: those who assert one invariably do so in order to silence opposition. Essayists who take a strong, clear position stake their integrity on the rigour of their arguments. Each of these essays sets its sights on Australian cultural hegemony, law and democracy, rejecting the status quo to champion profound change.

Marcia Langton's 2011 'Reading the constitution out loud' reminds us just how extensively successive Australian governments had prepared for the 2023 Voice to Parliament referendum. What had been a bipartisan approach over more than a decade was callously politicised at the last moment, shrieking over the careful work of community education to secure a political win. Langton sets out in valuable detail not only the long, detailed work behind recognising Indigenous Australians in the Constitution, but also, what happens when we take a good, close look at that document. Read aloud, the racist clauses that have never been removed from the Constitution must spur us all towards change.

And then **Manning Clark**, with his 1976 'Are we a nation of bastards?', expresses the shock of Australia and the shock of the world after the 'Ugly Australian', and the 'men with the hearts of walnuts', used constitutional powers to achieve a partisan and not political purpose. The constitutional crisis yielding the Dismissal of Prime Minister Gough Whitlam just months before should have triggered a constitutional reckoning. It didn't. Clark's polemic makes every single one of Marcia's words ring truer.

Today, Judge **Hilary Charlesworth** sits on the International Court of Justice in the Hague. Her 1992 'A law of one's own?: Feminist perspectives on equality and the law' sets out a strong, clear and accessible set of principles for a fairer legal system. Charlesworth challenges traditional understandings of the law as rational and neutral. Looking at equality as 'sameness', 'difference', and 'non-domination', she advocates multiple approaches to redressing inequality rather than assuming a 'monolithic conception of inequality'. Another of *Meanjin*'s most cited essays, Charlesworth's piece heralds a great era of significant Australian legal reform that would include the Mabo (1992) and Wik (1996) decisions of the High Court of Australia.[7]

Written in 2022, 'The act of disappearing' by **Amy McQuire** is an inheritor of the feminist framework advocated by Charlesworth. This essay was instrumental in changing the narrative from the 'unreliable' accounts of 'missing persons' who might have 'gone walkabout', to the *disappearing* of Aboriginal women—because without this necessary shift, 'the racial violence that disappears the women and their ties to country and community is left shrouded in silence.' A concept of 'Black justice' is needed, McQuire writes, that 'brings them back, and brings them closer, through acts of presencing.' We must 'listen to Aboriginal women.' Following the publication of McQuire's essay, the Australian Senate launched an inquiry into missing and murdered First Nations women and children, which is due to report shortly after we go to print. McQuire's sensitive, forceful essay also won that year's Hilary McPhee Award for essay writing that makes a fearless contribution to the national debate.

One of the mightiest pieces *Meanjin* has ever published, **Chelsea Watego**'s 2021 'Always bet on Black (power)' is a formidable exhortation. Read it aloud. Writing in both the first person and the universal voice, Watego makes it clear that her lived experience *and* scholarship *and* action are equivalent tools in her 'radicalism of Black power'—alongside both rage and love. 'It is not a fight for an alternative subjugation, for revenge or retribution,' she writes, 'but a call for a different society to be born'. This profoundly impactful essay introduces a new vocabulary for talking about race and anti-racism, power and Black power.

---

7. The two judgments—which feature in a number of our essays—are firstly, *Mabo v Queensland (No 2)* (1992), which rejected the notion that this continent was *terra nullius* (nobody's land), and recognised the existence of Aboriginal and Torres Strait Islander Native Title, and secondly, *The Wik Peoples v State of Queensland* (1996), which found that Native Title could coexist with pastoral leases.

Another mighty piece, **Michael Mohammed Ahmad**'s 2020 'It's shit to be White' also needs to be read out loud and in company—especially right now, when strengthening our vocabulary around race and anti-racism couldn't be more urgent. 'It's exhausting', Mohammed writes, 'constantly having to educate White people about a word that their own race invented to elevate themselves above the rest of us.' Writing with characteristic wog courage and pride, Mohammed sets himself the task of performing a valuable national service: 'Let's define White. Let's define racism. Let's define shit.' His essay analyses academic, journalistic and political language in ways that give us all the tools to shift the public conversation, side-stepping both 'White fragility' and 'White fragility fragility' towards a more realistic and respectful Australia.

In championing Lebanese Australian culture, Mohammed is another inheritor of a framework presented by a fellow *Meanjin* writer. **Sneja Gunew**'s transformative 1983 essay 'Migrant women writers: Who's on whose margins?' reminds us that 'Australia [is] a country which does not have English as a first language.' This was the first major essay to accord migrant women's work the respect and authority of rigorous analysis in the context of the world's foremost theorists. 'Looking at migrant women's writing is a way of questioning literary taxonomies', writes Gunew. 'Hurrah for anything that puts into question our hegemonic, monocultural assumptions.' This essay was an early achievement in what would become a magnificent, nation-changing career of global acclaim. Gunew's death, within just weeks of the conception of this book, calls us to honour her memory with deep respect.

Writing as a political act

The question of how and why writers write reveals a great deal about a culture. Writers make a lifetime commitment to their practice—and this means more than taking a position. It means crafting that position with great literary care. Choosing an authoritative mode of expression that balances the personal with the public. Asking questions that demand a response. This is a political act, and the ways we set out to understand it define the strengths of our culture.

Composer and writer **Nahed Elrayes**, writing in 2021 for the *Meanjin* blog, now *Meanjin Daily*, poses a series of devastating questions for our readers, each one demanding a carefully considered response. Elrayes's 'Gaza and the twenty-year War on Terror' was widely read and frequently cited on first publication, and given the atrocities the world is witnessing in Gaza today, this essay remains urgent reading. 'What if the stateless other—without legitimised, non-"terrorist" leadership—became an undifferentiable mass,' Elrayes asks, 'whose lives were thus disposable as statistics?' In an online environment where we are overwhelmed by the numbers of war fatalities, Elrayes implores us to slow down long enough to search our emotions, reconnect with our values, and recognise each one as 'a human life, worthy of grief', and worthy of our action.

Internationally acclaimed writer **Thea Astley**'s 1968 'A monstrous accent on youth' rankles with intergenerational intolerance—but when recognised as a comment on gender and class at a time of conscription during the Vietnam War, we readily understand how this essay changed Australia. Describing a clash between feminism and patriotism that she witnesses as a teacher, Astley finds herself experiencing a fear for the future, and she concludes: 'One is sorry life is so easy for the young and, because of this, so difficult.' Thea's piece was part of that edition's short essay set 'The Temperament of Generations', also the title of one of our past anthologies, which included AR Chisholm and Ian Turner trying to make sense of student activism and 'hippies' during the world's first experience of widespread political protest. As the world experiences another global student-led movement of action against genocide, Thea's piece is a timely read.

In his 1986 essay 'Why I write what I write', renowned Australian writer **Gerald Murnane** offers a deceptively straightforward account of what he writes: 'words', 'sentences', 'paragraphs' and 'chapters'. This is another work to be read aloud and savoured. 'Writing never explains anything for me', he writes; '—it only shows me how stupendously complicated everything is.' We also have Murnane to thank for two previous *Meanjin* anthologies: *The Temperament of Generations: Fifty years of writing in Meanjin* (1990), which he co-edited with Jenny Lee and Philip Mead, and *Meanjin Anthology* (2012), for which he wrote the foreword.

Sometimes prickly, often provocative, always polemical: no *Meanjin* anthology is complete without a piece by **Clem Christesen**. Foremost among Christesen's enduring contributions across all of his *Meanjin* writing are his articulations of the political role of the artist. His Spring 1945 editorial 'A quarterly of literature'—written for 'the first peace-time issue of *Meanjin*'—urges writers to commit even more deeply and passionately to their practice, seizing their responsibility 'to reveal and clarify our life by showing it to us through a vision different from ours and deeper.' This piece had a galvanising effect immediately on publication, and remains a valuable reference point for all artists. Writers are *responsible*, Christesen italicises, and so they must be well-informed, socially and politically connected, and attentive to their artistic integrity.

How do we come to understand that responsibility in contemporary Australia? Abundant arts coverage and criticism across all news media is a mark of a society that's curious and confident enough to recognise that all aspects of our culture—not just sport—are worthy of closer understanding. Today, argues Walkley Award-winning **Jane Howard** in her 2023 essay 'On criticism', its inclusion depends entirely on 'the belief of newsroom leadership in its inherent value.' Howard casts an eye across 150 years of Australian arts journalism and charts the consequences of its decline, looking at its media owners, platforms, technologies and means of production. This comprehensive essay is also a work of great national service, and the vociferous response it's received to date marks it as an essay already sparking change.

Writing this cultural moment

What does it mean to change Australia?

Change is generative, unsettling, invigorating—and always political. *Meanjin* writers have inspired us to ask new questions about who we are and why we do what we do. They've declared their sovereignty, mapped out our neighbourhoods, questioned our culture, defended their rights and called out injustices. They've edited the dictionaries, entered the news cycle, changed the conversation. If you want to learn about Australia's passions and preoccupations from the finest writers of the time, you go to *Meanjin*.

Each essay in this collection is among the most cited works we've ever published: they're quoted in news media, regularly drawn upon for academic research, and commonly referenced as authoritative exemplars. The nation-changing essays that are missing from this collection—and truly, there are many—are your invitation to leap into our archive, online or in print; *Meanjin* is also held in libraries across Australia and all over the world.

As you begin to leaf through this book, you'll notice that the essays are not arranged in the sequence my introduction has promised. There are so many ways to read each piece—so many conversations they're already having with one another. You're already beginning to notice the many ways their focuses overlap and diverge, seeing nationalism, feminism and urbanism rub shoulders with Black power, White privilege and wog pride. And why twenty? An arbitrary number for a portable anthology, offered not as a canonical set, but as provocations to withstand the test of time. Take it with you as you go about your day—and if you use the rear gatefold as a bookmark, you'll always know which *Meanjin* editor selected the piece you're reading. The place of essays within *Meanjin* has been dynamic over time as each editor has set their own agenda: we've seen themed editions, short essay sets such as 'The Temperament of Generations', and journal sections such as today's 'State of the Nation', 'The Year in…' and 'Australia in Three Books'. Each offers an entry point for writers and readers alike; a context for the arguments that follow.

Not all change is positive, of course, which is what makes *Meanjin* absolutely crucial as a space where arguments for change are advanced with rigour and care. *Meanjin* essays map the multiple trajectories that make up our culture, intersect in our democracy and clash in our politics. To refuse change is to align with inert positions that seek to guard their privilege, imposing a static understanding of history for a glib approach to the future. Only a venturous approach can create Australia's future.

Today, as from the very beginning, *Meanjin* offers the same invitation to all of our writers and readers: how will *you* change Australia?

‘Nothing has changed’

The making and unmaking of Koori culture

Tony Birch

Meanjin 51.2 Winter 1992

I

> You get somebody coming in, a foreigner at that, trying to tell us to rename our mountains.
>
> —Bob Stone, Stawell town councillor[1]

In March 1989 the Victorian Minister for Tourism, Steve Crabb, announced that the Grampians mountain range in western Victoria would ‘revert to their Aboriginal name, Guriward’ (which after further research was altered to Gariwerd). Although this initiative came from the Victorian Tourism Commission, and the local Koori community had not yet been consulted, the minister felt that he could already announce the names that would be ‘restored’:

> I expect that the Grampians will be known as Guriward, the Black Range as Burrunj, the Glenelg River as Bugara, Halls Gap as Budja Budja, Victoria Gap as Jananginjawi and so on.

The local white community did not share these great expectations. An ‘ex-Labor voter’ wrote to Crabb accusing him

1. *Melbourne Sun*, 27 March 1989.

of engaging in 'gutter level' politics, and warned of an electoral backlash: 'Remember Mr. Crabb the tax payer pays your salaries not the lazy, dirty, counter-productive black sector of Australia'.[2] The Mayor of Stawell, Peter Odd, claimed that behind the idea was a 'radical group' who had forced the proposal on the government:

> It seems to me more like a little group that can get what it wants like all the minority groups. The government just bows down to them and the government is ruled by the loudest noise all the time.[3]

Yet no 'noise' on the issue had come from the local Koori community. The five Koori communities in the Western District are represented by Brambuk Incorporated, which at the time was constructing the Brambuk Living Cultural Centre in the Grampians National Park. A spokesperson, Geoff Clark, criticised the government's continuing refusal to consult local Kooris on policies affecting their history and culture. Although he supported the 'refreshing and positive gesture' of the name restoration, Clark compared Crabb's approach with that of a fellow Scot: 'He and Major Mitchell are guilty of ignoring the Aborigines' past and present association and ownership of the Grampians area ... over thousands of years'.[4] Clark said that Brambuk 'would rename important features in the Grampians area with traditional Aboriginal names', regardless of any government initiatives.

In December 1990, without Steve Crabb's knowledge, signs carrying Koori names were erected at certain features to coincide with the opening of the Brambuk Living Cultural Centre.[5] Crabb objected; the community, he said, 'would be entitled to criticise any cost involved in erecting the signs bearing Aboriginal names before an official decision was made'. But Clark insisted that, as 'rightful custodians' of the region, Kooris 'had the authority to

2. Koori Tourism Unit file 9/7/76/3.
3. *Stawell Times-News*, 31 March 1989.
4. Press release by Geoff Clark, Chairperson Brambuk Incorporated, 29 March 1989, Koori Tourism Unit file 9/7/76/3.
5. Melbourne *Herald-Sun*, 11 December 1990.

erect the signs'. Clark asked: 'Will Mr Crabb, with his paternalistic attitude, expect those Aborigines among us with dark faces to be selling trinkets/beads and performing corroborees for his tourist industry?'[6] Brambuk was not opposed to involvement with tourism, but this had to be achieved 'without exploiting, and without becoming like the exploited'.[7]

The name change had been proposed in February 1985 by archaeologist Ben Gunn, who prepared a document for the Tourism Commission on 'Recommended Changes to Aboriginal Site Names in the Grampians'.[8] The region contains 80 per cent of Victoria's identified Koori rock-art sites, and Gunn suggested that these be given more appropriate names in line with the 'planned promotion of certain sites as public attractions'. He noted that the existing 'eurocentric descriptive names' (such as 'Cave of Ghosts') could produce 'inappropriate expectations in visitors ... disappointment or worse, ridicule'. Gunn proposed that Koori names be given to the sites in consultation with 'the local Aboriginal Communities'.

In 1988 an Aboriginal Tourism Survey alerted the Tourism Commission to the possibility of exploiting the region's Koori culture and history: 'Guided tours of Koori sites have the potential to be very successful. The opportunity is there to bring together the product and the potential customers.'[9] Immediately before Crabb's public announcement in March 1989, Ben Gunn conducted further research into alternative names for the rock-art sites, and for natural features of the region. He did not feel that it was necessary to consult with the local Koori community, as he regarded his research as 'an academic exercise, at this stage'.[10]

---

6. Ibid.; *Standard* (Warrnambool), 12 December 1990.
7. Geoff Clark, *Land Rights News*, October 1990.
8. Koori Tourism Unit file 12/2/6/3.
9. Koori Tourism Unit file 12/2/6/2: *Tourism and the Grampians Region* (Victorian Tourism Commission, 1990), p. 18.
10. RG Gunn, 'Alternative names for rock art sites and natural features in the Grampians National Park. A Report to the Victorian Tourism Commission', March 1989.

The minister's announcement two weeks later, however, was not an 'academic exercise', but a highly publicised media event.

Crabb demonstrated a typical European disregard for the Indigenous people of the area. To display 'art' was good for business, and to tag the sites with Indigenous names confirmed their legitimacy as artefacts of an 'ancient' culture. But it was not seen as necessary to consult the Kooris of the Western District about the marketing of the heritage that they had managed to retain through 150 years of oppression.

Soon after Crabb's announcement, the Tourism Commission appointed Ian Clark, a geographer from Monash University, to prepare a submission to the Victorian Place Names Committee. In his consultations with the groups that form Brambuk, he found that the Koori community regarded the absence of prior consultation as indicating 'a lack of respect and recognition of traditional ownership of the National Park'.[11] As a result, a representative of Brambuk, Lionel Harradine, was appointed to prepare the submission with Clark. The submission made four sets of recommendations:

> i.) that 21 incorrectly spelt Aboriginal place names currently in use be corrected, and that a further 10 Aboriginal names be retained;
> ii.) that the use of 44 known Aboriginal names of features more recently given European names be restored;
> iii.) that the traditional names of 11 places that do not carry European names be adopted;
> iv.) that the more appropriate names conferred on nine Rock Art Sites ... be formally adopted.[12]

The name restoration met opposition from a variety of groups. The Stawell Shire Council wrote to all local governments in

11. Koori Tourism Unit file 9/7/76/3.

12. 'A Submission to the Victorian Place Names Committee – The restoration of Jardwadjali and Djab wurrung names for Rock Art Sites and Landscape Features in and around the Grampians National Park' (Victorian Tourism Commission, 1990), p. 5.

Victoria, and gained wide support from both rural and urban shires. The Victorian Place Names Committee received petitions of protest with 60,000 signatures.[13] The Council of Clans regarded the proposal as a threat to 'Scottish heritage and pioneers'.[14] The Wimmera branch of the National Council of Women claimed that 'Aboriginals' did not 'know anything about the significance' of the rock art. The Balmoral Golf Club was concerned with the effect that the name restoration would have on its greens: 'Our Club is close to the Glenelg River & uses the water for irrigating the course'. A Horsham shire councillor, Don Johns, expressed similar concerns about Horsham's water supply.[15] Bruce Ruxton of the RSL stated the league's position in his inimitable style:

> In no way would we want the name of the Grampians changed to any other name whether it be an Aboriginal name or what...There is a real feeling of ill-wind prevailing over this proposal. [*sic*][16]

In a submission supporting the restoration, the Friends of the Grampians claimed that the League of Rights had manipulated opposition to the proposal, resulting in widespread 'racist hysteria'.[17]

The aesthetic and tourist value of the rock-art sites was also questioned. Many of the sites require protection behind cyclone-wire fencing, as they have been repeatedly desecrated by vandals.[18] Pat Reid of Bellellen Rise Host Farm, Stawell, claimed that visitors to her farm had 'little or no interest in our Aboriginal pre-history', and whatever there was 'dissipates completely upon inspecting Bunjil's cave (the most significant aboriginal art site in Victoria)'.[19] ER of Mt Waverley wrote directly to Steve Crabb, informing him that in twenty years of visiting the Grampians she had seen 'not

---

13. *Wimmera Mail-Times*, 16 October 1991.
14. This and the following letters are from Koori Tourism Unit file 9/7/76/3.
15. *Wimmera Mail-Times*, 20 June 1990.
16. Koori Tourism Unit file 9/7/76/3, 2 November and 28 July 1989.
17. A copy of this submission is in Koori Tourism Unit file 12/2/6/3.
18. Koori Oral History Program, Grampians Visit, 1 June 1989. Tape 46.
19. *Portland Observer*, 9 July 1990.

one Aboriginal person' and only 'a few miserable rock paintings'.[20] CS of Stawell wrote to 'point out some facts associated with Aboriginal myths of Dreamtime'. He denied a Koori presence in the region ('no Aboriginals ever entered the Grampians due to evil spirits') and claimed that the rock art was painted by 'a French artist who had a great appreciation of Aboriginal art of central Australia'.[21]

Steve Crabb apparently wants to promote the region as 'Victoria's Kakadu',[22] but he will have difficulty achieving this if people expect a replication of Kakadu 'art', ignorant of the regionally specific Indigenous culture and history of the Gariwerd area. An officer of the Victorian Archaeological Survey informed visitors to one of the shelters in 1989 that in the past 'people were disappointed in the art itself. They were expecting something like Northern Territory art.'[23] People not only expected to view the 'ancient', but also to see its readily identifiable signifiers, the art of 'real' Aborigines.

For visitors to appreciate the art, they must come to respect and appreciate Indigenous culture, both past and present, here in Victoria. An exploitative tourist industry will not achieve this. Denis Rose, a Koori cultural officer from Brambuk, feels that this will occur when the 'significance of the sites as places of occupation' is interpreted and understood.[24] The centre has attempted to do this by erecting signs that explain the spiritual significance of the art, and the Koori history of the area. The signs also inform visitors that 'If you wish to obtain more information about this site, its art or Aboriginal culture in general, please call at Brambuk in Budja Budja (Halls Gap).'[25]

20. Koori Tourism Unit file 12/2/6/3, 10 October 1990.
21. Koori Tourism Unit file 9/7/76/3, 10 May 1989.
22. Interview with Ian Clark, 21 October 1991.
23. Koori Oral History Program, Grampians Visit, 1 June 1989. Tape 46.
24. Ibid.
25. *Stawell Times-News*, 18 December 1991. Pat Reid incorrectly blamed Crabb's 'sheer arrogance' for the erection of the signs.

Some opponents of the name restoration also ridiculed Koori languages. Old racist slurs resurfaced: 'Aboriginal names all … sound the same, and in most cases, the spelling looks the same.'[26] The *Western District Farmer* claimed that the proposal pandered to 'pony-tailed basket weavers and banjo players', and the chosen names were 'totally unpronounceable to modern day black and white alike'.[27] Les Carlyon, in *Business Review Weekly*, complained that he could not 'pronounce let alone spell' the chosen names, and was concerned that the proposal was being considered when Victoria was 'paralysed by billions of dollars of debt'.[28]

The Grampians District Tourist Association strongly opposed the restoration proposal. The association identified 'Aboriginal cultural tourism' as a 'niche market' and therefore supported the upgrading of the rock-art sites.[29] Initially the association claimed that it wished to promote 'aboriginal culture' in the Grampians, and 'supported appropriate names for Rock Art sites and any unnamed features'. Yet it rejected an overwhelming majority of the proposed names. This included the proposed names for rock-art sites and previously unnamed features, which would not be acceptable unless they were altered (that is, anglicised) to something 'easily recognised and pronounced'.[30]

This cultural appropriation illustrates the attitude of many tourist operators, who regard Koori culture as a product that can be altered and re-presented in an acceptable form, as a commodity, but has little or no intrinsic value. The Tourist Association objected to the removal of names such as Mt Lubra and The Piccaninny. It felt that although such terms were 'possibly racist' they were 'not truly offensive as they are in common usage throughout Australia'.

26. *Wimmera Mail-Times*, 22 June 1990.
27. *Western District Farmer*, June 1990.
28. *Business Review Weekly*, 1 June 1990.
29. Koori Tourism Unit file 12/2/6/3.
30. Grampians District Tourist Association, submission to the Victorian Place Names Committee, 26 September 1990. By anglicised I mean corrupted, as was the case with some existing names, such as Cherrypool for Djarabul.

Bob Stone agreed: 'Piccaninny is a tribute to little Aboriginals,' he said.[31]

Some names were also rejected on aesthetic grounds. Ararat City Councillor Peter Wright stated that names that translated as 'pig face', 'base of spine' and 'phlegm' were 'not terribly good for a tourist area'.[32] Others related to excrement (such as Gunigalg), and 'would be more suitable for a sewerage treatment works'.

This European aesthetic ignores the relationship between naming and traditional Koori lifestyle. To reject such names is to reject their cultural significance, and to promote corrupt versions of Koori culture is not only appropriation but deception. Brambuk is disappointed that the Place Names Committee rejected some of the names on these grounds, denying the Koori community the opportunity to present and interpret the relationship to land identified in names that narrate spatial organisation.[33]

If white Australia is to move beyond a superficial appropriation of the Indigenous culture of this country, those in positions of influence—be they government departments, statutory bodies or tourist promoters—have to stop re-presenting Indigenous cultures in this way. If they are motivated by imperial possession, changes will not occur, as the motivation behind possession is the subjugation and control of the 'other'.

II

> Piper carries a pair of handcuffs slung round him as one [blackfellow] must be taken prisoner for the sake of obtaining native names of the places.[34]

---

31. Melbourne *Sunday Herald*, 3 June 1990.
32. *Ararat Advertiser*, 31 May 1990.
33. Interview with Ian Clark. Clark stated that the Place Names Committee also rejected Bugara, not because of nay distasteful translation, but because it 'sounds too much like bugger'.
34. 'The Journal of Granville William Chetwynd Stapylton', in L O'Brien and MH Douglas (eds), *The National History of Western Victoria* (Australian Institute of Agricultural Science, 1974), p. 95 (28 July 1836).

In his spatial history of Australia, *The Road to Botany Bay*, Paul Carter has written of 'how little value our culture attaches to names'.[35] This is because 'we', feeling imperially secure, and ignorant of the presence of another culture and history, see 'not a historical space' that may be contested, and may contain multiple histories, but a 'historical fact…as if it was always there'. The cultures of Indigenous people are relegated to 'prehistory' and the 'ancient', allowing only for metahistorical myths, located outside the boundaries of 'historical facts', which support imperial domination. As Chris Healy put it, 'true knowledge of the past was knowledge of white Australia and reserved for white Australians'.[36]

To name spaces is to 'name histories',[37] and also to create them. The process is accepted as natural, representing a 'given', that this country belongs to and is a white Australia. But this sense of security evaporates when the hidden history of colonial domination and Indigenous subordination is challenged by an attempt to alter the names of spaces.

Attaching names to landscapes legitimises the ownership of the culturally dominant group that 'owns' the names. Indigenous names themselves do not constitute a threat to white Australia. Houses, streets, suburbs and whole cities have Indigenous names. This is an exercise in cultural appropriation, which represents imperial possession and the quaintness of the 'native'. For the colonisers to attach a 'native' name to a place does not represent or recognise an Indigenous history, and therefore possible Indigenous ownership.

It is when names are restored to recognise earlier histories and cultures that the threat to ownership occurs. Imperial history cannot recognise the existence of Indigenous histories. A history of dominance is seen as the history of a 'nation'. An attempt to

35. Paul Carter, *The Road to Botany Bay* (Faber, London, 1987), p. 2.
36. Chris Healy, '"We Know Your Mob Now": Histories and their Cultures', *Meanjin* 49.3 Spring 1990, p.512.
37. See Paul Carter's essay in this issue. [Editor's note: 'Travelling Blind: A Sound Geography', *Meanjin* 51.2 Winter 1992.]

recognise the history of Indigenous people creates insecurity, paranoia, even hysteria. It 'wipes out over one hundred and fifty years of [British] history' and 'takes away that heritage'.[38] Existing names are 'recommended for consignment to the scrapheap of history'.[39] The features themselves can actually vanish: 'Ayers Rock is no longer'; 'GRAMPIANS, ARE THEY GONE?'; 'Familiar places or landmarks...would disappear from the map'.[40]

Many people of the Western District of Victoria cannot accept a Koori presence in the area, either in the past or present. If they do recognise an Indigenous presence, it is one that is long dead. They cannot accept a reality that makes a mockery of the racial theories and racist practices promoted for 150 years. In protest against the name restoration, BC, 'a former Halls Gap resident', dedicated a poem to Sir Thomas Mitchell:

> He battled through the heathery scrub and scaled the frowning wall
> To stand at last triumphant, on the topmost peak of all
> He named the range the Grampians.
> Why should we change it then?
> That traveller made our history, he and his stalwart men.

Of Mitchell's feats, and his place in history, she was certain. This was not so of Koori people:

> What the Coorie people called the hills we cannot ever know
> For they have gone like yesterday, with little left to show.[41]

Many opponents of the name restoration eulogised the nineteenth-century 'pioneers' who had 'developed the land using nothing but their bare hands and crude farm implements'.[42]

---

38. RS of Stawell, 7 April 1989, in Koori Tourism Unit file 9/7/76/3.
39. *Hamilton Spectator*, 22 December 1990.
40. BG of Horsham, 28 March 1989, in Koori Tourism Unit file 12/2/6/3; *Boort and Quambatook Standard-Times*, 29 May 1990; *Portland Observer*, 4 July 1990.
41. Koori Tourism Unit file 9/7/76/3, 31 January 1990.
42. PN Griffin, in *Stawell Mail-Times* (undated cutting).

Peter Wrigglesworth of Blackburn posed a question regarding the Indigenous peoples' relationship to the land: 'Did they strive to explore, to overcome danger, to improve their lot?' His answer: 'I don't know. There's no record. Who cares?'[43]

Even when their presence was recognised, the present Koori community in the district was often regarded as a 'cultureless remnant'. JR of Murtoa rejected the suggestion that the Kooris had 'some sort of culture', adding 'It's too late for all this nonsense.'[44] MW of Phillip Island asked:

> How many Western District Aborigines are there anyway? And what have they contributed to the progress of the area over the last fifty years or so? I'd guess, not many and not much.[45]

Philip Lienert of Horsham, in a letter to the *Wimmera Mail-Times*, argued for the need to put a contact history of 'murder, theft, rape, cruelty and ignorance' into its proper perspective: 'At what time in the world's history has one group of people not done that to another group?' He claimed that the Indigenous people of Australia were fortunate that they had been colonised by a civilised race: 'If Great Britain had not colonised Australia then someone else would have—and what would have been the fate of the Aborigines then?'[46]

Lienert is not the first to ask such a rhetorical question. Academic John Mulvaney has also asked 'a theoretical question but one which must be faced ... one wonders what French treatment would have been if France had been the occupying power'.[47]

The *Hamilton Spectator* urged Steve Crabb to 'leave history as it stands'.[48] By this the newspaper meant a dominant history that not only ignored the Koori history of the region, but was

43. Melbourne *Sun*, 19 April 1989.
44. Koori Tourism Unit file 9/7/76/3, 10 April 1989.
45. Ibid., 18 December 1990.
46. *Wimmera Mail-Times*, 22 June 1990.
47. *Overland*, 114, 1989, p. 8.
48. *Hamilton Spectator*, 13 May 1990.

also selectively amnesiac concerning the 'pioneer' history of the area. It was not a history of a civilised race, but one of ignorance, racism, greed, brutality and dispossession. Those who want to 'leave history as it stands' need to examine their own history with honesty.

III

> Australia is owned and run by white people not black. We took it and have fought several wars to keep it and our freedom.[49]

Popular Australian history has often been written about 'winners', who fought battles with the land before conquering it. Control of the Australian landscape is vital to the settler psyche. The victors' histories falsely parade as the history of Australia. These histories are those of absence: of *terra nullius*. In order to uphold the lie of an 'empty land', Europeans have either denied the Indigenous people's presence, or have completely devalued our cultures. These hegemonic histories take possession of others' histories and silence them, or manipulate and 'deform' them.[50]

This misrepresentation is now being challenged as Indigenous people confront the imperialist fictions that support political domination and racism. This upsets and displaces what Chris Healy has termed 'the seamless normality [of] a triumphal national history'.

Many Australian histories authenticate themselves by drawing on 'the available myths and discourses of national character and identity'.[51] These histories often speak of Australia's 'pioneer spirit', where the 'settlers' toiled in a harsh and empty land. They celebrate a hybridised Australian male: fiercely independent, but imbued with just enough British heritage to remain above the

49. Clive Johnson, *Wimmera Mail-Times*, 8 June 1990.
50. Janet Abu-Lughod, 'On the remaking of history: How to reinvent the past', in B Kruger and P Mariani (eds), *Remaking History* (Bay Press, Seattle, 1989), p.118.
51. Graeme Turner, *National Fictions* (Allen & Unwin, Sydney, 1986).

'natives', who hover around the fringe of such histories, or are disposed of in the 'prehistory' of the text.

Within academia, it is true, the debate has moved on. But outside the walls of the universities, where Indigenous people are fighting for land rights, cultural identity and the right to present and interpret our own histories, we are constantly forced to contend with an imperialist history that is really nothing more than 'a crude apologia for the status quo of the day'.[52] It is a history motivated by cultural and political domination. It disguises its own violence and oppression by presenting sanitised 'nationalist themes, grown cosy and thoroughly naturalized by repetition, [that] disguise or celebrate the actual history of imperial and colonial domination'.[53]

These histories may not be presented in the pages of a conventional text (although they often are). They parade themselves in the media and on film. They are evoked in political discussion of 'Aboriginal issues'. It is not surprising that many of these debates centre on the relationship to land.

In Perth, the Swan River Fringe Dwellers, Nyoongar people, have waged a struggle against developers and the state Labor government over the Old Brewery site on the Swan River.[54] They are attempting to protect a sacred dreaming track formed by Waugal, a serpent that created many of the landscape features in the area, including the river. The authenticity of their claim and their culture has been challenged by those who wish to build a recreation and cultural centre on the land. Although both the developers and government had difficulty accepting the Nyoongar belief in a 'giant snake', it did not stop them from trying to appropriate this creation story for their own purposes.

52. Rae Frances and Bruce Scates, 'Honouring the Aboriginal Dead', *Arena*, 86, 1989, p. 72.
53. Popular Memory Group, 'Popular memory: theory, politics, method', in R Johnson et al. (eds), *Making Histories* (Hutchinson, London, 1982), p. 213.
54. *Age*, 27 May 1991.

The original design for the redevelopment incorporated a 100-metre-long 'polychrome brick Waugal path'. The Nyoongars' right to protect their sacred land is being rejected by a government that attempts to deny their cultural identity. Steve Mickler has called this 'a colonialist disdain for the fallen "noble savage", the urban "half-caste"'.[55]

The simplest way to deny groups such as the Swan River Fringe Dwellers a right to their land is to deny their existence as Indigenous people. If such a denial of identity fails, some opponents revert to the *terra nullius* myth. In a recent newspaper article, a Victorian journalist opposed the Uluru name restoration, claiming that the area had been unoccupied by 'tribes of the desert … for centuries', with the exception of 'nomadic hunters' who visited the area 'in prolonged wet seasons'.[56]

At Echuca in Victoria, the local Yorta Yorta people had remains of their ancestors returned to them by the Museum of Victoria in 1990. The remains had been excavated at Kow Swamp between 1969 and 1972 by archaeologist Dr Alan Thorne. Professor John Mulvaney, a supporter of Dr Thorne, repeatedly claimed that the attempts to have the remains returned to the Koori community for reburial were 'the actions of a handful of radicals',[57] although the campaign to have the remains returned to the community was supported by the nine Aboriginal Land Councils of the Murray River Region, as well as Colin Walker, senior Aboriginal sites officer in the area and representative of the Yorta Yorta people.[58] Mulvaney and Thorne recognised the scientific value of studying the remains, but denied the historical and cultural relationship that present Koori people have with their ancestors. The remains were no longer a part of Koori history: they had become 'ancient

55. Steve Mickler, 'The Battle for Goonininup', *Arena*, 96, 1991. The Western Australian Government purchased the land in 1985.
56. 'ROCK ROBBERY', Don Petersen, Melbourne *Sun*, 15 October 1991.
57. See for example *Australian*, 21 August 1990.
58. Media Release, Murray River Region Aboriginal Land Council, 22 August 1990; *Age*, 3 August 1990. At the time Colin Walker had recorded 160 protected sites, and 'knew of many more'.

bones [that] belong to the world—not us'.[59] Thorne dismissed any ancestral link between Kooris living today and the bodies that he removed from their burial place, on the grounds that there were differences in anatomical features, while Mulvaney was concerned that 'we could face refusal to excavate any more Aboriginal sites'.[60]

Europeans continue to 'make' and 'unmake' Indigenous people. When we attempt to claim rights to land, or to the bodies of our ancestors, we are separated from an 'ancient past'. Steve Mickler believes that, as the appreciation (and possession) of Aboriginal art has increased, so too has 'the intensity of the denigration of practised or "lived" Aboriginal culture'.

This form of racism relates to what Renato Rosaldo has termed 'imperialist nostalgia', which makes racial domination appear 'innocent and pure'.[61] Having altered or destroyed the culture of the 'other', the colonisers then appropriate it for their own gain, or even mourn its passing, while at the same time concealing their 'own complicity with often brutal domination'.

Historically, Europeans expected to witness the eradication of the Indigenous people of this country, and Australian governments have attempted to erase the identity of Indigenous people by physical or cultural genocide, the latter often parading under the title of 'assimilation'. Despite their failure, 'imperialist nostalgia' is everywhere. The passing of an ancient culture is both mourned and celebrated. The collection of art, for example, can serve as evidence of the superiority of the imperialist culture, while allowing its owners the gratification of appreciating the 'beauty' in objects from a past time. James Clifford has noted the Western preference for collectables that are from an 'ancient (preferably vanished) civilisation'.[62] This is so for art and bodies. For

59. *Australian*, 28 July 1990, 6 August 1990.
60. Ibid.
61. Renato Rosaldo, 'Imperialist Nostalgia', *Representations*, 26, Spring 1989, pp. 107–122.
62. James Clifford, *The Predicament of Culture* (Harvard University Press, Cambridge, Mass., 1988), p. 222.

mourning to occur 'innocently and purely', without opposition, the possessed and commodified culture must be certified dead.

IV

> As much as guns and warships, maps have been the weapons of imperialism.[63]

We should fully recognise what nineteenth-century explorers and 'pioneers' accomplished in the Western District. In 1836 Major Thomas Mitchell passed through the land of the Jardwadjali clans in and around the mountain range that he named the Grampians. During this search for exploitable land Mitchell claimed that he was exploring a *terra nullius*—a no man's land—despite his having contact with local Indigenous people, some of whom his party murdered. Mitchell wrote:

> It was evident that the reign of solitude in these beautiful vales was near a close; a reflection which, in my mind, often sweetened the toils...of travelling through such houseless regions.[64]

He described these houseless regions as an 'Eden' awaiting 'the immediate reception of civilized man'. His second-in-command, Granville William Chetwynd Stapylton, had a fine understanding of the value of their speculative exercise. The area was an 'El Dorado' which would be 'at present worth sixty millions to the Exchequer of England', and hopefully result in 'a good fat grant' for the 'discoverers'.[65]

---

63. JB Hartley, 'Maps, knowledge, and power', in D Cosgrove and S Daniels (eds), *The Iconography of Landscape* (Cambridge University Press, Cambridge, 1988), p. 282
64. Major TL Mitchell, *Three Expeditions into the interior of Eastern Australia* (Australiana Facsimile Editions, 18, Libraries Board of South Australia, Adelaide, 1965, 2 vols), vol. 1, p. 174.
65. Stapylton, op. cit., p. 99.

Mitchell was a surveyor, taking control of the land by charting it on a map. By naming features, he placed a symbolic British flag on each of them. The land was charted, ordered and labelled, becoming a colonial possession. Mitchell eulogised his own feats: 'Of this Eden I was the first European to explore its mountains and streams.' His cartography and favourable reports to the British Government resulted in an immediate grab for land. He anticipated that his expedition would lead to the exploitation of 'those natural advantages [of the land], certain to become at no distant date, of vast importance to new people'. Such is the power of cartography.

Mitchell was able to map a 'socially empty space'.[66] Although the land had been occupied for thousands of years, by making a map Mitchell took possession of it for Britain. Elizabeth Ferrier has written that 'mapping determines the way landscape has been conceived'; it is described as an 'unfolded map'.[67] This is a powerful metaphor. The land that was possessed could literally be held in the hands of the invading colonisers. When Mitchell mapped his 'Australia Felix', a land without a recognised people or history was given a history—a British history. His maps conceal the presence and histories of the Indigenous people.

Opponents of the Gariwerd name restoration regarded it as an insult to Mitchell's 'memory and tenacity'.[68] And although the Koori Tourism Unit's submission highlighted the fact that Mitchell had only conferred ten of the forty-four European names at issue, it also said that 'Mitchell should be credited with advocating the retention of Aboriginal place-names', and had often done so: 'I have always gladly adopted Aboriginal names.' Steve Crabb, quoting the same passage from Mitchell's diary, said

66. On which see Hartley, op. cit.
67. Elizabeth Ferrier, 'Mapping Power and Contemporary Cultural Theory', in *antithesis*, 4, 1, 1990, p. 41.
68. For example, D. S. of Bentleigh, 30 March 1989, in Koori Tourism Unit file 9/7/76/3.

'the explorer went to great lengths to use Koori words when he named landscape features'.[69]

Although the Indigenous groups of the Gariwerd area followed Mitchell's party as it moved across the mountain range, they made little contact with him. Mitchell sometimes left the main party and 'explored' ahead with a smaller group, leaving Stapylton in charge. When visited by those from whom Mitchell wished to gain both knowledge and names, Stapylton recorded: 'I wish to detain them if possible until the Surveyor General returns, for by them we may obtain a great deal of knowledge of the intervening country'. Piper, a 'black' from New South Wales who accompanied the party, carried the handcuffs that would capture the Indigenous names. But Stapylton did not exactly put out the welcome mat:

> Blackfellows shot at and wounded today by one of the men in the bush. The native shipped his spear and was accordingly very properly fired at. Now to war with these gentry I suppose. They are encamped around us tonight. Tomorrow we will give them a benefit if they don't keep off.

Stapylton entered comments in his diary in reference to the Indigenous peoples: 'Their hollow resembles precisely the cry of some wild beast, which in fact it is'. On one occasion he disturbed a family who appear to have been hunting. He took great pleasure in the fear that he apparently instilled in them: 'these devils will always run if you give them the time'.

This is the man after whom Mitchell named Mt Stapylton. It was this feature that the Victorian Place Names Committee refused to restore to Gunigalg, apparently on aesthetic grounds.

In May 1836, north of what is now the Murray River, Mitchell's party had clashed with Indigenous groups. On 27 May Mitchell decided to take action 'in a war which not my party, but these savages had virtually commenced'. Mitchell set up an 'ambuscade'

69. Warrnambool *Standard*, 1 December 1990.

in order to surprise 'the vast body of blacks' that had been tracking the party. Realising that Mitchell's men were waiting for them, the group ran towards 'their citadel, the river'. Without waiting for an order from Mitchell, his men ran after the 'blacks', shooting them as they attempted to escape across the river. Mitchell later reported that seven had been shot. He accepted fully the decision of his men to chase and kill, 'for the result was the permanent deliverance of the party from imminent danger'. Mitchell commemorated the killings by conferring a name upon the site:

> I gave to the little hill which witnessed this overthrow of our enemies, and was to us the harbinger of peace and tranquillity, the name of Mt. Dispersion.

The massacre created enough 'ripples' to delay Mitchell's knighthood.[70]

To ensure that Mitchell's place in history is remembered, there are some fifty memorial cairns dotted along a commemorative track bearing his name.[71] This celebration of a 'great explorer' buries the dead and their histories. As Chilla Bulbeck has shown, 'most monuments avoid the sore spot of race relations'.[72]

Mitchell's exploration of the Western District had been pre-empted by the land-hungry Henty brothers, who occupied land at Portland Bay in 1834.[73] The way to gain free title to land was to exploit it vigorously. A claim was established by 'occupying it with sheep grazed in flocks from 500 to 1000 head, each flock

70. Manning Clark, 'Major Mitchell and Australia Felix', in Manning Clark et al., *Australia Felix* (Dunkeld and District Historical Museum, 1987), p. 79.
71. Ibid., p. 76.
72. Chilla Bulbeck, 'Aborigines, Memorials and the History of the Frontier', in J Rickard and P Spearritt (eds), *Packaging the Past? Public Histories* (Melbourne University Press, 1991), p. 170. See also Frances and Scates, op. cit.
73. MF Christie, *Aborigines in Colonial Victoria 1835–86* (Melbourne University Press, 1979), p. 24.

in the care of a shepherd'.[74] This had a devastating effect on the Indigenous population. When the Chief Protector of Aborigines, GA Robinson, arrived in Portland in May 1841, he discovered that only 'two of the tribe who once inhabited the country of the Convincing Ground are still alive'.[75]

Robinson's tour of the Western District uncovered large-scale murder by the European squatters, as well as Koori resistance. At Portland the Police Magistrate, Mr Blair, stated that the 'natives' of a 'tribe' that had killed a squatter and his shepherd 'should be exterminated'. He would 'shoot the whole tribe' if the murderer was not 'delivered up'. Two days later, one of the Henty brothers informed Robinson that 'the settlers were dropping them'. Blair, who was present, 'replied he hoped so', and added that 'he had no power to restrain the settlers from shooting the women and children'. At the Fitzroy River near Portland, a Mr Pilleau informed Robinson that 'the settlers encouraged their men to shoot the natives', and 'that for every white man killed 20 blacks were shot'. Robinson recorded that the settlers spoke of:

> ...dropping the natives as if they were speaking of dropping cows. Indeed, the doctrine is being promulgated that they are not human, or hardly so and thereby inculcating the principle that killing them is no murder.

He received information of the murder of two Koori women and a boy, who had been lured to their death with the promise of food. Other women were abducted, raped and beaten. On 26 June 1840 he was informed that 'an old woman' named 'Nar.rer.burnin' had been murdered at John Henty's outstation. She had been 'shot, kicked, and stabbed with a bayonet several times...and then buried in the ground'.

---

74. LP Peel, 'The First Hundred Years of Agricultural Development in Western Victoria', in *The Natural History of Victoria*, op. cit.
75. 'Journals of GA Robinson – May to August 1841', *Records of the Victorian Archaeological Survey*, 11, October 1980, p. 15.

At the Tulloh property near the Grampians, Robinson 'saw the corpse of a native on four sticks', apparently used as bait to lure and kill emus. Robinson despaired at 'the heartless manner in which Charles Winter and his ruffians [reacted to] the barbarous murder of this man'. Tulloh told Robinson that he and eight other men had previously gone to the Grampians 'in quest of blacks'. They found a child, laid it near the fire 'and roasted it or, to use his qualified expression, burnt it'. They also found a 'fine little boy', who bit one of the men who had abducted him. 'The ruffian then kicked the child to death'. A week later, following yet another attack on a native camp near Mt Sturgeon, Robinson could only state the obvious: '[this] would not be allowed in civilized society'.

In denying a Koori history, the people of the Western District have also conveniently denied their own history. This is a form of radical conservatism: the history is not unknown, but is repressed by building monuments to murderers. When this kind of façadism is threatened with exposure, the response is hostility and hysteria.

On 15 October 1991 Steve Crabb announced the Place Names Committee's decision on the name restoration. Forty-nine place-name restorations were accepted, fifteen were rejected and four required further investigation.[76] Most of the accepted names were given dual Koori/English names. The Koori Tourism Unit had publicly accepted this position during negotiations at least a year earlier: 'We have no objection so long as the Koori name goes first.'[77] But this did not happen. The National Park will be officially known as The Grampians (Gariwerd). The Koori name is therefore linguistically subordinated, 'handcuffed' in parentheses.

The local member for Lowan, Bill McGrath, promised that the names would be 'thrown out … as soon as the Opposition was returned to Government'.[78] Bob Stone, now Stawell's mayor,

---

76. *Wimmera Mail-Times*, 16 October 1991.
77. *Courier*, Ballarat, 20 October 1990.
78. *Ararat Advertiser*, 17 October 1991.

said that 'you won't have anyone around here using the names'. He believed that the signs would most likely be torn down, adding 'I wouldn't do it myself, as much as I'd like to.'[79] Geoff Clark of Brambuk, on the other hand, felt that on its own the name restoration was 'a poor attempt at some form of social justice', and would only amount to something of substance when 'the concept of land ownership [and] recognition of our cultural heritage within this particular area is recognised'.[80]

The name restoration may be a beginning or an end. The tourist dollar chases the 'niche market'. The marketers may one day target a Western District town as a 'Sovereign Hill'—perhaps Stawell, which has a gold-mining history. Its citizens may become artefacts, performing behind colonial façades, stuck in a local version of 'American Dreams'.[81] But if the market moves away from 'Dreamtime legends', the money may as well.

Koori culture is not a commodity. It must be interpreted in an educative fashion by those who live it—Koori people. To assist in this process the Koori names of landscapes in the region should be fully restored, not presented in a tokenistic fashion, or as a 'dead tongue'.[82]

The first publication to promote the newly named Grampians (Gariwerd) National Park informs us that 'There's a place in Victoria where time seems to have stood still. A place of Dreamtime legends.' The booklet tells of the Kooris, who 'roamed' the area, the coming of Mitchell, then the squatters, 'the farmers, the foresters, and the miners'.[83] It asks tourists to visit Brambuk

79. *Vox Populi*, SBS Television, 28 October 1991. This had occurred earlier in 1991 when a sign was erected at the newly named Yanga Nyawi National Park in the Mallee (*Wimmera Mail-Times*, 14 October 1991). It has since occurred in the newly named national park (*Age*, 14 December 1991).
80. Ibid.
81. See Peter Carey, 'American Dreams' in *The Fat Man in History* (University of Queensland Press, 1988).
82. Melbourne *Herald*, 31 May 1990: 'DEAD TONGUE SPARKS HOT WORDS IN THE GRAMPIANS'.
83. *The Grampians Gariwerd* (Victorian Tourism Commission, 1991), p. 3.

Living Cultural Centre, or possibly the 'Grand Canyon … Fallen Giant … Whale's Mouth … Jaws of Death'. Visitors to the park can experience 'the same panoramic views Major Mitchell marvelled at in 1836. Nothing has changed.'

In 1992, Fitzroy Blak writer **Tony Birch** was a postgraduate student at the University of Melbourne. Today, Professor Tony Birch is the University's Boisbouvier Chair in Australian Literature. He is the author of four novels, five short fiction collections, and two poetry books. Among many other prizes, Birch's work has been awarded the Queensland Premier's Literary Award, the Age Book of the Year for Fiction, the Christina Stead Literary Prize and the Steele Rudd Literary Award, and has been shortlisted for the Australian Book Industry Awards Literary Fiction Book of the Year, and the Prime Minister's Literary Award for Fiction. In 2023, Melbourne state school Preston High honoured Birch's contribution to literature and education by naming their new school library 'The Tony Birch Library'.

Creative City

David Yencken

Meanjin 47.4 Summer 1988

Emotionality or feeling is threaded through a person's day. It does not just appear at appointed times in pre-selected places; nor is it far oft. It is with the person all the time, contextualised and interwoven through their thoughts and actions.

—NK Denzin

WE GIVE MUCH attention to the efficiency of our cities, although they are sometimes far from efficient. We give some attention to the equity of our cities, although we could do much more to make them fairer. A creative city must be efficient; it should be a city that is concerned with the material well-being of all its citizens, especially the poor and disadvantaged. But it must be much more than that. It should be at the one time an emotionally satisfying city and a city that stimulates creativity among its citizens. What principles might guide us towards such a city?

In his essay 'A City Is Not A Tree', Christopher Alexander posed two central problems for those who are interested in cities. To illustrate the complexities of the interactions that take place in cities, Alexander first contrasted the mathematical forms of tree and semi-lattice: the tree a simple structural form with branches bifurcating into further branches, the semi-lattice a form with connections of different kinds between all its parts. He then drew on experiments with complex patterns to illustrate human inability to grasp or retain very complex forms and human propensity to simplify to reduce an overload of information and stimuli to manageable form.

The city is an extraordinarily complex system. Even if we can't fully grasp it, even if we are bound to simplify, we must hold on to that complexity, for it is complexity that gives cities richness, vitality, life and, significantly, health. In the same way that ecological variety and complexity give health to natural systems, so variety and complexity give health to social and cultural systems. People in different material circumstances, from different cultural backgrounds, of different ages, or of different temperaments, have different social and cultural needs. We cannot possibly list or envisage all these needs. They can only be expressed individually and satisfied by others responding to them in a myriad of different ways. Jane Jacobs, in *The Economy Of Cities*, has similarly drawn attention to the precariousness of cities that become too dependent on a limited range of industries and economic activities. So the first important principle for a creative city is to encourage variety and complexity.

We can also reach some understanding of complexity in another way, intuitively, by holistic thinking. Western education and logic systems do not, however, serve us well in teaching us how to think holistically, how to respond intuitively and how to work with rather than eliminate complexity. The system of logic that has dominated western thinking is based on Aristotle. In its simplest terms Aristotelian logic is concerned with the dichotomy 'it is' or 'it is not'. In contrasting western and eastern logic systems, Masao Kunihiro, a distinguished Japanese cultural anthropologist, has commented that 'In Kant's *Critique Of Pure Reason* he poses only one question concerning the limitation of self and the world: is it finite or is it infinite? Kant's reasoning', says Kunihiro, 'epitomises that of the west since Aristotle. The Western mind has established clear boundaries between light and darkness, day and night, nature and counternature.' In contrast Kunihiro cites the dialogue of Sanjaya in the Sen'yu-kyo scripture, which finds not two, but four answers to Kant's question: positive; negative;

positive and negative; and not positive and not negative. Sanjaya similarly finds four answers to the question whether there is life after death: there is; there is not; one can say both there is and there is not; and one cannot say either there is or there is not. Kunihiro notes that there are now other challenges to traditional western dualistic logic. The most recent theories in the fields of biology and quantum mechanics, for example, hold that the relationships between different entities are not fixed, but constantly changing. Kunihiro finally points out that the Japanese use both kinds of logic systems. For western-type analysis and dualistic contrast they use 'square words'. But when they wish to express their true feelings they use 'round words'. A second principle, then, is to encourage more holistic, intuitive approaches to our cities.

Through holistic thinking we can more readily find the appropriate balance between order and complexity, for a creative city must also have order. It must be legible, transparent and understandable. But the order must not be destructive of richness and complexity. This is a third principle.

It might also be noted that in Japan these different ways of thinking also seem to translate into somewhat different organisational systems, structures in which much time and effort is spent in reaching full agreement on new directions for the organisation before action is undertaken. This ensures that when the action begins there is clear understanding of the collective task and an enormous harnessing of collective energy. The senior managers' roles also appear to differ from those of their western counterparts. They are co-ordinators rather than individual leaders. Managers are also expected to spend much time in holistic scanning of the organisational environment. So we need to reflect on the way we have been taught to think, to look at problems, to appraise complexity and to act together.

The complexities of cities can be illustrated by looking at some of the more familiar ways in which they are perceived and understood. A city can be understood as an economic system with very intricate networks of economic flows. These can be expressed sectorally—as systems of exchanges and transactions—or spatially and socially—as having particular effects on particular groups in particular locations. A city can also be understood as a political and managerial system with particular sets of power-relationships, influenced by different groups and individuals. In recent years, for example, increasing attention has been given to the analysis of structural changes in ownership and control of capital and their influences on different groups in society.

A city can be understood as a set of social relationships and as a social network. Different societies and different groups within those societies have very different social networks. Understanding them is often very important. In many so-called slum-clearing projects it has been assumed that higher-quality physical conditions in new public houses or flats would lead to improvements in social conditions, while the significance of the social networks has been ignored. Preserving the social networks has later turned out to be much more important to many householders than physically improved housing in less accessible locations or with less attractive relationships.

A city can be understood as an ecological system. In many ways this is the most fundamental of all systems. Increasingly we have learnt how much damage we do to ourselves, to our environment and all our life-support systems by ignoring the ecological relationships—the earth's atmosphere, oceans, land masses, air and water quality, soils, trees and vegetation and habitats.

A city can be understood as a set of physical constructs—structures, physical forms and spaces and their relationships. Architects, engineers and landscape architects are particularly trained to look at cities in this way. A city can be interpreted as an expression of the past, as the tangible, physical evidence of the evolution of the city's history. Seen this way, the city is not just significant to historians, architectural historians or other groups and individuals involved in historic conservation. It also has strong psychic significance as the roots of our common culture and as the expression of the old, the comfortable and the familiar. Finally, a city can be perceived as a series of experiential relationships—events and activities and spaces and structures that generate emotions.

When we list these different ways of perceiving and understanding cities, two things are immediately apparent. In some sense we all experience cities in all these ways at different times, in different roles and in different moods. When we are reading newspaper commentaries on economic affairs or managing our personal or organisational finances, we are seeing the city as an economic system. When we are building our own houses or watching the construction of a large urban complex or reading the architecture critic at *the Age* castigating his fellow professionals, we are conscious of the city as a set of physical constructs. When we are voting, or reading with exasperation about our politicians' antics, or approving a political initiative that we strongly support, or trying to get a passport (especially if you happen to have been born, as I and many other Australians have, in a non-English-speaking country), we see the city as a political and administrative system. But when we list the different ways of looking at cities we become aware of how little we are rationally conscious of this variety of human responses. So we have to recognise that they are all perfectly valid ways of perceiving cities, and consciously value all of them.

We then need to understand that certain forms of analysis are of prime importance for certain purposes. If, for example, we judge that social justice is our prime objective, then political economy is likely to be one of the most effective ways of analysing the city—but may not be very helpful in telling us what to do about it. If we are preoccupied with economic growth, we will use quite different forms of analysis. We have to be able to use particular forms of analysis for the limited purposes of the projects and activities that most directly occupy us without losing sight of the whole. And, very importantly, if we are to have a creative city we must be sure that our notions of creativity extend to all the different dimensions of perception and understandings I have described and to the different systems and networks to which they relate. We have to be creative in every realm.

Another principle concerns our modification of environments. We are constantly modifying our environment, sometimes in very big ways, sometimes in small ways, sometimes well, sometimes horribly. It is not only *what* we do that matters, but how we do it. There is research evidence that animals and man in natural conditions select and modify, and that both show signs of stress when they are unable to select and modify. There is further evidence that the human stress of adaptation to a strange environment can be greatly reduced if the individual has some involvement in the initial change and some control over the later development and functioning of the environment. Choice, involvement and participation are thus important principles.

A further principle relates to stimulation and challenge. A creative city must excite and stimulate; but it must also have other qualities. Loren Eiseley, in his book *The Unexpected Universe*, likens the human quest to the Odyssean voyages of legend and science. In Eiseley's words,

> The almost three hundred year old epic the Odyssey possesses a perennial literary freshness that causes it to be translated anew in every generation. It can be read as an inward journey of reflection or as an outwardly active adventure. Throughout man's odyssey his technological triumphs have been constantly at odds with his hunger for psychological composure and peace.

In our creative city we thus need to balance stimulating environments with oases of peacefulness and calm. Each individual has to find his or her own inner peace or harmony. Some do it through music, some through meditation; some, the unlucky, never find it at all. But in our creative city we also have to provide places and spaces for sublimation, contemplation and healing.

The difficulty with oases and special places is that they can be very personal. I am reminded of a fine article called 'Treasure Island', published many years ago in *Architectural Design*. Several people were asked to list their magic places. One respondent answered that for him Euston Station in London would always be a magic place since the day he saw a man and a woman walk across the station towards each other and start to waltz. When I think about influences on me I think of places associated with water, distance, and wonderful harmony. In Melbourne I think of the end of Station Pier or the Botanic Gardens or of parts of the river. Are there common qualities in these places? I think there are. What we need to ensure is that places with these special qualities of peacefulness and harmony are to be found in all localities of the city.

It is also of critical significance that the cultural opportunities we present to people should be relevant to their own lives and experiences. Citizens in different places and in different economic and cultural circumstances have different cultural requirements, which need to be understood, supported and encouraged. This may sometimes require those involved in cultural administration to change their mindset. It is easy to assume that it is enough to provide opportunities for aesthetic experience through film, music, dance, painting, sculpture and literature and by encouraging individual or community creative activities. Certainly, the demystification of culture and high arts ought to be a major plank of arts policy—often the initiated would be as profoundly grateful for such a demystification as the uninitiated. But we also have to understand that for some people, particularly the most disadvantaged, there may be other priorities. We should, of course, ensure that those groups do have access to as many artistic and cultural experiences as possible. But when people are preoccupied with burning social issues, racial discrimination or oppression, poverty, unemployment, isolation and alienation, we should help them to find creative expression for these concerns, because it is likely that this is what is most culturally relevant to them. We should also help them to dignify their local histories, environments and work experiences. And when we create institutions that might help them to do these things, we should not have low expectations.

I was connected with the creation of the Living Museum of the West in Melbourne and have taken a continuing, if rather long-distance, interest in its progress and development. The Museum of the West was conceived as a museum without walls and without collections, a museum that would research, portray and illuminate working-class life in the western suburbs of Melbourne. It would be a mirror, and a dignifier, of the society of the west. It is a great regret to me that we missed the opportunity to lift institutions like the Museum of the West and Theatre West to new plateaux of quality and excellence in this bicentennial year. I mean no criticism of the admirable work of the people associated with those institutions. The criticisms are of those who distributed the bicentennial largesse. Let me illustrate. Some years ago my wife and I travelled half-way across Sweden to see a workers' play. Why? Because we had read an excellent review about it in a major Stockholm newspaper. That's equivalent to the *Australian*'s theatre reviewer writing a rave review of a workers' play in Port Pirie. We should help bodies like the Museum of the West and Theatre West to have a metropolitan, state and national profile equal to that of the best of our other museums and theatres. A major principle is thus the encouragement of relevant cultural experiences for all people in the city.

Furthermore, we must enrich *all* experiences. We cannot assume, for example, that it is sufficient to offer rich recreational opportunities in compensation for very poor working environments and conditions. There is now overwhelming evidence that the quality of work experiences colours—controls might not be too strong a word—the quality of leisure experiences. A six-nation UNESCO study on *Cultural and Working Life* eloquently documents the fact that a person with monotonous, repetitive or stressful work experiences is likely to have limited and relatively impoverished recreational experiences. Leisure opportunities cannot fully compensate for poor work conditions.

We are in a time of accelerating change. While for some people change is exhilarating, for most it is threatening and stressful. There is a deep psychic need for constancy in the midst of change. That is one reason for preserving the old and familiar—not only the best aesthetically, but also representative examples. In the older parts of the cities are the physical evidence of the past, our cultural roots. In the older parts of our cities there are forms, structures and spaces that we would not build today. They add variety to the physical experience of the city. Some are of outstanding quality. Once they are destroyed, we will never replace them. Thus a further principle is the need for conservation of our civic and architectural heritage, of the old and familiar and well-loved.

Another principle is that of fitness and local character. At a recent conference Marion Blackwell, a Western Australian landscape ecologist, described the building of mining towns in desert environments in the following terms:

> Such a town in the desert usually apes the ways, commodities and habits of its urban counterpart and completely ignores its natural surroundings. It tends to alienate its residents from the surrounding countryside. Some of them you find living completely isolated existences almost entirely within their air conditioned houses, hating the heat, the insects, the prickles and seldom if ever venturing outside the town precinct... Being unwilling to accept these new surroundings they concentrate on difficulties and on what are in their eyes deficiencies, spending their time pining for the things they were used to and which are not provided there.

Such towns can be planned and designed to fit and echo their natural surroundings rather than reject them. Careful education programmes can be devised to open residents' eyes to the grandeur of the landscape, to show them the delicacy of the desert wildflowers and the uniqueness of the wildlife and to suggest other ways in which deserts can be enjoyed. At Leinster, a nickel-mining town in the western arm of the Great Victoria Desert, when a programme of this kind was developed, not only was personnel turnover reduced to a fraction of that in other mining towns, but people were also given experiences that some expressed as being among the most memorable they had had in their lives.

Last on this list is quality. It seems so obvious, yet it regularly escapes us. We have to teach people not to accept impoverished places and environments. We have to use able designers more regularly. We have to teach architects that architectural egotism is a sin and that great architecture can be produced within the constraints of urban or environmental context. We have to train urban designers to work with local people in local environments. We have to use the very best designers in the most important places. We have to train developers to recognise the difference between architects who can design and architects who can produce buildings very efficiently; both are highly respectable skills, but they are not always combined. We have to get architects to accept, without any sense of loss of face, that they may have a skill in one area and not in others and should combine forces more often.

These are some initial principles that might inform our approach to creative cities. In the last part of this paper I want to return to the different ways in which cities can be perceived, and to concentrate on one of those—the experiential.

Why the emphasis on the emotional and experiential? One answer might be, 'Because it is an area that is most often neglected'. But there is another, more important. There can be few more significant objectives for a city than that of creating emotionally satisfying environments for all its citizens. Following Abraham Maslow's hierarchy of satisfactions, we know that certain other basic needs may have to be satisfied first. We know well we will never achieve such a lofty goal. But it is the objective to which we all intuitively aspire and towards which we should address our finest endeavours. Emotionally satisfying and stimulating environments—and in such environments I include events and activities as well as the places and structures—also work very well economically, administratively and politically.

Some people accept this with little persuasion. Marketers and politicians, for example, understand the power of emotion much better than accountants and bureaucrats. But they rarely see its full potential and mostly use it for very limited ends.

There are five groups of observers and performers who take special interest in the experiential: the scholars and commentators interested in changes in perceptions of space, structure, landscape and heritage; the environmental psychologists, scholars and commentators interested in human environment relationships; the marketers, especially the retail developers; the artists; and the architects, engineers and landscape architects. There are other groups—sociologists and psychologists, for example—whose work crosses into these areas, but the five groups I have chosen are perhaps the main ones concerned with the emotional experience of the city.

There is a rich tradition of study of historical and landscape perception. Different scholars have sought to trace changes in landscape perception in different times and different cultures. David Lowenthal, one of the most distinguished, has drawn attention to the changing attitudes to mountains and mountain scenery in European culture—from threatening and oppressive some hundred or so years ago, to grand expressions of nature today. He has also shown how, in the USA, historical environments have long been neglected in favour of nature and wilderness and how that is now changing. Some scholars have sought to find constants in human perception and valuation that can be isolated and used for classification of landscape values. Others, including Lowenthal, question whether there are such constants and argue that responses to environments are related to culture and time and background.

Others hold that there are different kinds of responses to environments—some genetically programmed, others culturally conditioned. One theory suggests that there are initial 'hard-wired' responses, lightning-fast initial appraisals, that are survival-related. For man in natural conditions, as for animals, these responses were a matter of life or death. There is then a slower, secondary review during which the environment is surveyed according to learnt cultural criteria.

Environmental psychology is now also a major field of study. It is concerned with human behaviour in different environments: how physical environments affect feelings and behaviour and invite or inhibit choices, and how people modify and affect their environments. It is an exceptionally important field for developers, planners, architects, designers and all those interested in urban change. Particularly noteworthy are the recent attempts to assemble the conclusions from this research and translate them into useful guidelines for practitioners. One pioneering work, *Housing As If People Mattered*, summarises all the literature on behaviour and satisfaction related to medium-density housing and draws from it a set of principles for planning and designing environments that will work for people. The authors are Clare Cooper Marcus and Wendy Sarkissian. Vischer and Cooper Marcus also carried out a delightful review of an architectural awards programme in British Columbia. They used criteria somewhat different from the architectural judges'—for example, whether people actually liked living in the places—and arrived at dramatically different conclusions. This is a cautionary tale for all designers.

The third category of observers is the developers and marketers. As we all know, the study of emotional and subliminal responses is a primary concern of advertisers and marketers, a concern on which billions of dollars hinge. But it is not only advertisers who are concerned with emotional responses. The most capable developers, particularly the retail developers, often have a superb understanding of the way people behave in different spaces. I recall a meeting with the US developer and philanthropist James Rouse, founder of the Rouse Corporation, builder of Columbia new town and creator of the Festival Market concept. He took me on a walking tour of Baltimore harbour. At each step he explained the ideal dimensions of waterfront boardwalks, plazas or interior corridor spaces to achieve certain kinds of people responses. 'I am concerned with detail,' he said, 'because it is the detail which makes the places work.'

The fourth group are the artists. Just as we need a judicious blend of stimulation and repose, so we also need the left and the right hemispheres, square and round words. Artists are the experts with round words. In a short essay called 'A Narrow Escape From Poetry', Anatole Broyard tells of an experience in Paris:

I was … on my way to dinner … the light was fading … through the gloom a man appeared … He seemed to want to speak to me so I slowed my pace … when he spoke it was in a light murmur '*La poésie, monsieur, ça vous intéresse?*' (Poetry sir, does it interest you?) For a wild moment I felt that I had come to Paris expressly to meet this man with his poems and his umbrella. How embarrassing poetry is I thought, like a blind date … '*Bien sûr*,' I said, 'Poetry interests me very much. But as you will notice, I am not at home in your language. Also I am still suffering from jet lag.'

In other words I excused myself, as most people excuse themselves from poetry, out of cowardice, with one rationalisation or another. What difference did it make that his poems were written in French? The difficulty would hardly be increased, for poetry itself is a foreign language. And one always feels jet lag in its presence—one has to travel so far, through such vast, threatening spaces.

Here was an opportunity and I had missed it. Even if his poems had been bad, his faith was good. We could have spoken of faith, for that's a kind of poetry too. We could have exchanged elaborate misunderstandings, which are perhaps the most poignant of all cultural transactions. To approach poetry you must start somewhere—in the dark, in the rain, in the shadow of a building, … on the way to some place else. You may not even need an umbrella.

Artists can also invest ordinary things with special meaning. So Bruce Dawe's poem 'Abandonment of Autos' begins with the news item, 'The City Council is reported to be concerned about the number of old cars being abandoned in city streets.' In Dawe's poem, the act of abandoning the car is transfigured:

It is the urban Arab's Farewell To His Steed,
Down to the final affectionate pat
On the near mudguard before turning away
To shoulder a passage through the indifferent crowds.
Made free in the moment of loss, the one true test.

Only the licence-plate which he carries with him
Into the new life stating as clearly
As any letter of recommendation:
'Here is one who senses the fitness of things.'

You see, there is no escape from poetry. We need the poets, painters and sculptors, the writers and musicians. We need the experiences and the challenges, since it is through the collision of their worlds of conjecture with the patterns of our daily thinking that we gain new insights and understanding.

The final group is the architects, engineers and landscape architects. They also bring very special skills and understanding to the making of the city. They are, indeed, the prime shapers of the city's forms. Some of them are also artists. Their insights and intuitions about human responses are often very sharp. But sometimes they are not. This is most often true of public spaces. Recently, when I was in Toronto, Michael Hough told me of a colleague who regularly took his Master's degree students at the beginning of the year to a natural stream in an unspoiled setting and asked them simply to describe it any way they chose. Each year he has found how much the engineers, surveyors, architects, landscape architects and other professionals have become the prisoners of their professional disciplines in the way they perceive and react to environments. This last year, as it so happened, he took one other person, a laboratory assistant without professional training, without a degree. He found that the laboratory assistant was the only person who gave a complete description of the river and its setting.

My purpose in describing each of these groups is, first, to draw to your attention how much each can contribute to the development of creative cities and, secondly, to stress the extent to which each has an incomplete understanding of human and emotional responses to places and situations—because the understanding is intuitive only, because it is limited in its scope, or because it is coloured and constrained by the way professionals have been taught to think. It is not hard to draw the obvious conclusion that all need to work together and to use their collective insights and skills. That is another principle to offer you.

It takes great skill to create emotionally satisfying environments. Both analysis and intuition are required. Many different kinds of environment are needed in a city; the designer/creator has to think carefully about the emotional experience he or she wishes to create. Many environments will work in ways quite contrary to our expectations or preconceptions, so we also have to be open, humble and willing to learn. And that is a final principle.

I recently passed through San Antonio in Texas. At first sight, San Antonio is an ordinary, awful American city. The central city is ringed by elevated freeways, blighted by empty sites used as parking lots. Walking through San Antonio, there is no immediate hint of the remarkable sub-surface world, the river. The river is a tiny, bijou environment, a few metres wide but delightfully planted and paved; much of it is adjoined by a host of small cafés, restaurants and shops.

Along a short stretch of the river is a series of different environments with different uses and designs. The first is the stretch along which the bars, cafés, small restaurants and shops are clustered. In the evening this is an area of extraordinary activity. It is hard even to move along the path, so many are the people strolling, eating, drinking, or browsing in the shops. There is a rich, soft quality in the planting, paving, stonework bridges and lighting, that relates perfectly to the informal café activities. In another area a river arm has been extended into a new shopping centre and hotel complex. This is also a high-activity area. Here the architecture is consciously rich but quite different from that of the informal café area. In an opposite arm a cultural centre has been built. This is the severe, formal architecture of high culture and established order. No-one walks here unless they are bound for a conference or concert. There are other areas of a quite different character, landscape environments of peace and repose—some partly man-made, partly remnant of the natural river, others new and consciously fashioned. So in a very small stretch of river there are areas of informal social activity, more deliberately planned areas of high-consumption activity, areas of formal culture and areas of peace and repose. The river is a microcosm of many different urban experiences. But it is not the world of all the residents of San Antonio.

On my night in San Antonio, I sat by the river and watched people in their thousands strolling, milling, drinking, eating. The next morning, very early, I went back for a walk along the river. I had it virtually to myself. The light was muted with the lazy promise of a very hot day. As I walked under the canopy of trees, past the flower beds, past three empty restaurants with the taller buildings dissolving into the sky above, past stretches of river landscape, I came to a tiny theatrette spanning the river. As I passed by, a voice behind me called out, 'Father, Father Priest'. I turned, and the voice called again, 'Father Priest is that you?' I saw an old Hispanic man standing with a broom. 'No,' I said, 'I'm not a priest.' I walked back to him.

He looked at me carefully and said, 'You are very like him. Many times I have walked the poor streets with him—for injustice.' We then laughed and shook hands. We talked about the performance that night and shook hands and laughed again. And I walked away. But I was very moved.

Notes

References cited, in alphabetical order, are: C Alexander, 'A City is Not a Tree', in *Design*, 206, February 1966; Anatole Broyard, 'A Narrow Escape From Poetry', in *New York Times*, 14 August 1988; C Cooper Marcus and Wendy Sarkissian, *Housing as if People Mattered* (University of California Press, 1986); K Cranham, 'Euston Station Discourse', in 'Treasure Island' *Architectural Design*, 7/6, June 1969; Bruce Dawe, 'Abandonment of Autos' in R Hall, ed., *The Collins Book of Australian Poetry* (Fontana/Collins, 1981); NK Denzin, *On Understanding Emotion* (Jossey-Bass, 1984); L Eiseley, *The Unexpected Universe* (Harcourt Brace & World, 1964); B Heurling, ed., *Culture & Working Life: Experiences From Six European Cultures* (UNESCO, 1979); J Jacobs, *The Economy of Cities*, (Jonathan Cape, 1970); M Kunihiro, 'The Japanese Language and Intercultural Communication', in *The Silent Power* (Simul Press, 1976); D Lowenthal, 'Finding Valued Landscapes', in *Progress in Human Geography*, Vol. 2, No. 3, 1978; J Vischer and C Cooper Marcus, 'Design Awards Who Cares', in *Places*, Vol. 3, No. 1, 1986, pp. 66–85.

In 1988 **David Yencken** (1931–2019) was Professor of Landscape Architecture at the School of Environmental Planning, University of Melbourne, and former Secretary of the Victorian Ministry for Planning and Environment. Yencken went on to become a prominent champion for excellence in the built and natural environment, promoting better outcomes for strategic policy, innovation design and practice across our cities and landscapes. His work was recognised with several Royal Australian Institute of Architecture awards, a special Australian Institute of Landscape Architecture Award, a Royal Australian Planning Institute Award, the Lord Mayor's Prize, the Queen's Silver Jubilee Medal, and the Planning Institute of Australia Lifetime Achievement Award. In 1982 he was made an Officer of the Order of Australia for services to conservation and history.

Reading the constitution out loud

Marcia Langton

Meanjin 70.4 Summer 2011

THE TRADITIONAL OWNER, an older woman with a tough grace, welcomed us to her land. Her words were plain and her voice was tinged with a sense of pride. Her group was one of the few in southern Australia to obtain a native title determination recognising the members as native title holders. They were now part of the social fabric of this small rural town in Victoria, and before the proceedings had commenced, one of the local dignitaries had engaged her in quiet conversation. I overheard a few of her words: 'next meeting', 'can't see any problem with the proposal', and 'good rain'. Everyone was talking about the rain. There had been more rain since January when the floods had hit, and all the waterholes and creeks were overflowing. It was still raining.

Here at the clubhouse at the local golf club in Horsham, a hardy few had come from the town and district in the freezing cold to hear me explain the work of the Expert Panel on Constitutional Recognition. A few town dignitaries were joined by retirees who had voted in the 1967 referendum; there were some town residents and others who lived on the craggy western side of the Grampians in native forests.

I began with the usual preliminaries. Julia Gillard, the Prime Minister, had made a commitment to hold a referendum during this Parliament's term on the question of recognising Indigenous Australians in the Constitution. Along with others, I had been appointed by the Prime Minister with the task of delivering to her a report in December 2011 with recommendations on a referendum question or questions on changing the Constitution to recognise Indigenous Australians. The panel includes members of parliament from all parties and one independent, Rob Oakeshott. Two constitutional lawyers, Henry Burmeister and Megan Davis, are members, and the remainder are leaders representing a matrix of issues; youth, gender and the Indigenous, corporate, legal, philanthropic and policy sectors. The terms of reference of the panel reach the highest standard of political correctness and political expediency in the era of 'Reconciliation'. The challenge had been accepted by the panel members, despite the costs to our professional and personal lives incurred as a result of the travel commitments.

We are required, in less than a year, to involve the public in discussion and debate on difficult constitutional matters and to report their views to the Prime Minister. This report must also advise on the level of support from Indigenous people and the broader community for each option. To date, panel members have visited more than seventy communities throughout Australia to ascertain the key concerns about this proposal, using the specifically developed communication aids such as a website (www.youmeunity.org.au), a DVD, a discussion paper, and a variety of informative papers. As of September more than 1000 submissions had been received. We have also appointed ambassadors and worked closely with the Australian Human Rights Commission, the National Congress of Australia's First Peoples and Reconciliation Australia.

Australians, I told the Horsham group, have approved only eight out of forty-four referendum proposals since Federation in 1901 and opinions vary on the likelihood of success for a question proposing recognition of Indigenous Australians in the Constitution.[1]

1. George Williams and David Hume, *People Power: The History and Future of the Referendum in Australia*, University of New South Wales Press, Sydney, 2010.

After this explanation, which drew satisfied murmurs from the men and women around the table, I faced the more difficult challenge of explaining what the Constitution states, what it does not state, and what it might state if a referendum were to succeed. My strategy to engage their attention, one I happened upon in Brunswick, Melbourne, when I found myself arguing with a beautifully youthful and idealistic Australian who had never read the document, was to read aloud particular sections, the historical versions amended by the 1967 referendum and the present versions.

The referendum held on 27 May 1967 involved three questions, two of which concerned the only two specific references made to Aboriginal people in the Constitution. The first question, referred to as the 'nexus question', is in Section 24 of the Australian Constitution, which required that the number of members in the House of Representatives be as near as possible to twice the numbers of members in the Senate. This section has the purpose of preventing the overwhelming of the Senate's power in the case of a joint sitting following a double dissolution election. The question was:

> Do you approve the proposed law for the alteration of the Constitution entitled 'An Act to alter the Constitution so that the number of members of the House of Representatives may be increased without necessarily increasing the number of Senators'?

This question was rejected by the Australian voters and did not achieve a majority of states in favour. The second question concerned two clauses, Section 127 and Section 51 (xxvi), which were the only references to Aboriginal people in the Constitution:

> 51. The Parliament shall, subject to this Constitution, have power to make laws for the peace, order, and good government of the Commonwealth with respect to:– … (xxvi) The people of any race, other than the aboriginal people in any State, for whom it is necessary to make special laws.

> 127. In reckoning the numbers of the people of the Commonwealth, or of a State or other part of the Commonwealth, aboriginal natives should not be counted.
>
> The question was:
>
> Do you approve the proposed law for the alteration of the Constitution entitled 'An Act to alter the Constitution' so as to omit certain words relating to the people of the Aboriginal race in any state so that Aboriginals are to be counted in reckoning the population?

In Horsham, reading this aloud had an effect even more galvanising than on my young combatant in Brunswick. Instead of shocked silence, there were outbursts of protest and disappointment. This was 'not what we voted for in 1967', one said. Several of the older people in the room explained that they had voted for Aboriginal rights in the 1967 referendum. It was revealed that they were retired and enjoyed living in the country, but remained in contact with their friends and colleagues in high places in Canberra, suggesting perhaps they were once public servants. Another stated, 'We thought we were voting for racial equality.' 'I had no idea that the Constitution said this.' They spoke fondly about the Aboriginal and other activists of the 1960s who had successfully waged the 'Vote Yes' campaign. Their campaign lasted for ten years.[2]

All states voted in favour and 90.77 per cent of voters supported the amendment. It is said to be the most successful referendum in Australian history. A critical factor in the success of the 1967 referendum was that the 'No' case was not developed or prosecuted as part of the referendum campaign.

---

2. For a brief account of this history, see www.indigenousrights.net.au; see also Bain Attwood and Andrew Markus, *The 1967 Referendum: Race, Power and the Australian Constitution*, Aboriginal Studies Press, Canberra, 2007 (previously published as *The 1967 Referendum, or, When Aborigines Didn't Get the Vote*, 1997).

In 1967 Australians almost unanimously agreed that the words 'other than the aboriginal people in any state' should be deleted so that, like all other Australians, the Australian Parliament could make legislation for them. By amending the 'race power', to remove the words excluding Aboriginal people from the clause at Section 51, which sets out the powers of the Parliament to make laws, it enabled the Parliament to discriminate against us. It now reads:

> **Part V—Powers of the Parliament**
> 51. The Parliament shall, subject to this Constitution, have power to make laws for the peace, order, and good government of the Commonwealth with respect to: ... (xxvi) The people of any race for whom it is deemed necessary to make special laws.

After the expression of the racialist undertow by Pauline Hanson, and the popular acceptance of her flawed logic, the removal of the 'race power' may yet prove to be the most difficult challenge in reforming our Constitution.

The silence about a tricky constitutional issue

At this point in the discussion, my impulse was to 'stick to the script,' that is to say, remain silent, about certain issues not mentioned in the discussion paper issued by the expert panel. Before I can explain this, I need to outline the propositions agreed on by the expert panel (to the extent that the complex of views of such a group can be represented accurately in such a document). The numbering of the ideas about how to change the Constitution may give the impression that the preference of the expert panel members is for a 'statement of recognition' and/or a 'statement of values' in a preamble to the Constitution, and a preamble without any legal consequence.

'Idea 1. Statement of Recognition' might involve recognition in a preamble of 'Aboriginal and Torres Strait Islander peoples', distinct cultural identities, prior ownership and custodianship of their lands and waters. This is followed by 'Idea 2. Statement of Recognition in the body of the Constitution', which seems straightforward but may not be; and 'Idea 3. Statement of Values in a preamble'. This last proposition has been formulated by members of the panel as a strategy for dealing with those who fear that the Constitution would no longer recognise them if it recognised Aboriginal people. Shades of Pauline Hanson.

The discussion paper states that this third option would involve 'recognition of Aboriginal and Torres Strait Islander peoples alongside a description of the Australian people's fundamental values, such as a commitment to democratic beliefs, the rule of law, gender equality, and acknowledgement of freedoms, rights and responsibilities'. It is also suggested that this statement could be 'similar to the pledge that new citizens are required to make when they become naturalised Australians'. This approach was adopted by Queensland in its constitution in 2010. In all the state constitutions that recognise Indigenous people, there is a clause that specifically states that no legal meaning will attach to such recognition.

A statement may have legal consequences, depending in part on form and content and the panel has sought legal advice on this. The expert panel has asked for contributions from the public on a statement that might be included in the Constitution. The expert panel's discussion paper goes on to elaborate the other ideas, only some of which are dealt with here. The paper states:

> *Many people, including Aboriginal and Torres Strait Islander representatives, believe that the amendment to the Constitution could and should go beyond a Statement of Recognition or Statement of Values and seek to address the potential for racial discrimination and lack of equality that they believe still exists in the Constitution. A final idea (Idea 7) contemplates inserting agreement-making powers between the Commonwealth and Aboriginal or Torres Strait Islander Australian communities in the Constitution.*

What the proponents of the Statement of Values or recognition proposal know very well, but fail to mention, is that the fate of the referendum proposal for a republic in 1999 involved a preamble.

It was drafted by the poet Les Murray, who had been appointed by John Howard, but whose language was so offensive to women and Indigenous people, that the only Aboriginal senator, Aden Ridgeway, was brought in to rewrite it. In any case, the question on this preamble to the Constitution was unsuccessful, achieving less than 39.3 per cent of the national vote.

It is when I came to the matter that many constitutional lawyers and politicians would prefer to keep in the Constitution—the 'race power'—that my script became unmanageable. Much of the following is what cannot be said to the usually kind and thoughtful people who have been consulted by us expert panel members. The simple question of whether to recognise Indigenous people in the Constitution would become lost in a maze of issues and obstacles of a constitutional, drafting and political nature.

The race power, preambles, silence and memory loss

In 1998 the federal government used its 'race power' to implement John Howard's so-called '10-point Wik plan' to extinguish native title in all pastoral leases; it also used it to allow the Hindmarsh Island Bridge in South Australia to be built. The Ngarrindjeri women, who asserted that they are custodians of a sacred site on the island affected by the bridge proposal, lodged a case in the High Court seeking to overturn that legislation.

The central issue, answered by the six Justices sitting on the High Court, in the Hindmarsh Island case, is whether the 'race power' can be used to pass laws to the detriment of Aboriginal people or whether it can only be used to pass laws for their benefit. As Justice Callinan removed himself from the Bench in this case because of his previous involvement in the matter, the answers provided by the remaining six Justices do not clarify the matter sufficiently to provide guidelines for other legislation. While it was acknowledged that Australia's Constitution was conceived with racist purposes, two Justices found that governments could not act with manifest abuse of power, and one, Kirby, found that no act could be racially discriminatory. The other three found that legislation enacted by a state could be amended. Another view is that a majority on the High Court found that the Constitution permitted laws to be made to the detriment of the people of any race—at least that is the interpretation of the judgment followed by the Howard government. This is a subject that the expert panel would prefer not to discuss for fear that the shock jocks and opinion columnists who generated public hysteria about Aboriginal 'women's business' during the Hindmarsh Island case may take up the cudgels again.

However, there is no unanimity among the expert panel members on these matters. Megan Davis is an Indigenous constitutional lawyer and legal academic with a sound grasp of the Australian Constitution and its failure to acknowledge the existence of Aboriginal and Torres Strait Islander peoples. Like many others, I agree with her on the most significant issue to be put to a referendum on the question of whether or not to recognise Indigenous Australians in the Constitution. Ten years ago, after reading the work of constitutional lawyer George Williams, I advocated in my Professorial Oration and the Centenary of Federation Alfred Deakin Lecture that the 'race power' should be removed. Davis puts it this way: 'One of the strongest cases for constitutional change is deleting or amending the races power. It is unacceptable for a modern liberal democracy like Australia to have a races power in the Constitution.'[3] She argues that it is most important to include a non-discrimination and equality provision in the Constitution and that this proposal is more likely to succeed at a referendum than other proposals.

This is in contrast to the mealy-mouthed proposal for a preamble that acknowledges the existence of Indigenous Australians but would have no legal effect. Legal advice to the panel members notes that a preamble 'may not be designed to explain anything that follows in the Constitution, given it would be inserted long after the rest of the Constitution was enacted'.[4]

3. Megan Davis is a professor of Law and director, Indigenous Law Centre, Faculty of Law, University of New South Wales.
4. Unpublished document in the hands of the author.

It could be an introduction to the Constitution with reference to historical fact and other issues, such as symbolic statements about the nation and its purported characteristics, such as 'values'. Both Julia Gillard and John Howard, the prime ministers who have supported constitutional reform to recognise Indigenous Australians, have stated their preference for a preamble.

> **Prime Minister Julia Gillard, 2010:**
> Now is the right time to take the next step and to recognise in the Australian constitution the first peoples of our nation; now is the right time to take that next step to build trust and respect, and we certainly believe that constitutional recognition is an important step to building trust and respect, it's an important step to building and acknowledging that the first peoples of our nation have a unique and special place in our nation.

> **Former prime minister John Howard, 2007, during the election:**
> My goal is to see a new Statement of Reconciliation incorporated into the preamble of the Australian Constitution … I would seek to enlist wide community support for a 'Yes' vote. I would hope and aim to secure the sort of overwhelming vote achieved 40 years ago at the 1967 Referendum. If approached in the right spirit, I believe this is both realistic and achievable.

'What will ultimately matter is the wording used,' the lawyers have advised. Further, as George Williams has pointed out, it would be more difficult to find the wording for such a preamble that would be agreed to by a majority. The left might oppose a preamble that used the word 'settle' rather than 'invasion' and the right might oppose a preamble that referred to the children forcibly removed from their families as the 'stolen generations'. Writers such as Keith Windschuttle and his supporters would oppose any reference to the history of violence against the first Australians. Fundamentalists from various religions might oppose a preamble that failed to mention a monotheistic god. Then we have the problem that some are arguing for a 'statement of values' in a preamble. The idea of a universally accepted 'value' is notoriously slippery.

We should not find it odd that the proponents of the preamble option rarely suggest that such 'values' include respect for human rights. The text of the preamble proposed in the 1999 referendum on the question of a republic should remind us of the danger of this course. The final version read:

> With hope in God, the Commonwealth of Australia is constituted as a democracy with a federal system of Government to serve the common good.
>
> We the Australian people commit ourselves to this Constitution proud that our national unity has been forged by Australians from many ancestries;
>
> never forgetting the sacrifices of all who defended our country and our liberty in time of war;
>
> upholding freedom, tolerance, individual dignity and the rule of law;
>
> honouring Aborigines and Torres Strait Islanders, the nation's first people, for their deep kinship with their lands and for their ancient and continuing cultures which enrich the life of our country;
>
> recognising the nation-building contribution of generations of immigrants; mindful of our responsibility to protect our unique natural environment;
>
> supportive of achievement as well as equality of opportunity for all; and valuing independence as dearly as the national spirit which binds us together in both adversity and success.

'With hope in God'? What if you are a Buddhist or Aboriginal, or a follower of some other non-monotheistic religion, or an atheist, or an agnostic? This Howard-era howler aside, and to give Les Murray his due, there are some nice turns of phrase, such as 'many ancestries'.

Some proponents of the preamble concept do not agree that the 'race power' is an unacceptable provision in the constitution of a liberal democracy. It has been proposed that the clause remain so that legislation could be passed by the Parliament to deal with matters of national security and other 'just in case' scenarios.

How it is proposed to identify the 'race' of any particular person is never explained, however, nor how abuses of power might be prevented if officials had a free hand. Some people speak in mumbled tones about 'Muslims'. When I point out to them that 'Muslim' is not a racial category but a religious one, they are strangely silent. An unknown number of Australian citizens and immigrants with permanent residency status have been held unlawfully in immigration detention centres by the federal government over the past ten years. There were a few high-profile cases involving Cornelia Rau, a German citizen with Australian permanent residency detained for months in a prison as a suspected illegal immigrant; Vivian Solon, an Australian who was unlawfully removed to the Philippines by the Department of Immigration and Multicultural and Indigenous Affairs in July 2001; and 'Mr T', a mentally ill Australian citizen originally from Vietnam who was detained three times. The federal government accepted liability for these cases, but the threat of such abuse of power by officials is a relevant issue in considering the 'race power', the findings of the High Court in the Hindmarsh Island case, and the question of how we, the citizens, would want our Constitution to read as the foundational document of the nation.

Section 25 Read Aloud

Section 25, which was not the subject of the questions put in the 1967 referendum, and which remains in the Constitution, is more difficult to comprehend. I read this aloud to the group at Horsham:

> 25. For the purposes of the last section, if by the law of any State all persons of any race are disqualified from voting at

elections for the more numerous House of the Parliament of the State, then, in reckoning the number of the people of the State or of the Commonwealth, persons of that race resident in that State shall not be counted.

According to constitutional law scholar Brian Costar, this 'obscure, puzzling, contested but largely neglected Section 25 of the constitution ... mandates not who should have the vote but how many House Representatives' divisions each state shall be entitled.' Some constitutional lawyers assert that it is 'a mild deterrent to discrimination on racial grounds', while others view it as 'odious and outmoded'. Costar's thinking on this clarifies the debate for those of us who are not trained in the dark arts of legal jousting:

> to assume that the Section has been voided by the passage of legislation deeming discrimination on the grounds of race illegal would be false for the simple reason that such legislation may be repealed or amended by parliament. Furthermore, the right to vote is not explicitly enshrined in the constitution and Section 30 has been interpreted as giving to the Commonwealth parliament the authority (subject to the constitution) to determine its electoral procedures. We can only speculate as to whether any future legislation restricting the right to vote on grounds of race, gender, class, etc. would be held by the High Court to be in breach of the 'directly chosen by the people' words of Sections 7 and 24. Given that uncertainty, a case can be mounted that Section 25 should be retained until the right of citizens to vote is unambiguously guaranteed in the written constitution or firmly embedded by judicial review in the unwritten one.[5]

5. Brian Costar, '"Odious and Outmoded"? Race and Section 25 of the Constitution', in J Chesterman and D Philips (Eds.), *Selective Democracy: Race, Gender and the Australian Vote*, Melbourne Publishing Group, 2003, 1 ed., pp. 89–99.

However, to bring the matter to a close, Costar, among many others, supports its removal for at least two reasons. He cites Justice Gibbs, who 'held in McKinlay's case (1975) that Section 25 could be interpreted in such a manner as to deny the franchise to certain people on the grounds of race. Second, "race" is now such a discredited biological and social construct that its citation in a democratic constitution is undesirable.'[6]

The odds: how to lose a referendum question

The most difficult work for the panel members is the development of the concepts for a referendum question or questions as to how the Constitution could be amended to recognise Indigenous Australians. We are required to report to the Prime Minister on the form of constitutional change and approach to a referendum likely to obtain widespread support, and the implications of any proposed changes to the Constitution. This has involved seeking advice from constitutional law experts.[7]

In her paper 'Indigenous Rights and the Constitution: Making the Case for Constitutional Reform', Davis succinctly recounts some of the background to the appointment of the Expert Panel on Constitutional Recognition of Indigenous Australians. Two previous prime ministers committed themselves to constitutional reform for such recognition: John Howard and Kevin Rudd.

> Recently, Prime Minister Kevin Rudd revived John Howard's 2007 pre-election proposal to amend the preamble to the Australian Constitution to recognise Aboriginal and Torres Strait Islander people. Rudd's announcement was prompted after Yolgnu and Bininj elders presented him with a Statement of Intent at the Federal Government's Community Cabinet meeting in Yirrkala, Northern Territory. Prior to that,

6. Costar, '"Odious and Outmoded"?'.
7. See Constitutional Recognition of Indigenous Australians, Expert Panel Terms of Reference, www.dss.gov.au/sites/default/files/documents/05_2012/constitutional_recognition6.pdf

constitutional reform had been raised by participants in the Indigenous stream at the Federal Government's 2020 Summit in Canberra and at the Barunga Festival in the Northern Territory. In fact, it has been a perennial focus of unfinished business between Indigenous peoples and the state.[8]

There are two dilemmas in this worthy goal, however, as Davis has noted. One is the desire of conservatives and naïve liberals to keep the 'race power':

> Given the presence of section 51 (xxvi)—the races power—in the Constitution that permits discriminatory legislation on the basis of race, it is a strange symmetry indeed to have a symbolic showcase like the preamble lauding the first peoples of Australia as being important to the Australian state, yet an operative provision that permits discrimination on the basis of race. Moreover, only eight out of 44 referendums have been successful in Australia's history and the difference between success and failure has been bipartisan support.[9]

There is also the fear, based on views expressed to date, that '... it will be acceptable as long as the Australian state doesn't have to give anything up. As Tony Abbott argued about the preamble proposal, he is supportive as long it is done "without in any way detracting from the role of the rest of us".'[10]

Given this state of affairs, there are some of us who would want to include among the concepts submitted to the Prime Minister at the end of this year, that a referendum not be held on this question if the outcome most likely is a preamble without legal effect, or Clayton's recognition of Indigenous people in the Constitution, along with the retention of the 'race power'. Davis notes in this

---

8. Megan Davis, 'Indigenous Rights and the Constitution: Making the Case for Constitutional Reform', papers.ssrn.com/sol3/papers.cfm?abstract_id=1402449
9. Davis, 'Indigenous Rights'.
10. 'Coalition concerned over Indigenous rights in the Constitution', *The World Today*, 24 July 2011, cited in Davis, 'Indigenous Rights'.

regard that 'the public conversation about the preamble proposal to recognise Aboriginal and Torres Strait Islander peoples is based on' the premise 'that recognition is acceptable as long as it has no effect or creates no legal rights'.[11]

There are several reasons for my own hesitation about a referendum proceeding on this matter. The obvious one is that, should the referendum question be defeated by the voters, it would not be put before the Australian voters again in my own lifetime. There is also the disappointment and bitterness that such a defeat would engender throughout Aboriginal Australia. Another reason is that to set the standard too low—to appear to be complicit in a referendum question that proposed only a preamble with no legal effect—would be, even if successful, a slap in the face for many Aboriginal Australians whose aspirations are for so much more. Take the Yirrkala Petition, for example, the latest in a litany of requests for respect for Aboriginal people from the Australian polity:

> **The Yirrkala Petition**
> We, the united clans of east Arnhem Land, through our most senior dilak 'elders', do humbly petition you, the 26th Prime Minister of Australia, in your capacity as first amongst equals in the Australian Parliament, and as chief advisor to Her Majesty Queen Elizabeth the Second, to secure within the Australian Constitution the recognition and protection of our full and complete right to:
> our way of life in all its diversity;
> our property, being the lands and waters of east Arnhem Land;
> economic independence, through the proper use of the riches of our lands and waters in all their abundance and wealth;
> control of our lives and responsibility for our children's future.
> These rights are self-evident. These rights are fundamental to our place within the Australian nation. We ask for your leadership to have the Commonwealth Parliament start

11. Davis, 'Indigenous Rights'.

the process of recognition of these rights through serious constitutional reform.[12]

That this process of considering constitutional reform would not achieve the goals of the Yolngu or similar Aboriginal goals elsewhere is not by itself a reason for delaying the referendum. The goals of the Yolngu would be more easily achieved by legislation and by continuing to reach agreements such as the mining agreement with Rio Tinto Alcan.

The process of a referendum

The timing of the referendum is also a strategic matter for the panel to consider. To amend the Constitution, a bill proposing the amendment must first be submitted to and passed by the Parliament. Between two and six months later the proposal can then be put to Australian voters at a referendum. For an amendment to succeed a 'double majority' is required. This means that a majority of voters nationwide need to vote 'yes' and a majority of voters in a majority of the six states must also vote 'yes' (territory votes are counted in the national total but not in any state figure). This timetable would appear to be unachievable given the state of national politics as I write. It was, after all, the Greens members of the House of Representatives and the Senate, who, in negotiating the terms of power when a 'hung' Parliament was the election outcome in 2010, extracted a commitment from Julia Gillard to hold a referendum on Indigenous recognition within this term of Parliament. The Greens politicians are amenable to altering this time table. It is conceivable, however, that the opposition would oppose the referendum question and argue a 'No' case,[13]

12. As cited in Galarrwuy Yunupiŋu, 'Tradition, Truth and Tomorrow', *The Monthly*, no. 41, pp. 32–40.

13. As explained earlier, the 1967 referendum is said to be the most successful referendum in Australian history, in part because a 'No' case was not developed or prosecuted. That there should be unanimous support from the political parties is critical to this matter being successful. In *People Power*, Williams and Hume show that the successful referenda—only eight of forty-four—have had in common the absence of a 'No' case.

or argue for a limpid preamble, as the election cycle closed and the likelihood of a landslide vote against the Gillard government, given the concerns about manufacturing industry, the carbon tax, the mining resource tax and the state of the economy—not to mention asylum seeker policy.

This is why the book *People Power: The Future and History of the Referendum in Australia* by constitutional lawyers George Williams and David Hume is essential reading at this time. Among their many findings based on detailed research of referenda voting, questions, patterns of voting and many other matters are several crucial points to be considered in framing a question for a referendum on Indigenous recognition. For instance, no referendum question has passed without bipartisan support. A 'Yes' campaign that is mismanaged, weak, smothered by other priorities, or not strongly supported by the government detracts from the chance of success. A referendum question that contains too many amendments to the Constitution has less chance of succeeding.[14] State governments can influence voting intentions, and are unconstrained in what they can say about referendum proposals. Three dissenting states can adversely affect strong overall national support as well as reduce the likelihood of recording the support of a majority of the states as required by the Constitution.[15]

Another critical matter is the cost of a referendum, estimated at present at about $70 million. This is why the preference of any government in our straitened economic circumstances would be to hold a referendum at the same time as a federal election. The next federal election, when voters consider whether or not to vote for the Gillard government again, is not the time to hold this referendum.

Labor's record of success at referenda is one from twenty-five attempts. This reflects Labor's history of proposing more referenda than any other party and a lack of bipartisan support

14. Williams and Hume, *People Power*, pp. 216, 211–14.
15. Williams and Hume, *People Power*, pp. 218–20

for Labor's proposals.[16] Williams and Hume list five keys to a successful referendum: bipartisanship, popular ownership, popular education about the proposal issue, sound and sensible proposals, and funding and neutrality issues (or bipartisanship and an absence of party preference for constitutional change) in the process. Reading their book has made me hesitate. Should we wait until after a popular education campaign on the complicated issues involved in the question of Indigenous recognition, one that would need to be at least as persuasive as the ten-year campaign leading up to the 1967 referendum by a coalition of Aboriginal activists and other Australians concerned about Aboriginal rights? At this stage, I am inclined to recommend that we wait.

Perhaps the most important work of the expert panel will be our encouragement of, and providing information to Reconciliation Australia to wage such a campaign in the coming years. If a referendum on this question does proceed now, the outcome is likely to be no more than a change to the preamble. It is our historical burden that we could expect nothing like the acknowledgement of aboriginal people in the Canadian Constitution Act 1982:

> **Part II—Rights of the Aboriginal Peoples of Canada**
> 35. (1) The existing aboriginal and treaty rights of the aboriginal peoples of Canada are hereby recognized and affirmed.

If I could return to Horsham and continue the conversation with the people I met there at the consultative meeting, I would want to say all these things and ask them what they think about them. They are not the people that some of our members and advisers fear; they are not the people who listen to Alan Jones and head to Cronulla Beach to have a 'race riot'. It is through explaining these issues to these kind and thoughtful people and others like them in far-flung parts of Australia that I have come to understand the difficulty of constitutional change, the problem of unintended consequence, and the invisible power of the idea of

16. Williams and Hume, *People Power*, pp. 226–7.

'race' in our body politic. But so have other expert panel members. At our last meeting, it was agreed not to proceed with the idea of a Statement of Values, and more serious thought was given to the 'race power' than in earlier meetings.

There is a logical approach to delineating the question or questions that we would put to the Prime Minister in our final report, and the logic is one that confronts the problem of 'race'. How could it be defined in the twenty-first century, hundreds of years after it was first developed in the imperial era as the British and Europeans ventured across the seas and discovered people of colour and classified them as the 'inferior races'. How, when the human genome has been thoroughly investigated and mapped, proving convincingly that we are one species with millions of variations, not just the crude categories of 'race' developed to justify colonialism: Negroid, Mongoloid, Caucasoid, and my favourite, Australoid.

The danger in saying all this is that a venal politician could insist that the referendum proceed, precisely so that it would fail at the polls. The balance of saying these things against silence is then not the question. The question is: how can we sustain the opportunity for a referendum on this question to be put to the Australian people and the states in circumstances that are not riven by 'dog whistle' issues in the racialist Australian politics that arise with each electoral season?

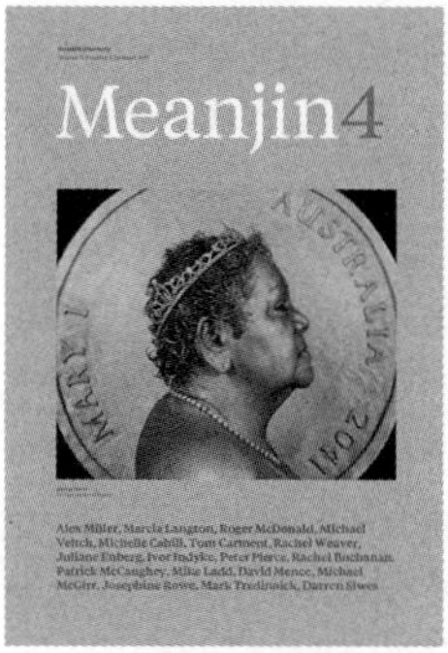

In 2011 **Marcia Langton**, of the Yiman and Bidjara nations, held the Foundation Chair of Australian Indigenous Studies at the University of Melbourne. Her work in anthropology and her advocacy of Aboriginal rights was recognised in 1993 when she was made a member of the Order of Australia. Today Professor Langton is also an Associate Provost at the University. She has advised several Australian governments as a member of the Expert Panel on Constitutional Recognition of Indigenous Australians, and is the author of many books including *First Australians* and *The Welcome to Country Handbook*. Langton is co-author of *First Knowledges Law: The Way of the Ancestors* and *Dhoombak Goobgoowana: A History of Indigenous Australia and the University of Melbourne, Vol. 1.*

Are we a nation of bastards?

Manning Clark

Meanjin 35.2 Winter 1976

TWO DAYS AFTER the dismissal of the Whitlam Government by the Governor-General I decided to drive past Parliament House searching as usual for what my children affectionately call 'Dad's historical atmosphere', and sometimes less affectionately 'Dad's excursions down memory lane'. This time two things caught my eye. One was the proclamation pinned on to the door of Parliament House proclaiming that the Governor-General had dissolved Parliament. The other was a booth on the lawns opposite Parliament House in which a man was selling souvenirs and post-cards. I wondered then whether the first portended the end not just of a particular parliament, but the end quite soon of parliamentary government, by which I mean the responsibility of the government to the group with a majority in the House of Representatives, the people's house, and the responsibility of the House of Representatives to the people. I considered, too, whether the appearance of that small shop perhaps meant the return of the 'money changers' to our temple of politics—whether an age of the accountants and the book-keepers was going to have a final brief, stormy period in our history before the angry young men of the Left swept them all into the dust-bin of our history.

These were gloomy thoughts. But a few weeks later on 13 December, when I happened to be in Derby in England, a town where the meanness of the English governing class sank to an all-time low, as DH Lawrence was fond of pointing out, a fruity noncommittal English voice confined my worst fears.

The Australian electors, bombarded for months by stories of the incompetence, the bungling, the corruption, the jobbery &c, &c, &c, of the Whitlam Government, had put back into government in our country a group of men who had the moral values of a troop of Boy Scouts, and the economic and social values which were rapidly disappearing off the face of the earth except in countries such as South Africa, New Zealand, Rhodesia, and possibly Spain. During the ensuing painful days I read, part in anger, part in agreement, editorials in the serious English, French and German papers which told their readers that 'the ocker', or the 'Ugly Australian' was still in charge 'down under'—that the 'ocker' had destroyed the man who, like Prometheus, had been trying to teach Australians that they could steal fire from heaven, that they were capable of better things.

The one great consolation in this time of shame for our country, in this period when we threatened once again to pledge ourselves to the past and to defend the old order of society, when a Prime Minister should glory in an idea of resurrecting the past rather than leading us into the future, was to know that other people were also shocked, bewildered, and even frightened about our prospects. They were fearful, that is, that we, too, like the other reactionary societies in South-East Asia and elsewhere, were about to be wiped off the face of the earth, that the peoples of the world, carried away as they were and are by a hope of better things for mankind, would not let us survive—that we always had been intruders here, and now, like the South Africans and the Rhodesians, and possibly much later, the white New Zealanders, we would either be eliminated and disappear off the face of the earth as though we had never been, or, mercifully, and with quite undeserved charity, be given a chance to return to the place whence we came, that precious grave-yard of the contemporary world, the United Kingdom and Western Europe.

The pity of it was that there were people in our society with ideas on what should be done. One was Charles Birch, who has been Challis Professor of Biology in the University of Sydney since 1960. In 1975, that year in which the money-changers and accountants—the men with a passion for interest rates seemingly as dionysiacal as the passion of some men for 'other things'—were to have their terrible day of triumph, a man dressed in the clothes of a bygone age, dismissed one of the greatest prime ministers this country has ever had, and then had the colossal effrontery later to tell the Australian people that history would vindicate his action. It was in that year that Charles Birch published his brilliant book on what mankind in general, and Australians in particular, had to do quite quickly if human life was to survive on this planet.

There was nothing startling or novel in what he had to say. The great distinction of the author, indeed his great gift, was that he combined within himself the mind of the scientist, the soul of the poet, and the gift of prophecy—by which I mean that power to see into the heart of what is wrong in any generation, and denounce that great evil with true moral passion. It was and is a magnificent book—a tract for the times, and a human appeal to all of us to 'gird our loins'. Birch has both common sense and a perception of the mystery at the heart of things. His book is all about how what we have generally understood by the term civilisation can survive.

The interesting thing, reading it down here on the far south coast of New South Wales where that other secular humanist, James Cook, first saw 'smook' in our country, and knew that the country was inhabited, is that no leader of either the Liberal or the National Country Party ever made one remark over the years during which Professor Birch was collecting his material to warrant inclusion in the book. The Labor Leaders, as Professor Birch points out, did have ideas. Gough Whitlam and Tom Uren appointed Mr Justice Hope to collect material and write a report on the 'National Estate'. That document stands as a monument of what must be done. It is now threatened with becoming a museum piece, or one of those documents historians of future generations will point to as examples of what might have been done if Labor had been given a chance to preserve Old Australia, and marry it, as it were, to the Australia of 1975.

But Labor was not given that chance—and hence Donald Horne's magnificent denunciation of the 'men in black', men with the hearts of walnuts, who were quite determined to use every card in the pack to stop Gough Whitlam and his government helping Australia get to 1975 before the progressive and hopeful part of the world took the next step forward. Gough Whitlam himself has called Horne's book the greatest philippic ever written in this country. Perhaps you can gauge the measure of its achievement, and the very high level of its performance, by the zeal with which the 'heart dimmers' and 'head shrinkers' have attempted either to belittle or to misrepresent what he has had to say.

It is a book about many things. It is a brilliant analysis of Kerr's possible reasons and motives for dismissing Whitlam. Donald Horne does not doubt for one moment that the Australian Constitution confers on the Governor-General the power to dismiss a Ministry or a Minister. The Constitution does not mention the circumstances under which the Governor-General should exercise that power; that is to say the Constitution lays down no guide lines. Donald Horne also points out that the Australian Constitution is based on an uneasy, clumsy union of two principles of government—the federal principle, and the responsible government principle.

As every student of our constitutional history knows, after somewhat tedious debates the Founding Fathers seemed to decide that wherever the federal principle collided with the responsible government principle, then the responsible government principle must take precedence. That was what Whitlam was arguing all through those agonising days in October and November after the 'men in black', and their much-bedizened women, went into their huddle at the Lakeside Hotel and answered, for themselves, Lenin's great question for any seekers of power: 'What's To Be Done?' I remember sitting on a sofa in the lobby at the Lakeside Hotel that Sunday afternoon, and sensing, my God, they are going to do it, they are going to use the powers (ill-defined as Donald Horne so rightly insists) to get rid of Gough Whitlam. But how will they do it? I did not guess then, nor did any of those with whom I discussed the question, guess that the Liberals only had to follow the advice of the old evangelical hymn: 'Ask the Governor-General to help you, comfort, strengthen and keep you. He is willing to aid you. He will carry you through'.

It is just because the Governor-General used his constitutional powers—those powers most people thought belonged to the days of yesteryear—to serve the interests of the Liberals rather than Labor that the men of good-will, men who may have been bothered by all those errors human frailty and folly had caused Whitlam and Co. to fall prey to, were filled with a righteous indignation. Similarly, it was the Governor-General's complete failure to let Whitlam, Hayden, Enderby and McClelland know the way in which his mind was moving which led to the charge of treachery against him. Those familiar with the human heart know that the memory of treachery lives on longer than any other human injury or evil.

Some cling to the hope that when passions die down history will be kinder to the Governor-General than his present attackers. Some even say that it is cowardly to criticise his action. So perhaps one should add that the history of mankind is written by the victors. As it seems now quite certain that 1975 was an aberration, a temporary halt in the people's march to victory, the Governor-General and his beneficiaries can expect little mercy from the historians of the people. It may be that in one hundred years' time some research worker in the early days of the 'People's Government' will come across Kerr's letter to Whitlam of 11 November, 1975, and see that there was a teeny-weeny case for Kerr. But, if one may judge from what happens to historians in the People's democracies of today, that historian would not be given the paper on which to write his defence, let alone the opportunity to publish it. The people's historians judge their opponents harshly. So there is no hope for the Governor-General from them: maybe God will judge him and all of us less harshly, but, according to Nietzsche, God is dead.

What is clear is that those historians of the future will find in Birch and Horne men of genuine moral passion. Their works will live on as testimony that we are not all 'bastards', not all 'ockers' who were out for a 'quick quid', and not all driven by some mad hatred against intellectuals and dole bludgers—all those people Whitlam tried to help. Now we will see what terrible things are in store for the creatures when God seems to have forgotten. Now for a while the world here will belong again to the men of brawn, the men with the terrible delusion that they are the only ones who work. So if the boy from Balmain had really wanted to impress the historians of the future, he might have been wiser to read, mark, learn and inwardly digest the moral of *Great Expectations*. The Joe Gargerys of his younger days would have proved that they, rather than Sir Garfield Barwick, are the children of light.

The books discussed in this article are Charles Birch, *Confronting the Future* (Penguin, Melbourne 1975) pp. 360, $2.95; Donald Horne, *Death of the Lucky Country* (Penguin, Melbourne 1976) pp. 115, $1.50.

By 1976, **Manning Clark** (1915–1991) had won the Fellowship of Australian Writers' Moomba Book Award, the Henry Lawson Arts Award, the Australian Literature Society Gold Medal and The Age Non-Fiction Award, was a Foundation Fellow of the Australian Academy of the Humanities, and had just been made a Companion to the Order of Australia. He went on to win the New South Wales Premier's Literary Award, and was awarded honorary doctorates by the Universities of Melbourne, Newcastle and Sydney. His six-volume *A History of Australia* (1962–1987) profoundly influenced scholarship. In 1980 Clark was named Australian of the Year.

A law of one's own?

Feminist perspectives on equality and the law

Hilary Charlesworth

Meanjin 51.1 Autumn 1992

THE TRADITIONAL ACCOUNT of the law has had remarkable power and resilience. This account, which I imbibed as a law student in the 1970s, is that the law is a 'seamless web', a system through which the golden thread of rationality runs, occasionally imperfect but always perfectible. Liberal theories about law, for example, assign law a special role that is separate from politics. This distinction invests law with authority: while politics concerns the negotiable and subjective, law deals in objective truths and standards that can be uncovered through the application of rational, abstract principles. The empire of law, says Ronald Dworkin, relies on arguments of principle rather than policy.[1] The basis of its authority is captured in the motto of the Western legal system, carved in stone on the walls of Harvard Law School: 'Not Under Man, But Under God and Law'.

This dominant theory of law as inherently objective and impartial, a scientific enterprise, has not gone unchallenged. The Legal Realists, Marxist scholars and the Critical Legal Studies movement, for example, have exposed in a variety of ways the intensely human and political agenda of much legal

1. Ronald Dworkin, *Law's Empire* (Belknap Press, Cambridge, Mass., 1986).

decision-making.[2] It is only recently that law has been subjected to a feminist critique that takes sexual equality as its focus. Feminist legal scholars have drawn on some of the existing critiques of law, but they have refined and redirected them.[3] The 1980s have seen a rich feminist legal literature develop. Some of it focuses on particular areas of law, from family law and rape to corporations and taxation.[4] Other feminist scholarship has proposed more general theoretical analyses of law, drawing on feminist writing in philosophy, literature and psychology. Much feminist legal scholarship is from the United States and displays particular concern with the American constitutional and legal system. The growing numbers of feminist lawyers in Australia, Canada and Europe have been influenced by this work, but have generally tended to pursue less local concerns.

In common with feminist work in other disciplines, the feminist project in law is pluralist: it has many methods and many voices. I will examine various feminist answers to the question of how the law should respond to inequality between the sexes. I describe three categories of responses, although many of the writers whose work I discuss use elements of all three in their analysis of the law's role with respect to sexual inequality. Feminists have also used approaches other than those outlined here to develop legal

---

2. See generally William L Twining, *Karl Llewellyn and the Realist Movement* (Weidenfeld & Nicolson, London, 1973); Hugh Collins, *Marxism and Law* (Clarendon Press, Oxford, 1982); Mark Kelman, *A Guide to Critical Legal Studies* (Harvard University Press, Cambridge, Mass., 1987).
3. For a discussion of the relationship between Critical Legal Studies and feminist legal thought see Deborah L Rhode, 'Feminist Critical Theories', *Stanford Law Review*, 42 (1990), p. 617, and Robin West, 'Jurisprudence and Gender', *University of Chicago Law Review*, (1988), p. 55.
4. For example, Frances Olsen, 'The Family and the Market: A Study of Ideology and Legal Reform', *Harvard Law Review*, 96 (1983), p. 1497; Christine Boyle, 'Sexual Assault and the Feminist Judge', *Canadian Journal of Women and the Law*, 1 (1985), p. 93; Kathleen A Lahey and Sarah W Salter, 'Corporate Law in Legal Theory and Legal Scholarship: From Classicism to Feminism', *Osgoode Hall Law Journal*, 23.4 (1985), p. 543; Judith Grbich, 'The Position of Women in Family Dealing: the Australian Case', *International Journal of the Sociology of Law*, 15 (1987), p. 309.

strategies to deal with inequality—for example, analysing the operation of the public/private distinction in legal thought.[5]

Equality as sameness

Some feminists accept the language and aims of liberal legal theory, couching many of their arguments in terms of individual rights. They reject any notion that the law should tolerate or recognise intrinsic differences between women and men. This approach characterised the first years of women's legal studies, and has achieved a certain level of acceptance. Legislation and legal doctrines explicitly providing for different standards of treatment to be applied to women and men are much less prevalent today than in the earlier part of this century. Some aspects of modern law in particular jurisdictions, however, continue to sanction discriminatory treatment—for example, legislation giving preference to war veterans in certain civil service positions, effectively precluding women from this work,[6] or legislation creating a presumption that women should not act as executors of estates.[7]

Liberal feminists' strategy is to require the law to fulfil the liberal claims for its objectivity and principled basis. They have worked for reform of the law, dismantling legal barriers to women being treated like men in the public sphere. In the United States, for example, feminists have put great energy into the (still unsuccessful) campaign to insert a guarantee of sexual equality in the Constitution (the 'Equal Rights Amendment'). In Australia the federal and State anti-discrimination laws are a product of this same spirit. Their goal is to achieve equality of treatment in the public areas of paid employment, market services and education.

The insistence that women and men be treated similarly falters when women and men cannot be equated. For example, feminists

5. For example, Katherine O'Donovan, *Sexual Divisions in Law* (Weidenfeld & Nicolson, London, 1985). For an excellent overview of the feminist project in law see Regina Graycar and Jenny Morgan, *The Hidden Gender of Law* (Federation Press, Sydney, 1990).
6. See Personal Administrator v. Feeney, 442 US 256 (1979).
7. See Reed v. Reed, 404 US 71 (1971).

have debated whether the ability to become pregnant should be legally acknowledged as a difference between women and men or regarded as a temporary disability like any other.[8] The absurdity of a limited 'equal treatment' analysis is illustrated by a decision of the United States Supreme Court in a challenge to a Californian law on disability insurance. The law was argued to have violated the equal protection clause of the Constitution because it excluded coverage of disabilities resulting from pregnancy. The Supreme Court rejected the challenge on the grounds that there was no sex-based discrimination because the law was simply distinguishing between 'pregnant persons and non-pregnant persons'.[9] This type of 'equality with a vengeance'[10] does not deliver equality at all.

Some versions of liberal feminism go beyond demands for formal equality and are concerned primarily with equality of outcome. Liberal feminism can be quite compatible with the prohibition of indirect discrimination and the requirement of affirmative action, if these are regarded as temporary measures to counteract inaccurate views that, given the same opportunities, women cannot perform exactly like men.[11] Special treatment is seen as ultimately promoting a neutral outcome.

Apart from this limited acknowledgement of the need for structural change to achieve equality, liberal feminists do not regard the legal system itself as contributing to the inferior position

---

8. For example, Wendy Williams, 'Equality's Riddle: Pregnancy and the Equal Treatment/Special Treatment Debate', *New York University Review of Law and Social Change*, 13 (1985), p. 325; Lucinda Finley, 'Transcending Equality Theory: A Way Out of the Maternity and Workplace Debate', *Columbia Law Review*, 86 (1986), p. 1118.
9. Geduldig v. Aiello, 417 US 484, 497 n. 20 (1974). See also Wimberly v. Labor and Industrial Relations Commission of Missouri, 107 S. Ct 821 (1987), where the US Supreme Court upheld a State law denying unemployment benefits to women out of work because of pregnancy.
10. A term used by Carol Smart in a talk, 'Feminist Jurisprudence', La Trobe University, Victoria, 2 December 1987.
11. Frances Olsen, 'Feminism and Critical Legal Theory: An American Perspective', *International Journal of the Sociology of Law*, 18 (1990), pp. 199–203.

of women. This approach adopts the vocabulary, epistemology and political theory of the law as it currently operates. First, it does not take issue with discrimination that occurs in areas deemed 'private'—for example, the family, religious institutions, private clubs.[12] Secondly, liberal feminism assumes that the law is ultimately rational, impartial and capable of achieving justice if it allows proper individual choice. Yet the interpretation of discrimination legislation in the courts indicates that the (overwhelmingly male) judiciary is reluctant to give a progressive account of the law. Interpretative discretion is usually resolved in favour of the status quo.[13] More problematic still is the androcentric and individualistic nature of the law designed to combat sex discrimination. It provides a remedy to women who attempt to conform to a male model, and offers little to those who do not. In dealing with individual cases of discrimination rather than structural inequality, equal opportunity law can at most solve a limited number of discrete problems. It fails to address the underlying causes of sex discrimination. The principle of equal opportunity, says Nicola Lacey, is 'inadequate to criticize and transform a world in which the distribution of goods is structured along gender lines'. It assumes 'a world of autonomous individuals starting a race or making free choices [and] has no cutting edge against the fact that men and women are simply running different races'.[14]

Equality as difference

Another strand in legal feminism is the acknowledgement of difference, which parallels work in other disciplines that has described, for example, a feminist theology or a women's

12. See Margaret Thornton, *The Liberal Promise: Anti-Discrimination Legislation in Australia* (Oxford University Press, Melbourne, 1990), pp. 103–42.
13. Ibid., pp. 198–206.
14. Nicola Lacey, 'Legislation Against Sex Discrimination: Questions from a Feminist Perspective', *Journal of Law and Society*, 14 (1987), pp. 411, 415, 420.

literature.[15] The work of the American child psychologist Carol Gilligan has had great influence in the development of feminist jurisprudence. In her book *In a Different Voice*, Gilligan reinterprets a dilemma used by her colleague Lawrence Kohlberg to measure moral development in adolescents.[16] Two eleven-year-olds, Jake and Amy, are faced with this dilemma: should Heinz steal a drug that he can't afford to buy in order to save his wife's life? Jake decides that Heinz should steal the drug. He construes the dilemma as a conflict between the values of life and property. He attributes a logical priority to life and thus solves the problem simply, describing the situation as 'Sort of like a math problem with humans'.[17] Jake's resolution is apparently rational and abstract: a judge sentencing Heinz for theft would engage in a similar deductive process and may well give a lighter sentence in recognition that Heinz's choice between two evils was logical. Amy, on the other hand, gives a much more complex answer. Amy is concerned to achieve the best outcome for all affected by the dilemma and to preserve continuing relationships. She places a premium on 'talking it through' to solve the problem. Gilligan terms Jake's method of analysis the 'logic of justice' and Amy's the 'ethic of care'. According to Kohlberg's scheme of six universal stages of moral development, Amy's responses rank a full stage lower in maturity than Jake's.

More generally, Gilligan notes the disparity between women's experience and the representation of human development contained in the psychological literature. The usual interpretation of this disparity was that it indicated problems in women's psychological development. Gilligan turns this analysis on its head

15. For example, Rosemary Ruether, *Sexism and God Talk: Toward a Feminist Theology* (1983), and Elaine Showalter, *A Literature of Their Own: British Novelists from Brontë to Lessing* (Princeton University Press, Princeton, 1977).
16. For example, Lawrence Kohlberg, *The Philosophy of Moral Development: Moral Stages and the Idea of Justice* (Harper & Row, San Francisco, 1981).
17. Carol Gilligan, *In a Different Voice* (Harvard University Press, Cambridge, Mass., 1982).

by arguing that the women's failure to fit existing models of human growth suggests a limitation in the notion of the human condition.

Although Carol Gilligan's conclusions have been criticised by some fellow psychologists,[18] her work has struck a strong chord with many legal feminists. The hypothesis drawn from Gilligan's research is that, just as traditional psychological theories have privileged a male perspective and marginalised women's voices, so too law privileges a male view of the universe. Many feminists have pointed out that law is part of the structure of male domination. Its hierarchical organisation, its adversarial format and its aim of the abstract resolution of competing rights make the law an intensely patriarchal institution. Law represents a very limited aspect of human experience. The language and imagery of the law underscore its maleness: it lays claim to rationality, objectivity and abstractness, characteristics traditionally associated with men, and is defined in contrast to emotion, subjectivity and contextualised thinking, the province of women.[19] The man in the Clapham omnibus, the benchmark of reasonableness invoked in many legal decisions, masquerades as a reasonable *person*.[20]

For legal feminists who describe the orientation of law as fundamentally male, traditional forms of legal reform are of limited utility. Indeed the language of 'equal rights' and 'equal opportunities' and the work of litigation and lobbying tacitly reinforce the basic

18. For example, Debra Nails, 'Social Scientific Sexism: Gilligan's Mismeasure of Man', *Social Research*, 50 (1983), p. 643, and Martha T Mednick, 'On the Politics of Psychological Constructs', *American Psychologist*, 44 (1989), p. 1118.
19. Frances Olsen, op. cit., note 11. Katherine Bartlett has argued that there is no sharp dichotomy between abstract and contextualised reasoning in either legal or feminist method: 'Feminist Legal Methods', *Harvard Law Review*, 103 (1990), pp. 829, 856–8.
20. In a critical review of two Canadian texts on legal remedies, which dealt inadequately with remedies of particular concern to women, Christine Boyle writes: 'I do not think that there is anything wrong with writing books of this nature, but they ought not to make a claim to universality. "Men and the Law" is tolerable as an area of intellectual activity, but not if it is masquerading as "People and the Law".' 'Book Review', *Canadian Bar Review*, 63 (1985), pp. 427, 430–1.

organisation of society.[21] The promise of equality as 'sameness' only gives women access to a world already constituted.[22]

Some feminist jurists have tried to devise methods of introducing a different, women's voice into the legal process. They have questioned the adversarial model of justice that assumes that the right resolution of legal disputes emerges from a contest between two parties, judged by a neutral decision-maker.[23] Some have proposed a model of feminist justice in which the decision-maker goes beyond adjudicating on the cases presented by the parties and can act creatively to avoid a win/loss situation.[24] Mediation and conciliation have been explored as alternatives to litigation. Other feminist lawyers have advocated broader notions of standing to pursue particular claims or wider conceptions of the evidence deemed to be relevant in a particular case. Feminist constitutional rights have been described, based not on the traditional respect for individual autonomy, but on communal values.[25] It has been argued that women judges could bring a 'new humanity' to the decision-making process.[26]

Celebrating the differences between feminine and masculine modes of reasoning in the legal system is not without problems;

21. Diane Polan, 'Toward a Theory of Law and Patriarchy' in David Kairys (ed.), *The Politics of Law* (Pantheon, New York, 1982), pp. 294, 300.
22. Clare Dalton, 'Where We Stand: Observations on the Situation of Feminist Legal Thought', *Berkeley Women's Law Journal*, 3 (1987–88), pp. 1, 5.
23. Lynne Henderson, 'Legality and Empathy', *Michigan Law Review*, 85 (1987), p. 1574.
24. Carrie Menkel-Meadow, 'Portia in a Different Voice: Speculations on a Woman's Lawyering Process', *Berkeley Women's Law Journal*, 1 (1985), p. 39.
25. For example, Kenneth Karst, 'Woman's Constitution', *Duke Law Journal*, 447, p. 1884; Susanna Sherry, 'Civic Virtue and the Feminine Voice in Constitutional Adjudication', *Virginia Law Review*, 72 (1986), p. 543; Catherine J Iorns, 'A Sexed Bill of Rights for New Zealand?', *Victoria University of Wellington Law Review*, 17 (1987), p. 215.
26. Justice Bertha Wilson, 'Will Women Judges Really Make a Difference?'—talk given at Osgoode Hall Law School, York University, Toronto, 8 February 1990. Compare Judith Resnick, 'On the Bias: Feminist Reconsideration of the Aspirations for Judges', *Southern California Law Review*, 61 (1988), p. 1877; Margaret Thornton, op. cit., pp. 143–70.

Gilligan's work has been referred to as a potential Uncle Tom's Cabin for feminist legal theory.[27] No challenge is offered to the mainstream legal system by a 'different voice' appearing in various isolated areas of the law. Indeed, some feminist jurists have pointed to the risk that 'feminine' methods of dispute resolution, such as mediation between parties in an unequal position with respect to skills, information and power, can in fact perpetuate inequality.[28]

The strategy of introducing 'women's voices' into the legal system could also support essentialist theories about women and men and relegate women to a caring, supportive, inferior sphere. It also fails to address the question of the cause of the difference between gendered modes of reasoning. The American lawyer Catharine MacKinnon has questioned the authenticity of the feminine voice documented by Carol Gilligan. The 'feminine', she argues, is defined by a patriarchal culture: 'For women to affirm difference, when difference means dominance, as it does with gender, means to affirm the qualities and characteristics of powerlessness ... when you are powerless, you don't just speak differently. A lot, you don't speak.' 'Take your foot off our necks,' MacKinnon says, 'then we will hear in what tongue women speak.'[29]

Equality as non-domination

A third proposal for dealing legally with sex inequality is to understand it as the product of domination of women by men: inequality as sexual in nature. Catharine MacKinnon has been the most consistent exponent of this approach. She argues that the common failing of theories associating equality with equal

27. Ann Scales, 'The Emergence of Feminist Jurisprudence: An Essay', *Yale Law Journal*, 95 (1986), pp. 1373, 1381.
28. Janet Rifkin, 'Mediation from a Feminist Perspective: Promises and Problems', *Law and Inequality*, 2 (1984), p. 21; Lisa G Lerman, 'Mediation of Wife Abuse Cases: The Adverse Impact of Informal Dispute Resolution on Women', *Harvard Women's Law Journal*, 7 (1984), p. 57.
29. Catharine MacKinnon, *Feminism Unmodified: Discourses on Life and Law* (Harvard University Press, Cambridge, Mass., 1987), pp. 39, 45.

treatment or with different treatment is that they implicitly accept a male yardstick: women are either the same as or different from a male norm.[30] MacKinnon views social relations between women and men as organised in such a way 'that men may dominate and women must submit'. The law, she says, keeps women 'out and down'[31] by preserving a hierarchical system based on gender. MacKinnon describes an alternative legal analysis of inequality for which the central question always is 'whether the policy or practice in question integrally contributes to the maintenance of an underclass or a deprived position because of gender status'. The law should support freedom from systematic subordination because of sex, rather than freedom to be treated without regard to sex.

MacKinnon's approach is not always easily applied because many of the relationships of subordination sanctioned by the law are so deeply ingrained that they appear quite natural. It involves looking 'for that which we have been trained not to see... [identifying] the invisible'.[32] If the issue of inequality is redescribed as one of domination and subordination, sex discrimination laws simply promising equal treatment are of limited utility. Instead MacKinnon has worked for an expansion of the ambit of the law to cover traditionally legally unrecognised harms of particular concern to women such as sexual harassment[33] and pornography.[34] She argues that the feminist project in law is to gain legal recognition of the real injuries women suffer in order to make them unacceptable.[35]

In this way gender relations can slowly be transformed. Using MacKinnon's analysis, other feminist lawyers have described discrimination in institutions, such as the workplace, where

30. Ibid., p. 34. See also Nicola Lacey, op. cit., p. 417.
31. Ibid., p. 205.
32. Ann Scales, op. cit., p. 1393.
33. Catharine MacKinnon, *Sexual Harassment of Working Women* (Yale University Press, New Haven, 1979).
34. Catharine MacKinnon, *Feminism Unmodified*, op. cit., pp. 127–213.
35. Ibid., p. 104.

practices are more compatible with culturally defined male life patterns than female ones. Christine Littleton has proposed defining the goal of equality as 'acceptance', so that social institutions could be required to react to gender differences by restructuring workplaces to fit women and their life patterns.[36]

Catharine MacKinnon's theories about law and inequality have been controversial both inside and outside the feminist community. Critics have wondered how MacKinnon can identify an authentic women's voice in a world she describes as utterly dominated by men.[37] MacKinnon's work has also been read as endorsing an essentialist position without regard to the influence of race, class or sexual preference.[38] The British feminist Carol Smart argues that MacKinnon concedes too much authority to law: although MacKinnon urges changing the values of the law, she nevertheless accords it considerable power, preserving its place in the hierarchy of male structures.[39] Smart and others have also questioned whether the construction of Grand Feminist Theory is useful in achieving equality between the sexes and whether such endeavours capture the contextualised and partial nature of our knowledge.[40] Moreover, MacKinnon assumes that if we get the legal theory correct, legal practice will follow. Australian experience with laws relating to sexual harassment indicates that the best-intentioned laws can be thwarted in practice if their interpreters do not appreciate why and how the prohibited behaviour contributes

---

36. Christine A Littleton, *University of Pittsburgh Law Review*, 48 (1987), pp. 1043, 1052. Similarly, Riki Holtmaat describes a feminist 'other law' that systematically takes women's needs into account: 'The Power of Legal Concepts: The Development of a Feminist Theory of Law', *International Journal of the Sociology of Law*, 17 (1989), pp. 481, 492–4.
37. Carol Smart, *Feminism and the Power of Law* (Routledge, London, 1989), pp. 75–7, 81, 88–9.
38. Deborah L Rhode, op. cit., pp. 624–5; Angela P. Harris, 'Race and Essentialism in Feminist Legal Theory', Stanford Law Review, 42 (1990), pp. 580, 590–601.
39. Carol Smart, 'Feminism', op. cit., note 37.
40. Ibid., pp. 70–2; Katherine Barden, op. cit., pp. 872–7.

to the subordination of women.[41] Smart argues that we should avoid general, abstract theories and focus instead on the realities of women's lives, studying the inconsistencies and contradictions in legal regulation:[42] the law does not operate in a monolithic way to oppress women and advantage men. She supports action at the micro-political level rather than the slippery path of law reform. It is better, Smart has said, to be a feminist journalist than a feminist lawyer.[43]

Feminist theories are still regarded as dangerous, or ridiculous, heresies by the legal establishment. Some lawyers react to even liberal feminism with skepticism or hostility because it requires the legal system to change to deliver ostensible equality. The more radical feminist critiques of the law meet more general opposition. Their implication that the law cannot claim real impartiality or objectivity strikes at the heart of legal mythology.

How should the law respond to inequality on the basis of sex? The fight against inequality must use all the approaches outlined above: inequality has both overt and subtle forms. 'Traditional' law reform can change the formal language of power and offer particular individuals limited remedies against inequality. Attempting to expose the thoroughly gendered nature of the legal system and balance it with other perspectives can alter a monolithic conception of inequality. And understanding the relations of power and subordination endorsed by the law can suggest methods of reform that will not fall into the same trap. At the same time it is necessary to remain realistic and somewhat skeptical about the importance of law in achieving social change.

---

41. The starkest example is the judgment of Justice Einfeld in Hall & Others v. A. & A. Sheiban Pty Ltd & Others, EOC (1989), pp. 92–250. See Margaret Thornton, op. cit., pp. 60–1 for a discussion of this case.
42. Carol Smart, 'Feminism', op. cit., note 37, pp. 68–9.
43. Carol Smart, 'Feminist Jurisprudence', op. cit., note 10. In a review of MacKinnon's *Feminism Unmodified* Frances Olsen defends MacKinnon's 'grand theory' as analytically useful and politically mobilising, even if oversimplified: 'Feminist Theory in Grand Style', *Columbia Law Review*, 89 (1989), p. 1147.

This essay is a revised version of a paper presented as part of the Gendering of Knowledge lecture series at the University of Melbourne in September 1988.

In 1992 **Hilary Charlesworth** was teaching in the law school at the University of Melbourne. She went on to build a distinguished career as an academic and jurist, making an exceptional contribution to the study and practice of international law through her research on peacebuilding, human rights law and international humanitarian law, international legal theory—particularly feminist approaches to international law—and the art of international law. Charlesworth has published over 130 book chapters and articles, and authored or co-authored 11 books. With co-author Christine Chinkin, Charlesworth received the American Society of International Law Award for Creative Legal Scholarship and the American Society of International Law's Goler T Butcher Award. In 2021, Judge Charlesworth was appointed to the bench of the International Court of Justice in the Hague.

Always bet on Black (power)

The fight against race

Chelsea Watego

Meanjin 80.3 Spring 2021

As a Blackfulla, I don't claim to speak for a people, but I do write from a place. A place of power. Mine.

I write this from a place in which I am meant to be powerless, literally.

At the time of writing this essay, I had just made the decision to withdraw a race and sex discrimination complaint I had taken against my employer, the University of Queensland, and two white male academics. The complaint lodged almost two years earlier had progressed through the Queensland Human Rights Commission and the Queensland Industrial Relations Commission conciliation processes, and failed settlement talks, each of which had taken up a considerable amount of my energy, intellectually and emotionally. And here I am walking away, like Craig David and Adam Goodes.

My decision to drop the case came just one week after National Reconciliation Week, having been threatened with a claim for costs by the university and having been abandoned by the National Tertiary Education Union, which also chose that time to tell me that I would have to find and fund my own legal representation. Up until this point, the NTEU had agreed to represent me, but despite being on the case for more than a year they had failed to pursue witness statements or discovery documents to build my case, which was now before the courts.

Not only did I make the decision to withdraw my claim but I also decided to relinquish a tenured position with the institution, a sandstone nonetheless.

My walking away could be narrated in all kinds of ways. Some might frame it as one of loss and a lesson on the futility of race discrimination processes, the racism inherent in calling out racism, while others might tell of this story as one of winning and the power of white supremacy prevailing.

But I didn't lose. You see, the place I write from—Yugambeh country, Lamington National Park—is a mountaintop, quite literally. And it is in this place that I am reminded of my power, one that is not derived from the vast and expansive views it offers over all other things, but instead via the roots that ground me to this place, culturally.

I've never been too impressed with the metaphoric mountaintop that Black race scholars and civil rights activists have typically been concerned with, of a promised land and a dream of one day transcending race as described by the good Dr Martin Luther King Jr (King, 1963). As appealing as it sounds, I don't believe that such a world will ever be possible in a settler colonial state. This is not because I don't believe we are powerful. I just know the place that they have built for themselves was established and is sustained by racial violence, and all of their institutions are unrelenting in their viciousness towards sovereign Black bodies.

Disentangling their violence from our power is a challenging task, but a most necessary one in the fight against race. Race, even in our resistance against it, remains inescapable. To take up a fight against racism marks a refusal to accept its terms, but in the fight against it we are nevertheless forced to engage on their terms, all the while taking the blows to our body. Yet here I stand in my power. To stand in one's power is not to ignore the violence visited upon us; it requires us to refuse their account of it, in which they deem it all of our making or imagining.

It is in this moment of walking away that I want to share what I've learnt in the fight against race. Some might argue that my walking away represents a giving up of the fight, but it is far from it. It represents a stance that demands a standing still and staying strong.

Mohawk scholar Audra Simpson (2014) has talked about the politics of refusal as an exercising of sovereignty, and certainly this is how I came to understand the stance that Adam Goodes took in his fight against race, from the moment he refused to play on having been racially taunted, to his refusal to accept the victory lap and Hall of Fame honours from a game that booed and bullied him week in and week out (Bond, 2016).

Refusal is indeed a most powerful stance in the fight against race, and my decision to walk away from UQ and the complaint process marked a refusal to allow them to exercise any more power over me than they already had.

So I come down from the mountaintop not to speak of winning the fight against race, but rather a strategising for a never-ending fight that is indelibly bound up in a sovereignty that also refuses to cede in what Singh refers to as 'sovereign divergence' (Singh, 2020). It is afterall our power, Black power, that forces us into this fight, but it too is Black power that sustains us in the midst of it.

To take up the stance of Black power in the fight against race is to fight on a battleground that has been strategically selected without the lofty elevations of white validation or affirmative white verdicts, but one that affords us the martial advantages of a grounded sovereignty. It is a stance that is embodied, and it is in this embodiment that we are reminded of our power. Kwame Ture, co-author of *Black Power: The Politics of Liberation* (1967), in his speech to the Student Nonviolent Coordinating Committee (SNCC) in 1966, argued that the significance of Black power, beyond the slogan, was in its ability 'to provide the community with a position of strength from which to make its voice heard'. It is this articulation of Black power that I draw from to articulate a Black power as I understand it here, in this fight against race.

Race must be named

> For once, Black people are going to use the words they want to use, not just the words whites want to hear. And they will do

> this no matter how often the press tries to stop the use of the slogan by equating it with racism or separatism … Black power can be clearly defined for those who do not attach the fears of white America to their questions about it. (Ture, 1966)

I remember the times when the University of Queensland rewarded me. It first welcomed me at the age of 17 as an undergraduate student through an alternative entry process to study Indigenous health. I would go on to graduate with first class honours and receive a medal for academic excellence. I continued to postgraduate studies and received a Dean's Commendation for my 'outstanding thesis', completed in under four years while having the eldest three of my children. I would later be rewarded with a Young Alumnus of the Year award, and soon after a tenured position, not in my discipline, but in the Aboriginal and Torres Strait Islander Studies Unit.

It wasn't until I received a prestigious Australian Research Council grant for a three-year early career fellowship that the institution suddenly became less welcoming. I was shifted around between two faculties and three different work units and I was no longer on the guest list for Indigenous events on campus, including Indigenous graduation ceremonies involving students whom I had supported. My son too, years later, would not be welcome, not even to an arts degree through an alternative entry process, although he would gain entry to a different institution.

I was deemed unappointable to a leadership position in an Indigenous health research centre where I had been leading all but one of the grants they administered and where I represented the public face of the centre across a whole range of activities. That leadership role was instead filled by a white male who was directly appointed despite having no track record in Indigenous health. He would be permitted to hold that position in a part-time capacity for some two years. At a time when I had invited keynotes to almost all of the national peak Indigenous health organisation conferences, as well as international Indigenous health forums from Aotearoa to the University of Oxford, the selection panel would claim that the scholarship of the only PhD-holding Indigenous academic in the centre did not align with its objectives.

You see, my scholarship, that prestigious fellowship I won, sought to explicitly examine how race operates in the production of Indigenous health inequalities. In speaking of race, even intellectually, I had become a problem, long before I spoke of racism in a legal frame. I was considered no longer deserving of the rewards the institution had bestowed, or even the most basic of entitlements afforded other workers some days.

Prior to this, my scholarship spoke mostly of culture, of identity, of strengths and health behaviours. I hadn't realised that all this time I had been rewarded for being silent about race. I also naïvely thought it was possible to fight race intellectually within an academic institution, much like those professors who are cast as valiantly fighting cancer. This was not the case. Mine it seems was not a just war deserving of the institution's support or approval.

But this is the very fight against race; it comes and is confronted when we name it. Those who claim to have found a way of fighting it through avoidance, or some form of excellence that demands they not speak of it, have not risen above or overcome their racial position. They have instead reinscribed it, in having agreed to trade it in their 'urge toward whiteness' (Hughes, 1926).

There is no way of dealing with race through diplomacy and non-violence. And, in fact, we must know that the violence they visit upon us in our fight against race is not reflective of a flaw in our strategising, but instead reflects the stuff of power bound up in notions of race. I now measure my success in the fight against race not by their awards or applause but by the weight of the blows they level against my body. Our power as a people is witnessed in the force of their resistance to us. When an institution directs so much of its energy and resources towards breaking us, it speaks to their fear of our power, and not our powerlessness.

To name race means a preparedness to relinquish their rewards and those mountaintop moments in return for dehumanisation and marginalisation. It means accepting that our scholarship, even in its excellence, will be dismissed as substandard, just like our racial positioning. Ture reminds us that our strategising cannot be one of self-preservation, of attaching their fears of it to our actions. We must stand in our own power, for it is only in knowing ours that we know the false claims of theirs.

This is Black power.

Rage must be the register

> There has been only a civil rights movement, whose tone of voice was adapted to an audience of liberal whites. It served as a sort of buffer zone between them and angry young Blacks ... An organisation which claims to speak for the needs of a community ... must speak in the tone of that community, not as somebody else's buffer zone. This is the significance of Black power as a slogan. (Ture, 1966)

I remember attending a national racism roundtable for Indigenous health researchers where one of the more senior non-Indigenous scholars suggested that 'when talking about the "r" word we should put "systemic" in front of it'. Her reasoning was that it would make people feel more comfortable about talking about racism, and by people, we can be certain that she meant white people. While at the time I thought this was laughable, I realised that in my fight against race I too had subscribed to a strategy that appealed to whiteness.

In lodging the race and sex discrimination complaint, I had agreed to fight in the register required of the Queensland Human Rights Commission processes. I had to make my articulation of race fit within their parameters, parameters so narrow that it could refuse all of my experience of racism and sexism, because despite having what I believed to be compelling evidence, countless witnesses and clear comparisons of differences in treatment on the basis of race and gender, there remained a requirement of 'motivation'. It is not enough to have experienced a negatively racialised outcome to prove that racism exists, the intentions of the perpetrators must have been expressed somewhere to someone. The additional requirement that I distinguish between race and gender, as though I didn't embody both at any one time, also spoke to the violence of the parameters of this process, which of course has been captured in Kimberlé Crenshaw's theory of intersectionality (1989).

In vesting my power in this process, I had largely been silent about my experiences of racism at work. I handed my story over to a process that refused to see me fully, including the full extent of the injuries I and my family had sustained. I persevered with the indignities and assaults in the process, I think because I was too invested in the idea of winning on their terms. But I realised that, even if I were to win, it would not be grounded in Black power, because so much had been ceded in an appeal to white sensibilities.

I am not suggesting that we don't use these processes to complain and to compel change; we must anticipate the lies and limitations that inevitably follow, especially clear in their supposed impartial adjudication. These limitations do not reflect the merits of our case, or our ability to articulate it. They speak instead to the violence of the battleground that they've designed for us to fight on.

This battleground is the mythical middle ground, and it has been the most brutal for Blackfullas. It presumes a level terrain and an impartiality and objectivity that simply don't exist in the fight against race. It is through a performance of objectivity, a trait deemed exclusive to white people, that the power of race is sustained to mark difference and to subjugate. It is always white people that are the arbiters of racism: in race discrimination conciliations, tribunals and court rooms, as coroners, commissioners and administrators. The clinical and judicial dispassion performed in these settings always works to the advantage of the perpetrator, who can assume the 'benefit of the doubt' or balance of probabilities inherent in the idea of dispassion.

I remember being relieved to discover a Black conciliator in my race discrimination case, yet unlike other occasions where I had a white facilitator, this Black facilitator found herself saddled with an additional co-facilitator who happened to be white and who was presumably there to ensure that dispassion did not give way to emotion. In other conciliation settings with white mediators, there had never been the necessity for an additional co-facilitator, even in my being outnumbered as the sole Black body in a room. It was not lost on me that this additional co-facilitator, a white woman, in her performance of objective mediation, would at the end of the failed deliberations offer assurance to me that the accused perpetrators, all white men, 'did respect me'.

It was here that she revealed how little difference there is between denialism and objectivity when it comes to the fight against race. And to take up the position of proclaimed objectivity is tantamount to taking a side, the wrong side. Those supposed neutral and impartial processes always seem to stack the odds against Black people, and their conclusions are always in solidarity with the perpetrators, and in harmony with the innocence they see in themselves. The idea that there is an objective take is one grounded in white universalism and supremacy, of seeing racism as occasional and aberrational, if one sees it at all.

Thus the fight against race is not well served by the processes the perpetrators have established to protect themselves and the register in which we are required to perform. We must reject their claims that theirs, filtered as they are through objectivity and impartiality, are better attuned to the prospect of change. bell hooks (1995) insists that it is Black rage that will bring an end to white supremacy. She argues, 'As long as black rage continues to be represented as always and only evil and destructive, we lack a vision of militancy that is necessary for transformative revolutionary action.' In honouring her own rage, hooks was motivated 'to take pen in hand and write in the heat of that moment'. Indeed, when I made the decision to drop my race discrimination claim, I too took my pen in hand to tell my story, here.

This is my rage. This is Black power.

White innocence is white supremacy

> Can whites, particularly liberal whites, condemn themselves? Can they stop blaming us, and blame their own system? Are they capable of the shame which might become a revolutionary emotion? (Ture, 1966)

Contrasted against Black rage is white innocence. It serves to sustain white supremacy and appears in the fight against race, more specifically in the fight against accusations of racism.

I remember 8 August 2019 when the crowds gathered on the lawns of the University of Queensland's Saint Lucia campus to celebrate Aboriginal and Torres Strait Islander culture as part of its NAIDOC Week festivities (UQ Aboriginal and Torres Strait Islander Studies Unit, 2019). It was the day on which senior executives were reported to have signed a Memorandum of Understanding (MOU) with the Ramsay Centre for Western Civilisation (UQ News, 2019). Having not been enlisted in any of the institution's Indigenous cultural celebrations, I joined a small number of academics and professional staff who gathered in protest outside the chancellery to voice our opposition. As the only Blackfulla there (at least from what I can recall), I got to see how effectively Indigenous peoples and culture could be deployed as a form of virtue signalling for Western civilisation. It would be one month later that I would lodge my race discrimination case against the university.

Angela Davis once said: 'In a racist society it is not enough to be non-racist. We must be anti-racist.' Apart from a human resources policy entitled 'Prevention of Racism', which is unaccompanied by a guideline or procedure that may give the policy substance, the institution doesn't appear to have a clear stance or strategy against racism (UQ, 2011). It is a signatory to a Reconciliation Action Plan (RAP) that claims to be a 'commitment to the building of respectful relationships and opportunities between Aboriginal, Torres Strait Islander and non-Indigenous peoples' (RAP, 2019). While some may argue UQ's signature on both an RAP and an MOU with the Ramsay Centre has a real Rio Tinto energy, it does tell a truth about the institution's position on race generally. If you look at their RAP, you will find not one reference to race or racism, beyond a quote from one of my postgraduate students who references my scholarship.

Within days of having threatened me for costs in my race discrimination claim, the institution would boast of its commitment to Reconciliation Week. On 27 May 2021, UQ's Faculty of Health and Behavioural Sciences executive dean, Professor Bruce Abernethy (*UQ News*, 2021), would announce the 'Yarning for Success' program, which claims to provide a supported career pathway program for a total of nine Aboriginal and Torres Strait Islander staff members in the faculty. These nine staff members were new appointments made through a recruitment drive in which Aboriginal and Torres Strait Islander people at any stage of their academic career were encouraged to apply for a position in any one of the faculty's schools and centres. Professor Abernethy in the media release stated the program would 'provide a safe space for Aboriginal and Torres Strait Islander staff, students and partners to fulfil their potential … with a focus on key leadership roles'.

In my time in that faculty, I did not know of any other Indigenous academics with PhDs, nor did I ever get a sense that there was to be such a substantial investment in boosting our numbers. The institution would likely claim that it was an expression of their commitment to its Reconciliation Action Plan, but I am also fairly certain that the story of this investment would have featured in their defence against my claims had the case progressed. White innocence is a key feature of resistance in the fight against race, and we see it deployed when we hear reference to intention, motivation and unconscious bias. I have no faith that white people or white institutions will ever be capable of expressing the shame necessary for disrupting the existing racial order of things. They have absolutely no shame.

But this is why we must take action to fight race not in the institution's internal processes but externally, whether it's legally or taking it to the public square. It is in their defence against being labelled racist that change occurs, not in the realisation or acceptance that they are indeed racist. As such, the beneficiaries of this defensive manœuvre won't be the victims of racism who had the courage to call it out, it will be all those who follow, who will be far greater in number than the lone and supposedly vulnerable complainant. That is Black power.

Black people must be believed and believed in

> Only Black people can convey the revolutionary idea that Black people are able to do things themselves. Only they can help create in the community an amused and continuing Black consciousness that will provide the basis for political strength. (Ture, 1966)

In the fight against race as told by them, the Black complainant will always be cast as the troublesome protagonist in the institution. And they will have no difficulty enlisting other Black people to reinforce our pariah-like status, for there are those who in their mediocrity will happily accessorise for the rewards afforded them. They will too happily speak in hushed tones about that troublesome Black who refuses to adhere to the racial order of things. 'They're too political,' they claim. 'What is wrong with them?' they ask. 'Stay away from them,' they insist.

Yet I feel not so much a sense of betrayal from Black people who stand in solidarity with white supremacy, but rather a sorrow. Langston Hughes (1926), one of the leaders of the Harlem Renaissance, explains the misfortune of 'the urge toward whiteness' as follows:

> One of the most promising of the young Negro poets said to me once 'I want to be a poet, not a Negro poet' meaning I believe 'I want to write like a white poet', meaning subconsciously 'I would like to be a white poet', meaning behind that 'I would like to be white'. And I was sorry the young man said that for no great poet has ever been afraid of being himself and I doubted then that with his desire to run away spiritually from his race this boy would ever be a great poet.

Never to know one's greatness is the real tragedy in all of this, rather than the Black complainant's supposed marginalisation in white spaces. It means a life of mediocrity, of constant disappointment and dissatisfaction as all kinds of opportunities are lost in the effort to appease one's oppressor. You see, despite having been cast out of the health and humanities faculties at my institution, I managed to lead a research team that secured another prestigious Australian Research Council grant, one far greater in value than the earlier one that first placed me in the fight against race. This ambitious $1.77 million grant involves the establishment of an Indigenist health humanities as a new field of research, building the very intellectual community that I could not find at the institution that employed me. This community is being forged through the values expressed in the Inala Manifesto (McInerney, 2019), a call to arms for carving out a transformative Indigenous health research agenda, reconfiguring the researcher's role as a public intellectual and change-maker. Here I came to learn of the power, not of my own making, but the power of a community brought together through a critical Black consciousness to build something that was beyond the imagining of the academy.

The institution struggled to deal with me, not as a problem, but in my excellence, failing for weeks to find a desk for me and my team to sit at, not even in the Aboriginal and Torres Strait Islander Studies Unit that I had been returned to. Eventually we would be housed in a building some distance from our organisational unit, on the floor that was home to crop scientists and a mixed bag of others who couldn't be situated in their work units, for one reason or another. Over the past three years, I had become accustomed to the stories explaining why my office wasn't in their school, on their floor or in the faculty in which I was employed. It didn't matter the location they reserved for me, it never altered the sense of my worth as a Blackfulla or as a scholar.

I always knew the institution would never appreciate the impact of my work, and it wasn't because it existed beyond their imagining or their reach, but because my work refused to be of service to it. The institution was the place where I went to work, but it was never the primary beneficiary of that work, because the fight against race lies in contesting the racialised knowledges they have produced.

Black power is not, however, derived from being believed, or believed in, by white peoples, processes or institutions. Some

Blackfullas will appeal for our sovereignty to be seen by them, but it need not be, because it just is. Black power is embodied by Blackfullas. It exists because it exists in the minds and the bloodlines of Blackfullas and it need not matter if it exists nowhere else. I am not speaking of a race transcendalism of pretending race isn't real, but instead I speak of a way of dealing with race head-on in our own damn heads, in refusing to accept their parameters for which they insist we exist. To speak of Black power as a place in our imagining is not to reduce it to an illusion or delusion. It must be as real in our heads as it is in our lands and our lives, and it must also be reflected in our work in the academy, intellectually, politically and culturally. This is Black power.

Black power is Black love

> Black people do not want to 'take over' this country. They don't want to 'get whitey'; they just want to get him off their backs, as the saying goes ... The society we seek to build among Black people, then, is not a capitalist one. It is a society in which the spirit of community and humanistic love prevail. The word love is suspect; Black expectations of a response from the white community, which failed us. The love we seek to encourage is within the Black community, the only American community where men call each other 'brother' when they meet. We can build a community of love only where we have the ability to do so: among Blacks. (Ture, 1966)

In strategising my fight against race, I must confess, I had entertained the idea of crowdfunding the costs of legal representation, to muster all of my energy to fight until the death. But I couldn't do it. I couldn't in all good conscience ask people to invest in a cause that was my own, that sought only to serve my interests, interests that weren't a matter of life or death. When mob are crowdfunding funerals and legal campaigns for loved ones killed in custody and the colony, I hated the idea of diverting scarce resources away from these most pressing causes. What I know about the fight against race is that me not securing a leadership role in a white institution isn't the real fight that I want to exhaust my energy on. But I did have to check my ego.

The radicalism of Black power in its rage is its love for Black people, a love that extends beyond the self, yet centres a collective Black self-love, unconditional and unwavering. Thus at the heart of the fight against race are not individual grievances, wins or wealth, or what Cornel West describes as installing 'Black faces in high places' (Reese, 2017). It must not be one of reforming violent institutions, of quotas on boards, of redrafting complaint policies, awareness-raising, diversity training or deck-chair shuffling tasks for committees or taskforces. It is not a fight for an alternative subjugation, for revenge or retribution, but a call for a different society to be born; one that is no longer structured according to race, but a genuinely shared humanity that, in reckoning with sovereignty, abandons the hierarchies that sustain white supremacy.

In walking away from the University of Queensland, I was not walking away from the fight against race, but instead I was choosing a battle more worthy of my time. Vine Deloria Jr insisted that 'the problems of Indians have always been ideological rather than social or political or economic' (1969). He states, 'it is vitally important that the Indian people pick the intellectual arena as the one to wage war'. And oddly enough during this time I was offered several alternative places to wage that war, with additional resourcing, including physical space not just for me but for this growing community, the combined value of which far outweighed what was originally being sought through the process of my race and sex discrimination claim. This war against race is not waged to gain an advantage or status or to exact revenge, but seeks to restore and redeem. This war that has been waged thus is one of love that builds an intellectual community committed to a Black humanity and is capable of advancing the interests of Black people instead of breaking them.

In the midst of this fight, I should acknowledge that there was a moment when it almost took me out. As the case progressed, my health was profoundly affected and my five children deeply impacted, all of which we are still attending to. So violent was the power of white supremacy, I almost lost sight of the significance of Black power. I am not ashamed to share this, as I know that racial violence is meant to break Black people; that it has always had a dispossessing function. But it was in this moment that I was reminded too of our sovereignty as unceded. And it wasn't at the mountaintop that I discovered this, but at the kitchen table of Aunty/Dr Lilla Watson in a series of conversations where she challenged the terms on which I had been operating in my fights.

Black power is not just a slogan derived from elsewhere, it finds itself expressed in Indigenous sovereignty. While I speak to the articulation of Black power and resistance to racial violence by African-American scholars and Indigenous scholars from elsewhere, our people have long articulated a fight against race through sovereignty, of a power derived from being the first peoples of this land. We witness this in JT Patten and W Ferguson's insistence of ancient bloodlines (1938) and Michael Mansell's articulation of a strength in adversity as evidence of an intact sovereignty (2007), to Aileen Moreton-Robinson's (2015) declaration that the bodies of Blackfullas in life and in death signify our title to this land, and to Cathy Freeman's account of her 2000 Olympic gold medal–winning run (Billiet, 2020), in which her opponents faced not just her but also her ancestors, the first peoples to walk this land.

When Blackfullas speak of power we speak to the power that is derived through our embodied relation to Black land. Black power originates from the place in which we became human and demands a humility not often expressed in the militancy of a Black power divorced from land. It is recognition of a power that is greater than ourselves, even at our most excellent. It seeks not a proximity to whiteness that is marked by myths of progress or of climbing racial mountains, walking or winning, but of standing in our own power. It is not a demand for theirs.

This standing in our own power is reflected in the cries of 'still here' and 'always was, always will be'. I never needed the coloniser's court to determine whether what I experienced was racist or sexist or both. It is in my experience that I come to know about race, the validity and veracity of which is charted in my scholarship, including the story that I am now free to tell. That is why silence can never be seen as a 'successful' resolution in the fight against race; it binds us to the perpetrators and renders us complicit in their violence, helping no-one, not ourselves, and most certainly not those who follow, who will never hear of it.

Hughes, in his rejection of ascending the racial mountain, speaks instead of 'the mountain free within ourselves' (1926). And I think that is one of the most foundational elements of a Black power as understood here. The most transformative Black acts have taken place at the margins, on the fringes of towns, among Black communities and collectives, Black minds, souls and hearts rather than at white centres, whether they be boardrooms or tearooms or university chancellories. The exiled location they insist we occupy is not the place of marginalisation they would have us believe, for this land is ours, all of it. And it is in knowing our place in this place that we are offered freedom, freedom to move, to coordinate, to innovate, to agitate and demand more, because we know that as Black people we deserve more than what they have begrudgingly offered us.

The realisation that I had received all of the things I had sought from the complaints process, but not achieved through it, offered the ultimate sense of freedom. It was in knowing it all came through our power, and not theirs that I came to see their battleground as little more than a playground that no longer amused me.

This realisation would never free me from their clutches. At the time of writing, the institution was still deliberating on whether to continue the fight for costs, and of binding me to them longer than I wanted and longer than necessary for them operationally. Thus, in their underestimation of our power, we should never underestimate *their* investment in the fight against race. It is after all, they who have the most to lose.

While I may not know what they will do, I will never forget the place from where I come. And that is Black power.

Acknowledgements: I wish to acknowledge Aunty/Dr Lilla Watson for reminding me of the power of Blackfullas, including my own, in what I once mistakenly believed were my most powerless of moments. I also would like to acknowledge the mentorship of Dr David Singh, who has helped me consider, intellectually and politically, the solidarities and incommensurabilities of critical race scholarship from a place elsewhere, in making sense of the fights I find myself in.

References

Laurence Billiet (dir.), *Freeman*, General Strike and Matchbox Pictures Production, 2020.

Chelsea Bond, 'Refusing to play the race game', *The Conversation*, 2016, www.theconversation.com/refusing-to-play-the-race-game-66043

Kimberlé Crenshaw, 'Demarginalizing the Intersection of Race and Sex: A Black Feminist Critique of Antidiscrimination Doctrine, Feminist Theory and Antiracist Politics', *University of Chicago Legal Forum*, 1989, no. 1.

Charles V Hamilton and Kwame Ture, *Black Power: The Politics of Liberation*, Vintage, 1967.

Langston Hughes, 'The Negro Artist and the Racial Mountain', in *The Collected Works of Langston Hughes*, University of Missouri Press, 2002.

Martin Luther King Jr, 'I've Been to the Mountaintop', Church of God in Christ Headquarters, Memphis, Tennessee, 3 April 1968.

Michael Mansell, cited in Aileen Moreton-Robinson, 'Introduction: Sovereign Subjects', in Moreton-Robinson (ed.), *Sovereign Subjects: Indigenous Sovereignty Matters*, Allen & Unwin, Sydney, pp. 1–11, 2007.

Marie McInerney, 'The Inala Manifesto: A call to arms for Indigenous health researchers', *Croakey*, 2019, https://www.croakey.org/the-inala-manifesto-a-call-to-arms-for-indigenous-health-researchers/

Aileen Moreton-Robinson, *The White Possessive: Property, Power, and Indigenous Sovereignty*, University of Minnesota Press, 2015.

JT Patten and W Ferguson, 'Aborigines claim citizen rights! A Statement of the Case for the Aborigines Progressive Association', *Publicist*, Sydney, 1938, https://nla.gov.au/nla.obj-241787110/view?partId=nla.obj-241788701#page/n0/mode/1up

Audra Simpson, *Mohawk Interruptus: Political Life across the Borders of Settler States*, Durham and London, 2014.

UQ News, 'Yarning for success', 27 May 2021, https://www.uq.edu.au/news/article/2021/05/yarning-success

UQ, 'Racism: Prevention of Racism—Policy', 2011, https://ppl.app.uq.edu.au/content/1.70.03-racism

UQ, 'Reconciliation Action Plan', 2019, https://about.uq.edu.au/files/535/UQ-RAP.pdf

UQ, 'UQ's Partnership with the Ramsay Centre', 2019, https://staff.uq.edu.au/update/projects-initiatives/ramsay-centre-partnership

In 2021, Munanjahli and South Sea Islander woman **Chelsea Watego** (formerly Bond) was Professor of Indigenous Health at Queensland University of Technology's School of Public Health and Social Work. Today Professor Watego is Executive Director of the QUT Carumba Institute. With over twenty years' experience in Indigenous health as a health worker and researcher, her scholarship has highlighted the role of race in generating health inequalities, and her advocacy is deeply committed to the survival of Indigenous peoples locally and globally, foregrounding Indigenous intellectual sovereignty. She is a prolific writer and public intellectual, having written for IndigenousX, NITV, *The Guardian*, and *The Conversation*. She is a founding board member of Inala Wangarra, an Indigenous community development association within her community, a Director of the Institute for Collaborative Race Research, and was one half of the Wild Black Women radio/podcast show, but most importantly, she is also a proud mum to five beautiful children. Her debut book *Another Day in the Colony* was published by UQ Press and met with critical acclaim.

It's shit to be White

Michael Mohammed Ahmad

Meanjin 79.4 Summer 2020

> When you're used to one hundred percent, ninety-eight feels oppressive.
>
> —Robin DiAngelo

I DIDN'T INVENT THE White Australia Policy. White people invented it. And they invented it to distinguish themselves from Aboriginals, Africans, Asians, Arabs and Pasifikas. And they didn't invent it to distinguish themselves in the negative; only in the positive, with greater rights to the stolen land on which they gathered than the rest of us. And while White people knew that they were not literally the colour white—most of their kind were somewhere between pink and beige—they did not seem confused about the term, fully aware that it referred to them and taking great pride in their sense of superiority over anyone that was 'not quite White'. White people took no offence in White's metaphorical nature, no offence in White's overgeneralisation, and they did not seek out any of their dictionaries to double-check White's definition.

So then, a few decades later, I was invited to do an interview with ABC Radio National about racism and White privilege in Australia. It was in response to the controversy surrounding a new book called *American Dirt*, about a Mexican mother and her son fleeing drug-cartel violence, which was written by a White woman. Jeanine Cummins received a seven-figure advance for the book and an endorsement from Oprah Winfrey's Book Club, guaranteeing her literary stardom. Meanwhile, Latinx authors who had been writing the 'authentic' experience of their identities for years were almost completely ignored by major publishers, reviewers, the media and the reading public.

There is always a bitter sense of irony, denial and shamelessness whenever a White journalist working for a White-run media outlet invites me to talk about 'the diversity problem' on their program: Whitey begins the interview by asking me, 'Does White privilege exist in Australia?' and I respond, 'How about you take a look around yourself and then you tell me.'

Fifteen minutes into the interview, I dared to begin a sentence like this: 'White people are …' Then I removed my headphones, exited the studio, caught the lift to the underground parking bay, and drove my car from the inner west back to the western suburbs of Sydney, where we poor brown folk lick the garlic sauce off our fingers. By the time I had arrived home, to the duplex that my cousin and I built when we both got married in our late teens, my email had been flooded with dozens of angry messages from White people. As it turned out, I was the actual racist, and it was their duty to educate me: White's a racist term! White's reverse racism! What's White anyway?

Define White!

I have a special folder in my email account called 'White Crap' where I save all these messages for my records. However, throughout my entire professional life, I have never once responded to any of Whitey's complaints. I'm usually too busy trying to run a literacy movement, write my self-hating novels, raise my half-White son and find a spare moment to wax my Arab armpits. That being said, I have always wondered if I've got the wrong attitude. Not the part about whether I'm the racist. That's dumb. But the other part. The part about me not responding. Maybe I owe it to the generous White people who helped me escape my shit-hole homeland and welcomed me into their wholesome country to explain why I've become such an ungrateful little wog. Well okay, let's do this. Just once. For that tinge of blond growing through my son's thick head of desert curls. Let's define White. Let's define racism. Let's define shit.

•••

In the mid '90s, a highly controversial political party called One Nation made headlines throughout the country. Led by conservative independent politician Pauline Hanson, One Nation represented a dissatisfied faction in the dominant White culture of Australia, who called for a reintroduction of the White Australia Policy, rejected Aboriginal land rights and raised concerns about an inevitable 'Asian invasion'. These policies first came to national prominence in Hanson's maiden speech in federal parliament on 10 September 1996. I was ten years old when I first saw Pauline Hanson on the primetime news, her red hair piercing my eyeballs as she declared that Australia would soon be facing a civil war. My father and his four brothers were huddled around our small flickering television at the time, which had a steel clothes hanger plugged in the back as an antenna. These five Lebanese men all looked deeply concerned, their dark olive complexions and large Bedouin noses casting a long shadow over our entire living room. Finally, my youngest uncle, Osama, said out loud, 'We just escaped a civil war; what does that bulldog know about civil war!'

> To someone of Lebanese background who has gone through part of the Lebanese civil war, like me, the day Pauline Hanson uttered the words 'civil war' in Parliament was truly of nightmarish quality, more so than anyone born in Australia can understand. If only the lady knew what she was talking about she would have realised how disgusting the very sound of those words is. (1998, p. 25)

In *White Nation*, Hage deconstructs Australia's fantasy of White supremacy, arguing that non-White communities in Australia are imagined, positioned and managed by the dominant culture as 'the other'. We might best understand the idea of 'other' here by drawing reference to the definition offered by Bob Pease: 'Othering is a method of portraying difference as if it were in some way alien to that which is normal' (2010, p. 13). In contrast, Australia's dominant culture constructs itself as the neutral, standard and default Australian identity. Hage calls this phenomenon the White Nation Fantasy—a belief among White Australians that they are completely 'in control' as the exclusive 'masters' of the nation. Few White Australians are exempt from participating in this fantasy: the White racist who says to the ethnic other, 'Go back to where you came from', and the White anti-racist who says, 'It's a multicultural country and we welcome everyone', both start from the assumption that Australia belongs to them as the 'true' and 'authentic' Australians. These fantasies of White supremacy exist in contradistinction to the multicultural reality of Australia—a literal society built on hundreds of cultural backgrounds and identities that exist and function as uniquely Australian in spite of (not because of) White control, dominance, tolerance, acceptance, policy-making and decision-making (1998, p. 18).

The first step in deciphering the White Nation Fantasy is to comprehend the difference between 'white', which is a colour, and 'White', which is a cultural category. In Australia, being fair-skinned, as is the case for some Aboriginals, Arabs, Asians and so on, might mean that a person looks 'white' or is 'white-passing', but it does not necessarily mean a person identifies as, or is identified as, or benefits from, being White. Usually when we refer to 'White Australians', we're generally referring to 'Anglo-Australians', but 'Anglo-Australian' does not fully encapsulate what it means to be 'White' in Australia either, for it leaves out many non-Anglo Australians who relate to, identify with, benefit from, and gain tangible and symbolic capital from the conception of Whiteness. For example, in recent history Australians of Irish, Scottish, French, German and Russian heritage have all been acknowledged as White. In consideration of these factors, Hage defines 'White' as the 'fantasy position of cultural dominance born out of the history of European expansion' (1998, p. 20). 'White' is recognised not as the literal physiology of a single race of people, but rather as a shared sense of identity among multiple groups of people that can be accumulated and utilised in the form of cultural, social, political and economic capital.

In order to understand how this definition of 'Whiteness' plays out in reality, we can juxtapose the media reportage on the Skaf gang rapes in the year 2000 to the media reportage on the rape, torture and murder of Anita Cobby in 1986. As a 'Lebanese' boy who was coming of age at the time of the Skaf gang rapes, in which thirteen young men of Middle Eastern background were convicted of multiple sexual assaults, I remember a relentless media frenzy among all the newspapers, radio stations and TV news networks. Every report attributed the crimes to a problem of Lebanese, Middle Eastern, Arab and Muslim culture, even though all the perpetrators involved in the crimes were Australians, and even though the crimes had nothing to do with the religion of Islam. In contrast, when researching the news reportage about the hideous atrocities committed against Anita Cobby, I could not find even one mention of the Irish backgrounds of the men who committed the assault. While White people had a history of racially demonising and vilifying Irish communities in Australia during the late 1800s (Gleeson, 2004), Collins et al. argue that Anita Cobby's murder was not seen as an 'ethnic crime', and politicians and newspapers did not refer to the incident as an 'Irish crime' because by 1986 the Irish were seen as part of the Anglo-Celtic majority and therefore normalised as White (2000, p. 9). This demonstrates that Whiteness is not defined by skin colour or country of origin, nor is it a fixed position. Rather it is a form of wealth, both fluid and malleable, that can be acquired and accumulated by any cultural group at any point in time. From this definition of White, we can begin to unpack Hage's argument that racism, as it exists in Australia, is not simply about race. It is about power and belonging, often manifesting through acts of nationalism and spatial management.

•••

Whenever a person of colour accuses a White person of racism, we usually get some form of the following response spat back at us: 'Everybody's racist' (Hage 1998, p. 33). Growing up in an uneducated and conservative Arab household, where none of my first-generation relatives had been given the opportunity to complete high school, I certainly appreciate the common-sense logic behind this counter-argument. Sure, Whitey called me a terrorist and a rapist and a drug-dealer, but my dad referred to Islanders as 'stupid coconuts' and my mum said Indians smell like 'curry-krishner' and my brother kept using the n-word when he sang the lyrics to his favourite Tupac song and all twenty-two of my aunts and uncles believe that Aussies like to fuck their own siblings, which is so much worse than Arabs, who draw the line at fucking our cousins.

Sorry, Jerry Springer—this ain't your 'gotcha' moment. Although most people may harbour some kind of distaste or prejudice towards a person or group because of their racial identity, the assertion that 'everybody's racist' downplays and normalises the higher degrees of racism that only some individuals and groups have the power to enact. Hage points out that racism is a structure in which decisions and policies can be made in consideration of, or in relation to, one's race. 'So ... while everyone is capable of stereotyping and essentialising others, not everyone is capable of using their racism to discriminate and subjugate others. Only the latter really qualifies as racism' (1998, p. 33). The same can be said for the classification of White supremacy. Layla F Saad argues that:

> White supremacy is a racist ideology that is based upon the belief that white people are superior in many ways to people of other races and that therefore, white people should be dominant over other races. White supremacy is not just an attitude or a way of thinking. It also extends to how systems and institutions are structured to uphold this white dominance. (2020, p. 12)

Within this framework, Australia's cultural minorities are rarely worried about the random bigot on the bus screaming, 'In our country, you follow our ways.' Our actual concerns relate to the power structures from the top down, which foster an environment for Whitey's bigotry to thrive. By way of example, let's examine the racial climate in New South Wales at the time of the 2005 Cronulla Riots. Following an altercation between a group of 'Lebanese' men and several 'Australian' lifeguards, five thousand White Australians marched on the beach in Cronulla, chanting 'No Lebs' and physically assaulting anyone they identified as Middle Eastern in appearance. In the nights that followed the riots, hundreds of third-world-looking young men stormed Sydney's beaches, attacking people, cars and shops that were seen to represent the Australian mob (Noble 2006, p. 2).

Now even though the riots revealed the hatred, anger, prejudice and violence that both White and Arab cultural groups could inflict upon each other, it was only the White Australian community that had the systems and institutions at their disposal to establish the Middle Eastern Organised Crime Squad in the months and years that followed the riots (Davies, 2007). This granted the Australian government the 'legal' authority to target the activities of one specific racial group in Australia with zero accountability. During a televised debate about the creation of the Middle Eastern Organised Crime Squad, renowned African-American rapper Napoleon, who was touring Australia at the time, explained it in a way that even a cracker could understand: 'I think having a task force just to target Middle Eastern people is like the most racist thing I've ever heard in my life' (SBS, 2007).

In 2016, I facilitated a creative writing workshop at Western Sydney University that was attended by a third-year student who introduced herself as a Tongan woman from the slums of Mount Druitt. Her name was Winnie Dunn. As the stand-out participant in my workshop, I invited Winnie to be the new general manager of Sweatshop, a literacy movement I had established that was devoted to empowering First Nations people and people of colour through reading, writing and critical thinking. In the coming months, as we ran workshops in schools and universities across Western Sydney, Winnie articulated to me the ongoing pain that

White people in the Australian arts sector had been inflicting upon her community since she was a small girl. While the mainstream television networks in Australia ignored Tongans completely, the so-called 'multicultural' networks who promote themselves as our allies were parading around in brown-face. For years the ABC had been supporting the White male actor Chris Lilley to apply bronzed make-up to his skin, wear an afro wig and don a stereotypical Islander accent to play a minstrel caricature in the series called *Jonah from Tonga*. In the context of this television program, Winnie did not hesitate to tell a culturally diverse audience at the 2018 Sydney Writers' Festival how she felt about the way Pasifikas had been represented by members of Australia's dominant culture: 'White people are shit!'

Although the simplistic definition of racism might argue that Winnie's statement was the racist component in all this, in practise her words were little more than a rhetorical generalisation. Firstly, it should come as no surprise that writers of colour have the creative capacity to be allegorical, metonymical, polemical and provocative in their use of language just as much as any White writers. Winnie's way of speaking happens to be hardwired into the flavour of the English language—when your late-night talk-show host says, 'the press hounded the pussy-grabber', you immediately recognise that in reality it was probably just a handful of reporters asking Donald Trump some questions; no one takes Stephen Colbert to literally mean that every journalist on Earth who is represented under this all-encompassing term called 'the press' was barking at the president like a dog. Secondly, words do not exist in a vacuum. Winnie's statement, 'White people are shit', was a response to the White supremacist systems and institutions that were designed to ensure that the only mainstream representation of Pasifikas we had ever seen in Australia was of a White man performing outdated minstrel theatre—a portrayal that upheld the ongoing stereotypes that Tongan men are hypersexual, hypermasculine, violent, sexist, homophobic, dyslexic and illiterate. It is precisely these kinds of representations from the top that filter down into the consciousness of the Australian public, eventuating in statements like those of the bigot on the bus—'our country, our ways'.

•••

Throughout my entire life branded an 'Australian Muslim', I have not found the Islamophobic yobbo commonly spotted on public transport anywhere near as annoying as the progressive White hippies who give me a condescending smile and say, 'You're welcome to follow whatever religion you like.' Ye know, because I'd been bowing to a statue of White Jesus five times a day, praying: Oh Aussie Overlords—please grant me your blessings to exist.

The White rhetoric of 'giving permission' falls into a category that Hage names the Tolerant Society as a White Nation Fantasy: the ethnic other is visualised as someone who must be offered the acceptance and tolerance of the dominant culture in order to carry on with their 'foreign' practises. 'To begin with, the popular language of acceptance, often encountered in the form "They're just as Australian as we are" or "They're Australian, too", reinforces the placing of the Anglo-Celtic Australians in the position of power they acquire within the discourse of tolerance' (1998, p. 102). Fantasies of tolerance and acceptance inflate the social, cultural and political status that White Australians have imagined for themselves—they are not simply one of many members of an intrinsically diverse society; they are the generous member of a monocultural society, who is willing to 'put up with' the customs and practises of the ethnic other as an act of kindness.

Ironically, one of the central traits of a 'tolerant society' governed by White people is its limited capacity to tolerate the other. Within such societies, the non-White values of a multicultural population are only accepted to the extent that they do not disrupt and discomfort the values of the dominant White culture—multiculturalism on the condition that non-White behaviour does not extend beyond speaking a little bit of durka-durka at home, dancing the dabke at your cousin's wedding, eating some dumplings at the Lunar New Year Festival and wearing a bright-red sari for your high school graduation. This explains why White definitions of 'free speech' have often made it very difficult for many White people in the West to genuinely tolerate and accept the more serious aspects of another culture and religion, such as the Islamic belief that it is a sin to depict the Prophet Muhammad in artworks, photographs, statues and films. In one particular video, Muhammad was portrayed as a blood-thirsty Arab, and included scenes in which he performed oral sex on his wife, leading to hostile demonstrations in Sydney on 15 September 2012. Following the protests, Australian Muslims were severely criticised by the White Australian media and politicians for holding placards that stated, 'Behead all those who insult the Prophet'. In response, Barry O'Farrell, then Premier of New South Wales, argued that the protests revealed the 'unacceptable face of multiculturalism'. This mirrored a similar expression voiced by the Australian government's opposition leader at the time, Tony Abbott, who said, 'I don't believe we saw an acceptable face of Islam yesterday' (Gridneff & AAP, 2012).

It's no coincidence that O'Farrell's and Abbott's responses to the protests were both framed around the language of 'acceptability', tying them directly to the fantasies of 'tolerance' and 'acceptance' identified in White Nation. Before Whites can assert what is unacceptable for the rest of Australia, as did our premier and soon-to-be prime minister, they must first buy into the illusion that the values of non-Whites require their acceptance. Their fantasies are not just based on the belief that there's an originally White alternative to multicultural Australia that can magically be re-implemented if non-Whites misbehave, but also that they are in control of that alternative, and ultimately decide what is an acceptable standard of Australianness for non-White citizens. In reality, whether O'Farrell and Abbott accept or do not accept the many faces of multiculturalism and the many faces of Islam makes no difference; we are Australians either way and that can never be undone.

O'Farrell and Abbott were not the first politicians to show me the White Nation Fantasy in action. Throughout the late '90s and early 2000s, as my nose tripled in size and my bumfluff grew into a full-blown terrorist beard, I witnessed a relentless news-media campaign that attributed a series of drug deals and drive-by shootings in Western Sydney to the 'ethnic' backgrounds of the perpetrators (Collins et al., 2000, pp. 1–7). Within this climate, the then NSW premier, Bob Carr, did not hesitate to blame 'Lebanese' people for the crimes, with statements such as the following: 'Police investigators have revealed that a Lebanese gang involved in drugs and car theft has been identified in relation to recent disturbances ...' (Collins et al., 2000, p. 3). A few months after Carr had begun making these statements, I arrived home from school and immediately switched on the television—my usual routine of X-Men cartoons and two-minute noodles before I started my homework. Professor X said, 'I strongly believe in the peaceful co-existence between mutants and humans,' and then the episode cut to a commercial. Straightaway Premier Carr appeared in a newsflash, face like a lump of cauliflower, bumbling voice reverberating through my skull: 'Obey the law in Australia, or ship out of Australia.'

This sentence was one of my earliest indications that my leaders did not see me as a real Australian. I knew that Carr would never have suggested a solution as ridiculous as deportation for dealing with White Australian criminals. When he said, 'obey or ship out', he was specifically referring to people like me, whom he'd imagined as foreign, alien, ethnic, unfamiliar and exotic. Carr's fantasy was based on the obvious oversight that these so-called 'Lebanese gangs' comprised Australian-born citizens who weren't going anywhere, and also his belief that if we didn't obey the law, he actually had the power to kick us out of our own country.

That following Eid, I discovered just how deluded Premier Carr was about his mastery over the ethnic communities of New South Wales. It was the end of the Holy Month of Ramadan and thousands of Muslims had gathered outside of Lakemba Mosque to conduct their morning prayers—the street had been closed off in order to make room for a sea of hijabs and monobrows. From the crowd, I watched as Premier Carr emerged beside the grand mufti at the head of the stairs to the mosque, offering us his support and well-wishes. A moment later one of the mufti's disciples, a Santa Claus-like figure with an enormous gut and a long orange beard, took the microphone. He gave the premier a grin and said with a firm nod, 'Thank you, Honourable Mr Carr.' Then he turned to the thousands of worshippers below and instructed us in Arabic not to ship out any nonbelievers just yet—they still had their uses.

•••

Every time I drive the speed limit down the Hume Highway, I'm eventually overtaken by an angry Holden Commodore with a bumper sticker on its arse that says: love it or leave it. Phrases such as this play an acutely important role in the White Nation Fantasy—revealing the association between racism and nationalism. In a chapter titled, 'Evil White Nationalists', Hage suggests that we need to examine more carefully the movement of the hand that tears the scarf off a Muslim woman's head. 'There is a dimension of territorial and, more generally, spatial power inherent in racist violence that categories deriving from the concept of "race" cannot by themselves encompass' (1998, pp. 28–36). Although negative opinions about the hijab—such as the assumption that hijab-wearing women are inherently oppressed—might generally be considered racist, there is nothing in that opinion that would necessarily lead to an attack against the hijab. Hage explains that such attacks have more to do with a desire to control the national space: 'Unlike notions of inferiority, undesirability certainly implies, and propels actions. The subject acts because he or she sees in the scarf, through whatever it may symbolise to him or her, a harmful presence that affects their own well-being' (1998, p. 37).

Here 'undesirability' reveals itself to be a relative concept. Some people may consider it undesirable to have women wearing the hijab in Australia, while having little to no concern about women wearing it in their 'own' countries. This attitude prompts the classic racialised statements that go, 'I don't care what you do in your country, but in this country, you follow our ways.' Remarks like these are only concerned with race in relation to spatial management—what is 'too many' and 'undesirable' in one place is easily viewed as 'not enough' and 'desirable' in another. This is why in the interviews Hage conducted with those who had torn off a Muslim woman's hijab, the issue of there being 'too many' of these hijab-wearing people often came up (1998, pp. 37–38). It is not so much that the subjects considered Muslims to be inferior (though they probably did); what they found more troubling was the idea that too many of these people might eventually lead to all Australian women being forced to wear the hijab. In one particularly infamous incident, the sheer presence of Muslim activist Yassmin Abdel-Magied on the ABC's *Q&A* prompted independent senator Jacqui Lambie to glare at her dark skin and colourful hijab and then scream in front of a live audience: 'There is one law in this country and it is the Australian law … it is not sharia law, not in this country. Not in my day' (Robertson, 2017). Similar to forms of homophobia, this kind of reaction is based on the contagion model; an attack against the hijab, both literally and figuratively, is an attempt by members of the dominant culture to prevent contamination of, and maintain control over, a territory that they imagine as their exclusive property.

Whenever I think of spatial management as a form of racism, I am often taken back to my time in school. I attended Punchbowl Boys High School between 1998 and 2004. During these years, 95 percent of the student population identified with some combination of Lebanese, Arab, Middle Eastern and Muslim. There were nine Mohammeds in my class alone; ten if you included me! Grossly underfunded and understaffed, Punchbowl Boys regularly appeared in the mainstream media—on television and in the newspapers—as the state's most troubled school (Rolfe, 2013). The students' cultural likeness, and in some cases their direct affiliation, with the 'Lebs' out in the streets who were involved in violent shootings, drug-dealings and sexual assaults, transformed every Punchbowl Boy into a wanted criminal. Very quickly, we found our fences surrounded by barbed wires and our walls covered with cameras. It wasn't long before the school earned its nickname: Punchbowl Prison.

A few school boys with terrorist-sounding names does not mean Australia is about to become an Islamic State. Nevertheless, there is certainly good reason for anyone who declares themself a White supremacist, White racist or White nationalist to try and keep us contained. Since 1788, ongoing waves of migration, as well as increasing awareness of Indigenous histories and human rights, have continued to transform Australia into a visibly more culturally diverse society, provoking many White Australians to believe they are a 'dying breed'. Hage refers to this phenomenon as the Discourse of Anglo Decline: 'This discourse either passively mourns or actively calls for resistance against what it perceives as a state-sanctioned assault on the cultural forms that have their roots in the British colonisation of Australia' (1998, pp. 179–180).

The Discourse of Anglo Decline is built on paranoia and speculations that an 'ethnic takeover' could happen, regardless of whether there is any visible evidence of it, but also on … conspicuous shifts in the cultural make-up of suburbs, schools, work-places, etc., which members of the dominant culture interpret as losing control of spaces that once belonged to them. Hage points out that 'it is primarily a lived reality for some Australians who, because of their specific social and cultural background, have not been able to incorporate into their national fantasy space the migrant presence that has resulted from the immigration of the 1970s, 1980s and 1990s' (1998, p. 210).

Whitey, sincerest condolences: my family is responsible for the lived reality of your dying breed. During the early '70s, my four grandparents and their 24 children migrated from Tripoli, northern Lebanon, to Redfern, New South Wales. Twenty years on, our family would increase ten-fold, as my parents and aunts and uncles gave birth to an army of Arab-Australians. We could no longer fit inside the crammed heritage-listed houses of Sydney's inner west, nor could we afford to keep living in a suburb that was going through an aggressive process of gentrification, so my entire generation, including my grandparents, parents, aunts, uncles, all their husbands and wives, my siblings and all my cousins, relocated to a suburb in south-western Sydney called Lakemba. And we weren't the only Lebanese there—the area had been so heavily flooded by our kind that we affectionately came to call the neighbourhood 'Leb-kemba'.

On my street alone, there was a Lebanese family in every house except for one, which was occupied by an old skip who owned a pink-nosed pit bull. Each morning my siblings and all our Lebo friends walked past his orange terrace on our way to Lakemba Public School, speaking passionately to each other in a mixture of English, Pig Latin and Arabic. The old skip would always be sitting there on his veranda, massaging his dog's chin as he bellowed across his lawn, 'I remember when the young fellas around 'ere used to speak Aussie!' I never felt any anger toward that peckerwood, only sympathy—he died before he ever saw his suburb return to the days of the Weet-Bix Kids.

A Lebanese family bought his house, tore it down, and built a duplex in its place. The entire street belonged to us now.

•••

As discussions about race in Australia and around the world have intensified, specifically within the context of the Black Lives Matter movement, the general fantasy among White people that they are under attack and in decline has been identified as part of a condition called 'White fragility'. Writing in first-person plural, Robin DiAngelo explains that White fragility is when a small amount of racial stress in White people becomes intolerable:

> The mere suggestion that being white has meaning often triggers a range of defensive responses. These include emotions such as anger, fear, and guilt and behaviours such as argumentation, silence, and withdrawal from the stress-inducing situation. These responses work to reinstate white equilibrium as they repel the challenge, return our racial comfort, and maintain our dominance within the racial hierarchy. (2018, p. 38)

One of the best examples of White fragility I have witnessed was the audience reaction to Winnie Dunn's 'White people are shit' remark in 2018. During question time, a White woman accused Winnie and the other panellists, who were all Indigenous or people of colour, as being the true racists in the room: 'I just want to know what you think you have to gain by calling me "shit". Everything you're suggesting we do to you, you are doing back to us, and I just want to know what you think you have to gain by that.' Next the White woman threatened to withdraw her support for the panellists' writing and books unless they were willing to be nicer to White people. When the panellists refused, the White woman began to sob, attracting a significant amount of attention, affection and support from the other White people in the crowd, who consoled her as she left the theatre in tears.

This incident was examined in a renowned *Guardian* article by author and journalist Ruby Hamad, who identified the audience member's behaviour as part of a historical pattern in which White women use 'strategic tears' to derail conversations about race and avoid their accountability and complicity in racism and White supremacy: 'White women are equally aware their race privileges them as surely as ours condemns us. In this context, their tearful displays are a form of emotional and psychological violence that reinforce the very system of white dominance that many white women claim to oppose' (Hamad, 2018).

In recent years, not only have White people demonstrated their inability to discuss Whiteness, but also their inability to discuss White fragility. Shortly after Hamad's article was published, it was shared on social media by African-American broadcaster Lisa Cooper. After two White female co-workers saw Cooper's post and reported her to management, she was permanently suspended for 'creating a hostile work environment based on race and sex' (Hamad, 2018). Consider the shameless cycle that White people have created here in an attempt to obscure any criticism of their privilege whatsoever—they cry when their racism is called 'shit', and they cry when their reaction to being called 'shit' is called 'fragile'. Diagnosis: White fragility fragility.

•••

It's exhausting constantly having to educate White people about a word that their own race invented to elevate themselves above the rest of us. It's even more exhausting constantly having to prove to White people that they are the benefactors, not the victims, of their own Whiteness. Twenty-two years since she delivered her maiden speech in parliament, and amid the recent push from Indigenous people and people of colour throughout the world for greater equality across the racial spectrum, Pauline Hanson has sustained her sense of White victimhood. In 2018, she declared her concern that 'anti-White racism' is on the rise and attempted to pass a motion in federal parliament that stated: It's OK to be White. In all fairness, she was just defending herself from the angry brown girl out in the ghetto who called her 'shit' that year.

When I first heard those words spoken out loud—'White people are shit'—I was immediately reminded of a similar turn of phrase I'd encountered as a young man. The Lebs at Punchbowl Boys were on their usual mission to derail our English teacher's Shakespeare lesson, and they were collectively asking her, 'Miss, why'd you get divorced?' and 'Miss, why don't you get re-married?' Ms Lombardo, an obese woman of Italian background, did not respond to any of these questions at first. She held our anticipation for several minutes until we all quietened down, and then, once the room was silent, she stood up, glared upon us with her deep-black eyes wide open, and said firmly and matter-of-factly: 'Men are shit.' Upon hearing these words, the Lebs did not accuse our teacher of personally attacking them; they did not call her a misandrist or a reverse sexist; they did not go running to the principal in tears, playing the victim and pretending to be traumatised by her foul discriminatory language; they did not attempt to have her fired for creating a hostile classroom environment based on sex and gender. Instead these 25 teenage boys quickly identified that throughout this poor woman's life, a handful of men had probably done some really awful shit to her. And they proceeded to ask her the obvious questions: 'What happened, miss?' 'Are you okay, miss?' 'Is there anything we can do to help, miss?' 'Want me to knock out your ex-husband, miss?'

So, here's a little riddle: Why is it that some dumb Lebs from Punchbowl Prison, who apparently come from the most patriarchal race and culture on Earth, are emotionally mature enough to be told that 'men are shit' without whining that they are the true victims of gender inequality, but when you tell some middle-class members of the dominant culture that 'White people are shit' they convince themselves that reverse racism is a greater problem than racism? You wanna know why? Because White people are …

References

J Collins, G Noble, S Poynting and P Tabar, *Kebabs, Kids, Cops and Crime*, Pluto Press Australia, Annandale, NSW, 2000.

J Cummins, *American Dirt*, Tinder Press, Hachette UK, London, 2019.

A Davies and J Norrie, 'Crime squad's new wave', *Sydney Morning Herald*, 7 April 2006, http://www.smh.com.au/news/national/crime-squads-new-wave/2006/04/06/1143916659479.html

R DiAngelo, *White Fragility: Why it's so hard for white people to talk about racism*, Beacon Press, Boston, 2018.

K Gleeson, 'From Centenary to the Olympics: Gang Rape in Sydney', *Current Issues in Criminal Justice*, vol. 16, no. 2 (2004), pp. 183–201.

I Gridneff and AAP, 'Sydney violence has no place in our country, Gillard says', *Sydney Morning Herald*, 16 September 2012, https://www.smh.com.au/national/nsw/sydney-violence-has-no-place-in-our-country-gillard-says-20120916-25zyq.html

G Hage, *White Nation: Fantasies of White Supremacy in a Multicultural Society*, Pluto Press, Annandale, NSW, 1998.

R Hamad, 'Could sharing an article about "white tears" be read as hostile?', *NITV*, 24 August 2018, https://www.sbs.com.au/nitv/article/2018/08/24/could-sharing-article-about-white-tears-be-read-hostile

R Hamad, 'How white women use strategic tears to silence women of colour', *The Guardian*, 8 May 2018.

A Mansour, *Not Quite White: Lebanese and the White Australia Policy 1880 to 1947*, Post Pressed, Teneriffe, Queensland, 2010.

G Noble, *Lines in the Sand*, Institute of Criminology Press, Annandale, NSW, 2006.

B Pease, *Undoing Privilege: Unearned Advantage in a Divided World*, Zed Books, London, 2010.

J Robertson, 'Q&A: Jacqui Lambie and Yassmin Abdel-Magied in heated clash over Islam and sharia law', *The Guardian*, 14 February 2017, https://www.theguardian.com/australia-news/2017/feb/14/qa-jacqui-lambie-and-yassmin-abdel-magied-in-heated-clash-over-islam-and-sharia

D Rolfe, 'A matter of principal', *Sydney Morning Herald*, 31 January 2013, http://www.smh.com.au/nsw/a-matter-of-principal-20130121-2d2ej.html

LF Saad, *Me and White Supremacy*, Quercus, Hachette UK, London, 2020.

SBS Television, *Insight*: 'True Colours', 2007.

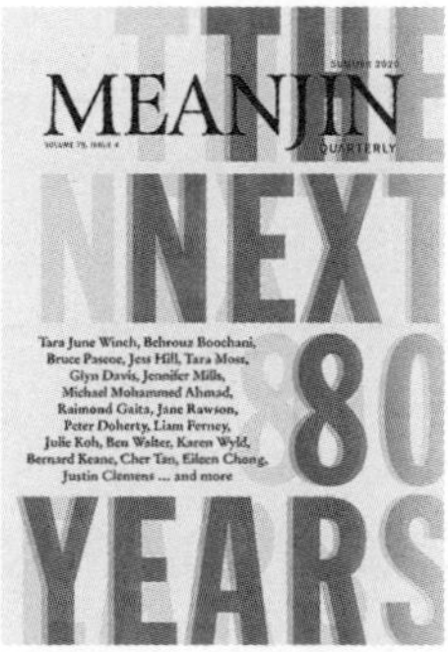

Multi-award-winning author **Michael Mohammed Ahmad** is the founding director of Sweatshop Literacy Movement. Mohammed's debut novel, *The Tribe* (Giramondo, 2014), won the 2015 *Sydney Morning Herald* Best Young Novelists of the Year Award. His second novel, *The Lebs* (Hachette Australia, 2018), won the 2019 NSW Premier's Multicultural Literary Award, and was shortlisted for the 2019 Miles Franklin Literary Award. Mohammed is also the editor of several critically acclaimed anthologies, including *After Australia* (Affirm Press, 2020). His memoir piece 'Life of a Folk Devil', published in *Meanjin* 82.1 Autumn 2023 and illustrated by Matt Chun, won the Woollahra Digital Literary Award. Mohammed received his Doctorate of Creative Arts from Western Sydney University in 2017, and is a tireless champion of the voices and the rights of culturally and racially marginalised writers.

Migrant women writers

Who's on whose margins?

Sneja Gunew

Meanjin 42.1 Autumn 1983

> No theory can develop without eventually encountering a wall, a practice is necessary for piercing this wall.
>
> We ridiculed representation and said it was finished, but we failed to draw the consequences of this 'theoretical' conversion—to appreciate the theoretical fact that only those directly concerned can speak in a practical way on their own behalf.
>
> —Gilles Deleuze[1]

THIS ESSAY WILL be about theory and practice as these relate to territorial boundaries, and about that 'voice of experience' and whether it can be authenticated.

Why should our concerns be with *migrant* writing?

For the time being let us assume that 'theory' translates, in this instance, into the territory of Australian writing, which in turn has long been a Tasmanian poor relation to British (Anglo-Celtic) writing. Not in the least does one wish to blunt that point, this shaft of practice which has pierced the walls of that institutional fortress, 'Brit. Lit.' Hurrah for anything that puts into question

1. From 'Intellectuals and Power: a conversation between Michel Foucault and Gilles Deleuze' in M Foucault, *Language, counter-memory, practice* (Cornell University Press, Ithaca, 1977), pp. 206, 209.

our hegemonic, monocultural assumptions. But perhaps the time has come also to question the category of 'Aust. Lit.' since it too has become a 'discursive formation' in Foucault's sense of the term. It too is now an institutional practice.

As a critic recently stated, Aust. Lit. is often loosely categorised as a 'corpus of travellers' tales … footnotes to the *Odyssey* and the *Aeneid*'.[2] This conjures up not just the picaresque Münchhausen yarns, but a whole coracle fleet of lone voyagers surrounding the unknown great southern land of the psyche. In turn, the interpersonal relations of voyagers and ocean have now spawned a new archipelago, that of migrant writing, a further set of cousins. But, as Jacques Derrida has pointed out (in *Of Grammatology*), the problem with supplements is that they tend to take over, insofar as they point to a lack or absence within the plenitude, in this case of the theory/territory of Australian writing. If something requires an addendum then it was incomplete from the beginning, and the supplement ends up supplanting the original. Here then, in the case of migrant writing, we discover a further set of travellers' tales which put into question, but also reinvigorate, the Australian literary paradigm of the exodus/adventus—the *Wanderroman* or *Wandergeschichte*.

The very term 'migrant writing' has been bestowed from within the *nouveau riche* walls of Australian writing. But how precisely was it arrived at and what is the nature of its taxonomic genealogy?

> It is perfectly possible to argue that some distinctive objects are made by the mind, and that these objects, while appearing to exist objectively, have only a fictional reality. A group of people living on a few acres of land will set up boundaries between their land and its immediate surroundings and the territory beyond, which they call 'the land of the barbarians'. In other words, this universal practice of designating in one's mind a familiar space which is 'ours' and an unfamiliar space beyond 'ours' which is

2. Ian Reid, 'What is an Australian Literary Work?' Unpublished paper delivered at ASAL Conference, Adelaide, May 1982.

> 'theirs' is a way of making geographical distinctions that *can be* entirely arbitrary ... Yet often the sense in which someone feels himself to be not-foreign is based on a very unrigorous idea of what is 'out there', beyond one's own territory.[3]

One of those 'fictions' underpinning the them-us binary opposition is the one which asks on just what authority 'they' speak to 'us'. Since the beginning of story-telling there has always been this question of *auctoritas*: who is licensed to hold us with a glittering eye? Invariably the answer comes: the witness, or, the simulacrum of one. As Deleuze reminds us, the direct voice, the authority of experience is the most compelling. But as we also know, from seeing endless documentary interviews and being bored by lack of editing in the agonising search for 'what really happened', there are conventions for truth-telling. The use of the first-person mode is no guarantee of anything but that a convention has been mobilised.

Which brings us to the further refinement of why this is an essay on migrant *women* writers. That women writers have privileged access to truth or to the confessional mode is an assumption underlying much of what gets published in recent women's writing, so much of which is cast in the first person. The glittering I and its relation to the hitherto suppressed, to the voice from the other side of the barbed wire, is what permeates the following discussion concerning the nexus of migrant, women, and writing.

Until very recently migrants, like women, have signalled their oppression largely through their silence, at least for those who were prepared to hear it. Certainly both migrants and women have long figured as the metaphoric caryatids of many myths. The problem with this subordinate position is that it suppresses specificity. The line from a recent fine example of migrant women's writing comes to mind; 'For all persecuted people look like Ghetto Jews to me'.[4] But the sameness about the oppressed and marginal voice

3. Edward Said, *Orientalism* (Vintage Books, New York, 1979), p. 54.
4. Maria Lewitt, *Come Spring* (Scribe, Fitzroy, 1980), p. 268.

is largely the result of the undifferentiated way it has been situated by the dominant culture. It comes back to the question of who issues the licence to speak and under what conditions.

One of the seductions of speaking in the first-person, in one's 'own voice', is that story-telling, narrative shaping, gives an illusion of power and control over one's life. The last few decades have seen a proliferation of writings from the oppressed, the marginal, which have been 'adopted' by dominant cultures. Why not? Is this not another version (as Edward Said has shown in his study of the discursive practice of Orientalism) of colonialism? And isn't the central metaphor, once again, that of sexual conquest?[5] The first-person account conveys both strength and vulnerability. As Foucault has most recently demonstrated (in *The History of Sexuality*), hearing confessions can also be an exercise in sexual politics.

One can generalise (as Said does) about the oppressed position as having invariable affinities with the female condition but this generalisation, or homogenising process, is in fact a large part of the process of oppression: as a character in a novel by Antigone Kefala puts it, 'to steal one's perspective was equal to killing a person'.[6] The blending process finally serves only to reinforce the normative, what we already know. Look, for example, at the whole notion of 'multiculturalism' which was heralded as a necessary successor to the oppressive concept of assimilation.

Multiculturalism is the patented supplement, the addendum to Anglo-Celtic mono-culturalism. But what really does it offer? Edward Said's contention that Orientalism (Europe's discourse about Islam and the Arab world) is an enclosed space, 'a theatrical space affixed to Europe', may cast new light on the domain of multiculturalism. Don't certain folkloric puppets glide easily into one's memory in the space reserved for migrants? For most New Australians growing up now and after the second World War, wasn't the acknowledgement of their difference palpably

5. See for example *Orientalism,* pp. 207, 309.
6. *The Island* (to be published by Hale & Iremonger in 1983).

recognised in a song and dance act in some school auditorium? And now can't we fill that theatrical space with even more public manifestations of multiculturalism—with multicultural television, for example? Contrary to the first conception of this project we have so far been offered very few *local* migrant voices. Instead the extra-Australian world has been ransacked for 'entertainment' which is defined by its alien and exotic characteristics. Even more than in the past the local migrants become further projections of this eternal repetition of the colourfully costumed singing dancing migrant. That's entertainment—with subtitles. And that whole issue of sub-titling, interpretation and translation deserves an essay in its own right.

From 'a whole world of migrants' we turn to another system of catching and classifying the authentic voice of migrant experience. A recent annotated bibliography of migrant writing[7] being promoted in secondary schools has chosen to include only those writers born outside Australia in a country which does not have English as a first language. The rationale for the publication is that it will promulgate cultural diversity and that 'it will have the ring of truth about it'. The venture is to be applauded but one cannot suppress the uneasy query: whose truth? By choosing to include only those authors born outside Australia and the English language it may be that the editors have, in spite of their stated intentions, guaranteed a limit to diversity. For example, for a writer who needs to break into not only a culture but also a language, success may well be synonymous with *writing like the Australians*. Success may mean *not* rocking the boat, abiding by the prevailing conventions in order to prove one's competence, not being master but mastered. Then the authority of experience will amount to suffering in distant parts and relief at being here in a safe territory—the will to assimilation in fact.

7. P Lumb and A Hazell (ed), *Diversity and Diversion: an Annotated Bibliography Australia Ethnic Minority Literature* (Hodja Press, Richmond, 1983).

A more empirical objection to the bibliography is that one of the finest accounts of children passing from one culture to another, Zeny Giles' *Between Two Worlds*[8] has not been included because Giles (Zenovia Doratis) was born here, though of Greek-Cypriot parents. Also excluded, because not so 'accessible', was poetry. The innovative language experiments of poets like π.O. and Ania Walwicz, who interrogate prevailing linguistic conventions far more profoundly than on the merely thematic level, are absent. This is another version of the blending process which shepherds migrant writers through a narrow gateway of the authentically ethnic.

If an enterprising publisher catches the bona fide migrant from overseas, the witness for the *Wanderroman*, then the most readily recognisable (and presumably saleable) mode of truth-telling is the first-person account. Even better if the illusion is heightened by the further subtitle that this is an auto-biographical account. (What writing is not?) Further, the desire to associate the first-person with the autobiographical in the sense used above is so strong that it will not be deterred by overt expressions to the contrary. For example, in that same bibliography a reviewer of Antigone Kefala's novella *The First Journey* persists in seeing the narrator (whose name is Alexi, amongst other references to the masculine gender) as a 'girl' on the sole evidence, one assumes, that the story is in the first person and the author is a woman. But the first person is open to anyone:

> The I is an empty signifier available to anyone. The mere use of I does not answer the question of who or what that I actually stands for.[9]

That 'I' guarantees nothing, just as the fact of being born overseas into a language other than English does not guarantee

8. Published by Saturday Centre Books, Cammeray NSW, 1981.
9. Nelly Furman, 'Textual Feminism' in *Women and Language in Literature and Society,* ed. by S McConnell-Ginet et al. (Praeger, New York, 1980), p. 50.

that one speaks from a place different from that taken by writers placed within the host language. Writing from a female position, writing from a migrant position, need not be coincident either with being biologically consigned to the female of the species, or with having come in on a foreign passport. One is not thereby magically freed of the conventions associated with the way the migrant is metaphorised in writing. Both women and migrants internalise the process whereby the culture constructs them, and it requires a great deal of self-conscious analysis before they are able to step (and only ever in part) outside these constructs. Therefore, as has been suggested, the pressures to conform are inevitably much stronger in the case of migrants of the first generation. Nonetheless, returning to Deleuze, theory needs to be pierced or extended by a practice and such a practice does derive from a material reality, among whose elements are both lived experience and its mediation by conventions of representation. There are no 'right answers' for detecting the authority of authenticity, I am merely advocating a skepticism towards equating certain conventions with truth-telling. Rather than expending energy on the quest for a pure-bred or authentic migrant voice, perhaps there is more to be gained by pursuing another kind of lateral approach, Foucault's notion of the transgressive.

> The limit and transgression depend on each other for whatever density of being they possess: a limit could not exist if it were absolutely uncrossable and, reciprocally, transgression would be pointless if it merely crossed a limit composed of illusions and shadows...
>
> Transgression carries the limit right to the limit of its being; transgression forces the limit to face the fact of its imminent disappearance, to *find itself in what it excludes* (perhaps, to be more exact, to recognize itself for the first time), to experience its positive truth in its downward fall?...
>
> Transgression, then, is not related to the limit as black to white, the prohibited to the lawful, the outside to the inside, or as the open area of a building to its enclosed spaces. Rather,

their relationship takes the *form of a spiral which no simple infraction* can exhaust.[10]

It is possible that it is not so much a question of 'being' a migrant but of writing from a migrant position, and this in turn could be a matter of choosing to interrogate—a will to alienation. Admittedly this is also, in the long run, going to mean being subject to metaphorisation since anyone can mimic forms of rebellion. It is not just a matter of which 'I' but of what sustains the various 'Is': what are the conditions of speaking? 'I paid for this. I am pleased. I am my own ... When I open the door, I open me'.[11] How many 'Is' are offered here? The authentic voice, the practice which extends the theory, is always a problematic category which can only ever be partially defined. In the case of migrant writing it is not synonymous with the discursive formation of 'multiculturalism'. Neither is it merely reducible to the rhetoric of conviction, the first-person mode. It is not exhausted, for example, by the voices of migrants contained in the oral history collections by Lowenstein and Loh.[12] If it were, we would never need to move beyond such oral history. It is only one area of the archipelago of migrant writing.

To explore other aspects, I would like now to focus on the work of four writers, to show their differences from each other as well as their difference from Australian Anglo-Celtic writing. Antigone Kefala is a Rumanian Greek who emigrated to and spent her youth in New Zealand before moving to Sydney. Zeny Giles (Zenovia Doratis) was born in Sydney of Greek-Cypriot parents. Ania Walwicz was born in Poland and arrived in Australia in her adolescence. Anna Couani is a second-generation Australian of Greek-Polish extraction (a Polish grandfather arrived here

10. 'A Preface to Transgression' in *Language, counter-memory, practice*, pp. 34–35.
11. Ania Walwicz, 'I' in *Mattoid*, 13, p. 22 (available from the School of Humanities, Deakin University, Victoria, 3217).
12. M Loh, *With Courage in their Cases* (F.I.L.E.F. Coburg, 1980). W Lowenstein and M Loh, *The Immigrants* (Penguin Australia, 1977).

in 1860). On the face of it Couani does not belong in the category of migrant women writer yet she chooses to speak from various migrant positions, as we shall see. All four writers are transgressive in ways that interweave the voices of women and of migrants: testing the limits of languages, the limits of gender.

Unity is conferred by the gaze of the other, the parent culture. This corresponds to the homogenising process we have already observed. But the notion of a unified subject is very much in dispute in recent times. Where, if not in marginal territories, might we seek conventions which represent the fragmented subject, the splintered ego? If it is to succeed in being compelling, the glittering eye must, at the very least, reflect the eye of its listener. Here, as in so many other places, Lacan's account of the mirror stage in the formation of the subject is helpful, in this case, for understanding the notion of the fragmented subject.[13] In this fiction, the child's first encounter with the mirror endows its fragmented sense of self with a spurious unity; endows but at the same time imprisons and at the cost of several other aspects of the potential 'I' which need subsequently to be suppressed. The mirror stage is analogous with that process which includes the entry into language, into socialisation, the prescriptive gaze of the other which succeeds in splitting the subject into perceiver and perceived, subject and object. That schizophrenic perspective, sometimes overtly attached to the image of the mirror, but always indicating the network of contradictions which invade the enunciating subject, is a trope of migrant writing. One common manifestation is in connection with names, those social labels for the unified subject which, when questioned, or changed, or mutilated, throw everything concerned with identity into question.

> She could see that Manoli was right—they had to learn to live in two worlds. At school they would answer to Nina and Herb. They would speak English, trying to copy every characteristic of the accent around them. They would join in lessons and

---

13. Jacques Lacan, *Écrits: a Selection* (Tavistock, London, 1980).

> sport and play with their Australian friends, trying in every way to fit in. But as soon as they stopped at the back door of their house, they were different people. Herb would become Manoli, Nina would become Finnaki or Chrisaphina, as Father called her. (Giles, *Between Two Worlds*)

How does one project the self onto a world when the prime signifier, the personal name, has either disappeared or become multiplied? Mirrors, as in Lacan's account, reflect more than surfaces.

> And I stayed alone in my room watching my face in the mirror. Caged in myself. Petrified in this frame out of which I could never hope to come except by a definite act. A positive act of will that would destroy me at the same time. And in the meantime the other one stayed inside me unimpressed. For there were always two inside. The one that moved and laughed, cried and was angry, had attitudes and demanded things and was stubborn in wanting, that felt the vacuum and was afraid. And there was the second one. The one that undermined every effort towards an involvement. The one that dwelt somewhere at the roots of my being and knew with an absolute certainty that everything was futile. That I was making far too much noise about all these not very important matters. The second one that could see through everything. That was merciless. Absolutely indifferent. That watched the very movement of people with a sharp clinical eye, when I, the other one, was totally involved. So that the moment became split, between a doer and a watcher, and the watcher being the stronger, the doer tried to maintain such a level of concentration and involvement leaving no room, no crack, for the second one to insinuate itself. (Kefala, *The First Journey*)

That second 'I' perceives the fragility of the constructs of the self as they impinge on the equally fragile surrounding world. In Giles' *Between Two Worlds* the mirror functions to confirm a past socio-cultural self that has been interrogated too soon.

> Before he'd started school in Australia, he had always fitted in so comfortably that he'd never even thought of what he looked like. He didn't remember even bothering to look in a mirror in Castellorizo, except perhaps to pull a funny face. Now he would stare into the bathroom mirror and he was ashamed of his brown skin and his short black hair. He was determined never to allow Maria to cut his hair again. But most of all he hated the old-fashioned knitted suit Maria had bought in Port Said, it made him look so different from the others. He had been at school for well over a month and he still dreaded the time each day when one bully or another would poke fun at him. And the terrible part about it was that although he despised these bullies for making fun of him, he wanted to be like them. He wanted light hair and fair skin and, most of all, he wanted to wear not-good clothes. (Giles, *Between Two Worlds*)

Implied in both these quotations is the arbitrary nature of these social images which in turn reflect, or cast doubts on, the nature of the larger social structures which prescribe certain convention of behaviour and speech. Compare this with Ania Walwicz's two prose poems: 'I' and 'Sitting Pretty'.[14] In the latter there is once again the splintering of the self into the social selves of certain kinds of female stereotypes: an amalgamation of doll and child. Again, as in the Kefala extract, there is the caged self but in this case, paradoxically, because the images are so definitive, so definable, it is possible to escape them. The enunciating 'I', from a third place (not doll, not child), discards them. 'And I was nice and quiet and no trouble to anyone. And clean and tidy. And I left me.' In the poem 'I' there is a reverse movement of Rabelaisian (or Whitmanesque) inclusiveness where the 'I' finally (and in a fundamentally truthful phenomenological sense) engulfs everything, but also remains 'I'. 'My objects are pieces of me … They speak my words. I wrote them.' Although it embraces the

14. A Walwicz, *Writing* (Rigmarole, Melbourne, 1982), p. 27.

universe, the 'I' is subject *and* object still. Compare this with the fifth section of Couani's prose poem, 'Untitled'.

> The two white chiffon curtains are being blown into the room by the wind from the open window. They are twisting like cigarette smoke and obscure the view which is of a hazy grey block of a building. Through the open doorway to the next room can be seen a mirror which reflects the mattress on the floor and some pillows, sheets and clothes. There is a small tinkling sound and then a door closing softly. The curtains are blowing over the table just touching the top of a glass without moving it.[15]

Here the 'I' is displaced by the description of objects, akin to the putative objectivity of a camera eye. Gradually, in succeeding sections, across the fixed frame of the mirror, there drift further details, including limited human statements. In this case it is the reflected listener, the reader, who is left free to draw connections between these fragments. In a later poem sequence in that volume, 'The View', the various sections keep re-playing the same perceived sequence of events in order to tease out various meanings. In this case more of the process is completed for the reader but, nonetheless, there is never a total unification or closure. The ends are not tied up. It is never a question of a unified perspective mediating or enclosing an event. This refusal of closure, this interrogative approach, reinforces the notion of language itself as a network of territories where boundaries keep shifting in accordance with prevailing ideologies. *These transgressions query constantly the concept of a 'natural' language in which one gains competence.* 'You step outside convention and then you forget it. The convention seems arbitrary—for anyone who does it anywhere in the world.'[16] Amongst other things the migrant voice can alert readers to the arbitrary nature of place, that the mother or father land amounts to an imaginary territory perilously shored

15. A Couani, *Italy* (Rigmarole, Melbourne, 1977), p. 11.
16. A Couani, *Were all women sex-mad?* (Rigmarole, Melbourne, 1982), p. 20.

up by conventions which may melt away on close scrutiny. In an interview about her writing, Ania Walwicz stated:

> As both woman and migrant I have been given no sense of belonging in the world, no set place. I have to state my identity. I have to reconstruct the world ... I join me to the world.[17]

This awareness, that the 'world' comes into being through the 'I' is echoed by the narrator in *The First Journey*:

> The old fear in me again that they might all disappear some day because of a negligence of awareness on my part. A moment when I would fail to lend them my *constant* support as an onlooker, that gave substance to their limbs.[18]

At the same time since communication needs to involve the recognition of a shared base, that 'I' is the result of construction in and through language. In *Between Two Worlds*, Manoli is unable to articulate his sense of self in the alien language but breaks through when he recognises a familiar place in the universal language of numbers (p. 50). Later, the book includes an important section where Greek and English words are juxtaposed so that the shared base is extended by means of this either/and rather than either/or approach. In Kefala's story 'Alexia' the eponymous protagonist is introduced to the vagaries of the English language by a teacher who demands:

> 'Are you happy?'
> Alexia went immediately into a panic. For she felt HAPPY to be an Enormous Word, a word full of flamboyant colours, which only people who had reached an ecstatic state had a right to use. She saw it as the apotheosis, so to speak, of a series of events which, as far as she could see, lay totally outside her life. But she could not explain this, for everyone on the Island

17. Walwicz, *Mattoid* 13, p. 14.
18. A Kefala, *The First Journey* (Wild & Woolley, Sydney, 1975), p. 27.

kept asking, as if this Fantastic Word was the basic measure of their days—
...
And the more she thought about it, the more confused she became. Did Miss Prudence mean:
Was she happy eating her mashed potatoes?
Being in the house with the grandfather clock chiming?
Happy living on the Island?
or
Happy living in the world?
There she was, with the salt cellar in her hand, which she had been asked to pass on to Mary, not knowing what to say, getting more and more confused between Happiness and Salt.[19]

What can be more transgressive than such comedy? Almost comparable in the sardonic confusion of meaning and representation is Lucija Berzins' story 'The Berlitz Method'[20] in which an earnestly conducted English language class is anarchically sustained by the promise of a strip-tease.

Edward Said has explored in detail how the Orient becomes an object constructed by the Orientalist. So too the migrant becomes an object constructed by Australian culture, in particular, by its officialdom. Paternalistic institutions reduce the migrant to the status of child as is seen in Walwicz's poems 'So Little'[21] and 'helpless'[22]:

before they were big i was small they could do things more than me they were something now they are nothing he was a doctor of animals now he was learning to speak properly he talked funny they made mistakes she was clumsy she works in a factory he cleans the floors of the serum laboratory now life can be everybody clean and nice and we are all wrong

19. 'Alexia' in *Mattoid* 13, pp. 38–43.
20. M Jürgensen (ed), *Ethnic Australia* (Phoenix, Brisbane, 1981).
21. *Mattoid* 13, p. 19.
22. S Gunew (ed), *Displacements: Migrant Storytellers* (Deakin University, Victoria, 1982), p. 2.

> here i was the translator i was the mother of my mother they were more helpless they were useless nervous didn't know what to do i was too serious for me it was too early to be like this we walked lost on the street we were looking for John street i was bigger than them my parents were again small old children they were heavy for me they couldn't do much you are helpless useless.

So that another trope in migrant writing becomes, not surprisingly, the government institution, be it a hospital (as in Kefala's 'The Waiting Room'[23], Walwicz's 'Hospital'[24], or even the academy, as in the following extract from Kefala's unpublished novel, *The Island:*

> I spoke. One could see from his face that he had not the faintest idea what I was saying, the meaning stopped somewhere mid air between us, he incredulous that he will ever understand me, I incredulous that he will ever understand me. He was busy swallowing thin mouthfuls of vinegar, watching me with preoccupied eyes, rubbing his hands as if drying them of sand, trying to get rid of it. One could see in his whole attitude the immense surprise of being confronted, here in his own room, at the University, by something as foreign as myself. The implied extravagance of my voice, the rapid nervousness of my movements, my eyes that looked too directly at him.

As well, however, there is a reversal of this process of objectification when the migrant, in turn, transforms the Australian experience into an object. Compare, for example, Walwicz's poem 'Australia'[25]: 'You big ugly. You too empty. You desert with your nothing nothing ... You don't like me and you don't like women' and its counterpoint poem 'Wogs'.[26]

---

23. D White and A Couani (ed), *Island in the Sun 2,* (Sea Cruise Books, Glebe, 1981), pp. 58–59.
24. Walwicz, *Writing,* pp. 20–21.
25. Walwicz in *Island in the Sun 2,* pp. 90–91.
26. Walwicz, *Mattoid* 13, pp. 16–17.

> you can't speak to them why don't you learn to speak english properly they are not like you or me they're not the same as everybody they change us is your child educated by an australian? is it? do you know if? you don't know what they think you don't know what they can do here they change us they paint their houses blue green have you seen blue houses who ever heard of that they live too many together they're too noisy they

In a sense the 'you' addressed in the former is the speaker of the latter, in the former the speaker is oppressed, migrant and female and attacks the assumptions of the 'you' which is loosely defined as Ocker and male but also, strangely, oppressed. 'You go to work in the morning. You shiver on a tram.' In the fourth chapter of Couani's *Were all women sex-mad?* there is a long section of Australia as object for scrutiny by, presumably, the 'citizen of the world' mentioned elsewhere:

> It's unique I'll say that. Anyone can feel at home there because it has a strange character or atmosphere which is like an absence of character, a kind of neutrality. I think it's very tolerant or maybe just very anonymous. No really, I do *like* Australia. When I lived there I liked it. But I realize coming away again that there's some strange pressure there. It's subliminal, very subtle. I don't think I could describe it exactly because it's an abstract quality which pervades everything there, the work situation, the politics, the social life. It's a place that gets you down. The amount of drinking the people do is phenomenal. And it's as though everyone's bitten by the same bug—some kind of desperation or hysteria which is never expressed. They're stoics, the Aussies. The most cynical people in the world. Beyond morality—like the English but more sophisticated because they never say *anything*.

And later, even more damning:

> But now it's changing a bit at last. They're starting to come in from the cold like the old stockman returning to the bright

> lights of the station after 2 weeks riding the fences in the cold and the dust. While he's away he has to remember the warmth and light of his home but when he comes back he can forget it.
> —He says, And then I get home and wouldn't you know—the wife started her period today. Forget it.
> —I think you're starting to understand.

Looking at migrant women's writing is a way of questioning literary taxonomies. Such writing speaks from positions which interrogate socio-cultural conventions, notions of linguistic competence, and gender certainties. Migrant, and women's, and migrant women's writing are the 'excess' of Anglo-Celtic writing, a luxury which is an index of what? Civilised skepticism? The mining rights to an unknown territory? New histories for new subjects?

> He claimed that in order to understand history, one needed a type of vision that only people placed at the crossroads could provide. That is, people that lived between cultures, who were forced to live double lives, belonging to no group, and these he called 'the people in between'. This type of vision he maintained, was necessary to the alchemy of cultural understanding. (Kefala, *The Island*)

For those inclined to take territorial metaphors for certainties, migrant writing indicates that Australia is really off the planet.

In 1983 **Sneja Gunew** (1946–2024) was teaching literature at Deakin University. She was the editor of *Displacements: Migrant Storytellers* (Deakin University Press, 1982) and had recently completed two video films on migrant narratives. Gunew went on to become a nation-leading campaigner for cultural diversity in the arts, and one of Australia's most innovative literary critics and theorists. Her pioneering work founded a significant area of creative and critical endeavour, bringing multiculturalism in from the margins to become a defining feature of Australian literature. After Gunew's recent death, Wenche Ommundsen, Emeritus Professor, University of Wollongong, and Gunew's literary executor, reflected: 'Sneja Gunew leaves behind a vast legacy: pioneering work on feminism and multiculturalism in art and literature together with large numbers of former students, colleagues, research associates and friends who have greatly benefited from her intellectual and personal generosity.'

On criticism

Jane Howard

Meanjin 82.4 Summer 2023

> The great weakness of criticism in Australia is that it is not in itself a profession. Journalism is a profession. But to be a critic is to write a column in one's spare time.

That was theatre critic Katharine Brisbane writing in *The Australian* in 1971. Most critics, she went on to say, 'have another job—usually a journalistic or academic one—at which they earn their real living; and a visit to an exhibition or a performance is a diversion of their weekly routine'.[1]

I, like most critics working in Australia today, have always had a day job where I earn my 'real living'. If there was ever a dream I could make a living from criticism, it was quickly quashed when faced with the realities of the industry. Arts journalism is a niche field; criticism is a niche within a niche.

Arts journalism in our mainstream news publications exists largely due to the belief of newsroom leadership in its inherent value. More Australians might engage with art than sport,[2] but more people are at your average AFL game than your average night at the theatre. It stands to reason a sports story will get more eyeballs than an arts story.

---

1. Brisbane, K (2005). *Not Wrong—Just Different*. Currency Press, 177–181 (original work published 10 July 1971).
2. Debritz, B (2020, February 27). 'Sorry, sport, but the arts are winning the numbers game'. *InQueensland*.

It is easy—and possibly smart—to be pessimistic about the place of arts coverage in Australian news organisations. Already this year, *The Canberra Times* has stopped commissioning reviews (and axed its 101-year-old bridge columnist, which feels especially churlish) due to cost-cutting measures.[3] *The Adelaide Advertiser* severely cut back its reviews coverage of the Adelaide Fringe.[4] The ABC will no longer have a specialist, stand-alone arts desk.[5]

But this pessimism is nothing new. The history of criticism in Australia is one of an industry perennially in crisis.

'Australian art-criticism is a joke among artists of any consequence, but the joke is on the Australians,' wrote a columnist in *The Bulletin* in 1934. 'They are getting what they deserve, and they will continue to get it till they begin to take an interest in art which is in some degree comparable to the interest they take in sport.'[6] Sydney's art critics can be divided into two camps, wrote *The Bulletin* in 1881, 'the bad and the very bad'.[7] Music critics are 'dishonest or ignorant', wrote R Minton Taylor in the letters page of literary journal *The Triad* in 1926.[8] Australian theatre criticism is 'utterly incompetent and sickeningly servile', said the same journal the following year.[9]

Why so much disdain? Much criticism of the critic over the past hundred years appears to stem from how these writers come to their positions.

'With one or two exceptions,' said a JD in *The Bulletin* in 1933, 'the highly technical business of criticising pictures is given

---

3. Meade, A (2023, June 29). 'Shuffling the deck: Canberra Times drops 101-year-old bridge columnist as part of cost-cutting drive'. The Weekly Beast, *Guardian Australia*.
4. Marsh, W (2023, February 23). 'Adelaide Fringe: Stand-off between festival and the News Corp-owned The Advertiser'. *The Sydney Morning Herald*.
5. Eltham, B (2023, June 19). 'The ABC sacrifices arts coverage in latest staff cuts'. *Crikey*.
6. 'Criticism in Australia'. (1934, April 4). *The Bulletin*, 5.
7. 'Curious criticism'. (1881, May 14). *The Bulletin*, 13.
8. Minton Taylor, R (1926, November 1). 'A Good (?) Australian Hits Back at Mr. Gerald Simpson'. *Triad*, 11(13), 34.
9. JVD (1927, January 8). 'The Theatre in Australia'. *Triad*, 13(1), 46.

to some member of the staff who is not yet old enough to be trusted with the law reports or racing.'[10] The average critic and his employer, wrote John Lloyd in the journal *Manuscripts* that same year, 'apparently has been unaware that the work requires a special training'.[11] There is a 'growing trend', wrote Cameron Williams in *RealTime* in 2017, 'where editors and producers aren't looking for experienced critics to provide arts coverage'.[12]

Arts coverage is 'a sad trailer to politics, economics and general feature writing' (1984);[13] newspaper critics 'know about as much of dramatic criticism as a professional politician knows about common honesty' (1926);[14] Australia's newspapers hire expert economists, politics academics, former international sports stars and yet 'there are only two directions in which the dailies depart from their rule that none but experts need apply—art criticism and book reviewing' (1933).[15]

'Criticism is valueless when most newspapers neither want good criticism nor are prepared to pay for it,' wrote the ABC's theatre columnist Geoffrey Thomas in 1953 in the broadcaster's weekly print magazine.[16] 'The state of art criticism in Australia has never been worse,' said Paul McGillick, director of Sydney's Institute of Contemporary Art, in 1977.[17] 'I'm quite optimistic about the future of music journalism because it is currently about as bad as it can get,' said musicologist Matthew Lorenzon in 2017.[18] Newspaper hiring sends a clear message, said writer Shirley Le

---

10. JD (1933, May 17). 'Criticism in Australia'. *The Bulletin*, 5.
11. Lloyd, J (1933, August). 'Criticism in relation to Australian literature'. *Manuscripts*, 6, 15.
12. Williams, C (2017, June 6). 'Triple J & arts criticism in crisis'. *RealTime*.
13. Griffiths, G (1984, March 1). 'Theatre Reviewing in Australia'. *Meanjin*, 43.1, 186–193.
14. Russell, E (1926, November 1). 'Barrie versus dramatic criticisms'. *The Triad*, 11(13), 39.
15. See footnote 10.
16. Thomas, G (1953, December 12). 'Can art thrive without criticism?' *ABC Weekly*, 15(50), 14.
17. McGillick, P (1977, January 22). 'Congrats to the critics'. *The Bulletin*, 5.
18. Eslake, S (2017, May 25). 'What is the future of Australian arts journalism?' *CutCommon*.

in 2020, that 'the monocultural face, voice and gaze of the Australian arts reviewership is here to stay'.[19]

As far back as 1869, newspapers were bemoaning that Australian literature critics 'judge colonial productions more favourably, criticise them more leniently, deal with their faults more mercifully, praise their merits more warmly' than books from England.[20] 'There is a widespread tendency, which can do Australia nothing but harm, to condemn as anti-Australian any critic who refuses to pretend that mediocre Australian works are good ones,' opined a *Sydney Morning Herald* editor's note in 1945.[21] In 2004, in *Metro*, film critic Paul Byrnes said, 'If you apply different standards to an Australian film you're not doing the film any favours.'[22]

In 2019, theatre critic Alison Croggon described the 'product-driven consumer review, which is more often a function of public relations than of serious intellectual enterprise'.[23] 'It is a disturbing phenomenon when the reckless and vindictive critic is suddenly embraced when a favourable notice appears', wrote critic Murray Bramwell in 1994.[24]

Management at the ABC, said Keith Gallasch in 2004, seems to have 'a suspicion and dislike of the arts as difficult, and a total lack of vision'.[25] An ABC specialist this June said the redundancy of their digital arts editor speaks to 'a lack of conviction in arts coverage by ABC management ... Why do we have to beg for a dedicated arts reporter for online when there must be a multitude covering sport?'[26]

---

19. Le, S (2020, May 6). 'Pardon your expression'. *Overland.*
20. Henbiots (1869, February 27). 'Colonial criticism'. *The Australasian*, 264.
21. 'Book reviewing criticised'. (1945, October 9). *Sydney Morning Herald*, 4.
22. Cenere, P (2004, September 6). 'Film Criticism ... Somebody's Got to Do It'. *Metro Magazine.*
23. Croggon, A (2019). 'Criticism, Performance and the Need for Conversation'. *Currency House.*
24. Bramwell, M (1994, September 1). 'Critical Conditions'. *Meanjin* 53.3, 447–454.
25. Gallasch, K (2004, June 1). 'The arts, ecologically'. *RealTime*, 61, 4–5.
26. See footnote 5.

'Really, why does an intelligent and informed public put up with this sort of nonsense?' exclaimed academic Gareth Griffiths in *Meanjin* in 1984.[27]

So, after 150 years of consternation, what of reviewing in Australia today?

When the critic has to earn their 'real living' outside of review writing, they are only able to interact with a small minority of the art in their field. When 'most newspapers neither want good criticism nor are prepared to pay for it', the number of commissions is diminished.

Over the past two decades, we have lost specialist arts magazines, column inches in newspapers, and much of the street press where the critics of my generation cut our teeth. Some online publications entered the fray and have lasted; others turned out to be a flash in the pan—to say nothing of the once vibrant and flourishing culture of theatre blogs where we learnt our craft and found our community.

Australian book reviewing is in a healthier place than most. A recent report into literary journals in Australia found 29 contemporary publications, with some (such as *Australian Book Review* and the *Sydney Review of Books*) primarily publishing book criticism, and many publishing reviews alongside essays, poetry and fiction.[28]

Book criticism benefits from a natural synergy between writers in other genres and critics, and a natural synergy between the readers of books and readers of reviews. Many writers in these journals also find a home in the generalist press, where many publications offer both short-form reviews in the form of recommendations and longer, more considered pieces. There is also a commercial industry of booksellers that drives reviewing, from specialist publications like *Books+Publishing* to bookshop websites.

27. See footnote 13.
28. Menzies-Pike, C, & Ryan, S (2023, July). *Literary Journals in Australia*. Writing and Society Research Centre of Western Sydney University.

The nature of books—unlike, say, a theatre production or a gallery exhibition—means they work on different timelines and aren't geographically constrained. There are more spaces to retrospectively consider the big books from three years ago, or the smaller books that were lost.

There are a handful of Australian visual art magazines and, while writing might not be the primary artform for visual artists, many artists will have a critical literary lens they occasionally lend to the work of others. For all other artforms, there tends to be a sharp divide between your artist and your critic, and the collection of specialist, professional publications drops precipitously. There are a couple of generalist arts publications covering as much of the local industry as they can, but it is a big job for these small organisations.

When we turn our eye to generalist news organisations, most publications have an arts desk and specialist editors, if more rarely specialist journalists. Some publications place everything under an arts and/or culture umbrella, with a handful of news organisations also having specialist literary or books editors. Editors (including myself, as arts and culture editor at *The Conversation*) have to balance the commissioning of reviews with news and broader cultural analysis. There is never enough staff to cover all we should be covering.

Unfortunately, this means it is often independent productions, smaller gallery shows and films without a wide release that are less likely to be reviewed. It's in these spaces—the collectives of emerging theatre makers, the artist-run initiatives, the pub back rooms—where you often find the most exciting art. They are the artists pushing the form forward, asking new questions in new ways. They deserve considered criticism—but so few places have the time or space to dedicate coverage to this work. With every click measured on the internet, it becomes harder to justify the work required to give these pieces of art the consideration they deserve.

But it's not just independent shows that aren't being covered. A critic might once have covered every show in a state theatre company's season. Now, the critic and their editor are often only covering a handful of shows in a season. It's critical damnation by omission.

The internet, while offering new publishing opportunities for many, is still on constantly shifting ground. Referrals to news websites from social media are shrinking as algorithms (and legal landscapes) change.[29] We're now anxiously watching on as Google's increasing use of artificial intelligence could stymie click-throughs to news pages.[30] In this landscape, it is easy to imagine how criticism, already less popular than news, will find it harder to hold on. And it's not just arts desks we need to be thinking about: it seems all specialist positions could be at risk. Earlier this year, *The New York Times* disbanded its sports desk, instead sub-contracting content to its subsidiary publication *The Athletic*.[31]

In Australia, a lot of arts journalism (and almost all criticism) is done by freelance writers. Where this isn't the case, some non-arts staff will cover arts stories. There are many writers, especially at local and regional ABC stations, who are passionate about covering the arts in their community. But speak to these journalists and they will frequently talk about how they had to 'fight' to publish these stories.

Arts journalism and criticism are still in a period of adjustment in the internet age. We critics have never been less relevant to the marketing and awareness of new productions or publications. There is no need to turn to the local paper to see what theatre shows are on if you can go to a website—or, even easier, follow the company you like on social media. Arts organisations are more in control of their narrative; arts criticism, in particular, is often regarded as superfluous.

Digital tools mean theatre performances can be easily videoed for archival purposes—there is no need for a critic to write this

29. Majid, A (2023, May 4). 'Facebook referral traffic to news sites: How it has plunged'. *Press Gazette*.
30. Owen, LH (2023, May 11). 'Google is changing up search. What does that mean for news publishers?' *Nieman Lab*.
31. Klein, C (2023, July 14). '"There Hasn't Been Empathy": NYT Staff Frustration Spills Over After Sports Desk Closure'. *Vanity Fair*.

first draft of history. This is all well and good for established artists, but what does this mean for the random discoverability of a new band, a new gallery, a new theatre director? What does this mean for how we understand art because of the context it is made in if we have no outsiders to consider that context?

For more commercial, popular media—such as blockbuster cinema and pop music—the questions have already been asked and answered: corporations behind this art want cheerleader 'influencers', not serious cultural criticism.[32] This boosterism is, unfortunately, not rare enough when it comes to criticism of other artforms—even if the junkets, merchandise or cultural cachet comes up short. What does the critical critic do in the face of such cheerleading?

There are values prescribed to arts criticism that we, as outsiders to the productions, rarely talk about. A July article in *Dance Magazine* detailed how the lack of reviews is impacting visa applications for dancers and touring groups in America;[33] recently, a local producer told me they had used my words in an application for a UK visa for their artists. Where does this leave artists—especially those emerging artists—who might be looking to take their work overseas?

These are all questions we should be facing. But the biggest difficulty facing Australian criticism today is how rarely criticism in Australia appears in dialogue. What do we make of the theatre critic who isn't seeing every show; of the art critic who isn't going to every exhibition? What do we make of the book that received only two reviews; of the book that received none? How do we understand a critic if we're not regularly seeing their name and understanding their tastes?

Good criticism thrives in the complexity of its environment. Each review sits in conversation with every other review of a

32. Lazic, M (2023, August 1). 'Who needs film critics when studios can be sure influencers will praise their films?' *The Guardian*.
33. Whittenburg, Z (2023, July 5). 'How a Lack of Dance Criticism in the U.S. Affects International Dancers' Visa Applications'. *Dance Magazine*.

piece of art, with every other review the critic has written. The shrinking space for considered criticism and professional careers as critics means more and more artworks won't get written into our history—unless by the marketers.

Cultural critic and humorist Sydney Smith (1771–1845) reputedly said, 'I never read a book before reviewing it; it prejudices a man so.'[34] It's worth meditating on this in light of the recent accusations of plagiarism, published by Mary Garden in this journal, against Ross Fitzgerald regarding his reviews in *The Australian*.[35]

People have long been floating the idea that reviews should be objective. The mid-2010s' violent 'Gamergate' movement ostensibly started against 'unethical' and objective games journalists.[36] Read: critics (mostly women) who dared to bring themselves, and their biases, into the way they approached a review.

So, as Smith joked, is the ideal review sent on high from a place of objectivity, in which case perhaps the best review is an amalgamation of all that came before? I think not. The best review is a much messier affair. And strangely, after diving into the archives and reading Garden's piece, it is in this messiness where I find my strongest strains of hope for criticism in Australia today and into the future.

To review is to grapple with a piece of art, yes. But it is also to grapple with yourself: how do you see the world, and how does the world see you? What are the biases you bring to life and to art? Who are you, experiencing this piece of art, on this day, in this place?

What I enjoy so much about a lot of Australian arts criticism today is in the tangle of these questions. Critics aren't afraid to put themselves—their chaotic, biased selves—into their writing.

---

34. Ratcliffe, S Ed. (2017). 'Sydney Smith'. *Oxford Reference*.
35. Garden, M (2023, July 19). 'Plagiarism, cobbling or accidental inclusion?' *Meanjin*: meanjin.com.au/latest/plagiarism-cobbling-or-accidental-inclusion/
36. Romano, A (2020, January 20). 'What was Gamergate? The lessons we still haven't learned'. *Vox*.

'A critic cannot be fair in the ordinary sense of the word,' wrote Oscar Wilde. 'It is only about things that do not interest one that one can give a really unbiased opinion, which is no doubt the reason why an unbiased opinion is always absolutely valueless.'[37]

Art is relational. It means nothing in a vacuum, and so criticism means nothing in a vacuum. To take the human—sitting in the theatre, walking through the gallery, turning the pages of the book—out of the equation is to take away from criticism the only thing that matters.

My favourite critic is not the writer I always agree with. It is not the writer I trust to send me forward into my next piece of art. It is the critic who is honestly themselves. I do not trust their opinion to guide mine. I trust their opinion to be in dialogue with mine.

The great joy of criticism in Australia right now is how many excellent people we have writing it, in all of their messy complexities. There is Cassie Tongue, who comes to musical theatre with her whole heart. Jini Maxwell, who makes the virtual worlds of games feel tangible and real. Sheila Ngọc Phạm, who connects her book reviews not only to who she is today but also who she was as a child and all the pieces in between. Timmah Ball, who captures the visual arts with sheer exuberance.

The joy is in Elias Greig exploding the narrative of *Bruny* by Heather Rose into a much broader discussion of art in Australia,[38] Catriona Menzies-Pike considering Trent Dalton not just on the page but also in how we read him,[39] and Declan Fry on a group show at Gertrude Contemporary and the contradictions and tangents of our brains we experience in the presence of art.[40]

It is wonderfully, gloriously easy to list off the brilliant critics working in Australia today. I am so often energised by the reviews

37. Wilde, O (2019). *The Critic as Artist*. Thames & Hudson (Original work published 1891).
38. Greig, E (2022, Summer). 'Tasmania first: ecofascism and the settler invasion fantasy'. *Overland*, (249).
39. Menzies-Pike, C (2022, May 16). 'Critic Swallows Book'. *Sydney Review of Books*.
40. Fry, D (2023, June 3). Octopus 23: 'The Field'. *Memo Review*.

I read and the complex grappling with art their authors undertake. It's a more diverse field of writers than I can remember, and they're making us pay attention to the diversity of art created in Australia, too. The prestige of the critic at the daily newspaper has long gone—and so too has the stereotype of the old, white, male critic. That person is no longer the average art critic in Australia—and nor should he be. (Although, as an aside, I was devastated to open *The Weekend Australian Review* and read David Stratton was 'on leave' for Barbenheimer's opening week.)

I am passionate about arts criticism because of the way it allows me to grapple with the world. To write about art is to write about climate change and politics and beauty and trauma. It is writing about childhood and history; today and tomorrow; drunken conversations and unignorable truths. It is writing about those parts of ourselves we thought no one else saw and those parts of others we have never observed before.

It's a privilege to spend time observing the world through the eyes of artists, to gently tease apart someone's creation and to build it back up again in another form. I'm interested in reviewing the ephemeral, and capturing what it was like to sit in the theatre that night or walk through the gallery on that day. I am passionate about reading arts criticism because I think it is a form which, at its best, shows us our humanity.

I cannot say what the future of criticism looks like in Australia. But I am looking forward—perhaps naïvely—with a sense of hope.

There is not enough, but what there is is often very good. It's unevenly distributed—around the country, across artforms, within artforms. Too often, in a small community in a small country, writers are not truly writing without fear or favour. It is still, as Brisbane observed 50 years ago, not a profession.[41] But the voices, finally, that are creating Australian criticism look a bit more like the artists, and the artists look a bit more like Australia.

Perhaps paradoxically, the fact that criticism isn't a career—that jobs aren't monopolised by staff writers, or even freelancers

41. See footnote 1.

with any sense of job stability—means we get to have more voices, each with their own internal complexities and contradictions and their sheer interest in art.

It is a genre of writing in desperate need of more support. This support needs to come from newsroom leadership, from readers speaking up for the coverage they enjoy, and in better funding for arts publications, both literary journals and beyond. We—as writers, editors, artists and audiences—need to have a fuller conversation about the value and place of arts criticism in Australia and how we can make sure there is space for it. We need to have a more holistic view of what is being left out of the critical conversation, and consider how to broaden our remit.

But I remain hopeful. Anyone choosing to really spend time engaging with art in Australia, and then choosing to write considered criticism, could never be described as disinterested. They are extremely interested; and that's what makes their work interesting at all.

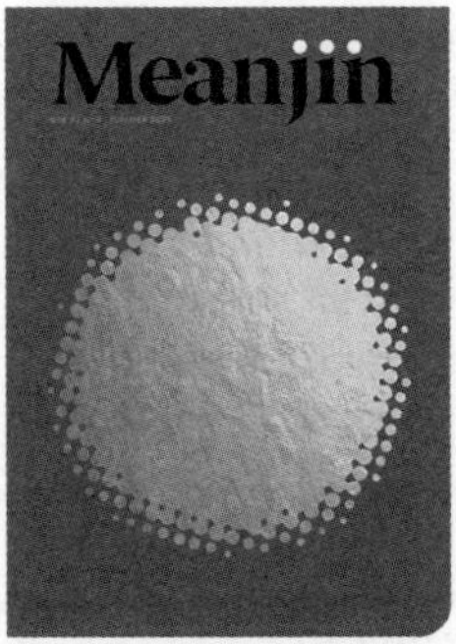

Walkley Award-winning **Jane Howard** is one of Australia's leading arts journalists and the editor of arts and culture at *The Conversation*. Her work for news and specialist publications such as *The Guardian*, *RealTime* and *The Conversation* have set new standards in criticism and journalism. Howard is also the recipient of numerous prizes awarded by press clubs, arts organisations, festivals, philanthropic trusts and writers' peak bodies. Howard's past artistic and collaborative projects include *The Importance of Seeing Earnest: A Critical Experiment*, *Simple Art Transfer Protocol* and *Excess Thoughts*, and she is a former Director of the Digital Writers' Festival, an initiative of the Emerging Writers' Festival. Howard is currently working on the non-fiction book project *The Exhaustion of Sadness*, exploring the intersection of art and grief.

Why I write what I write

Gerald Murnane

Meanjin 45.4 Summer 1986

I WRITE SENTENCES. I write first one sentence, then another sentence. I write sentence after sentence.

I write a hundred or more sentences each week and a few thousand sentences a year.

After I've written each sentence I read it aloud. I listen to the sound of the sentence, and I don't begin to write the next sentence unless I'm absolutely satisfied with the sound of the sentence I'm listening to.

When I've written a paragraph I read it aloud to learn whether all the sentences that sounded well on their own still sound well together.

When I've written two or three pages I read them aloud. When I've written a whole story or a section that you might call a chapter, I read that aloud too. Every night before I start my writing I read aloud what I wrote the night before. I'm always reading aloud and listening to the sounds of sentences.

What am I listening for when I read aloud?

The answer is not simple. I might start with a phrase from the American critic Hugh Kenner ... *the shape of meaning*. Writing about William Carlos Williams, Kenner suggested that some sentences have a shape that fits their meaning while other sentences do not.

Robert Frost once wrote: 'A sentence is a sound on which other sounds called words may be strung.'

Robert Frost also had a phrase, 'the sound of sense', to describe what he listened for in writing. Frost likened this sound to the pattern we hear when the sound of a conversation, but not the sounds of actual words, reaches us from a nearby room.

Robert Louis Stevenson had a different notion of what a sentence should do.

> Each sentence, by successive phrases, shall first come into a kind of knot, and then, after a moment of suspended meaning, solve and clear itself.

I don't say that I swear by any of these maxims that I've quoted. But each of them lights up a little part of the mystery of why some sentences sound right and some don't.

A word I haven't mentioned yet is *rhythm*. A lot of nonsense is talked about rhythm. Here's something that is far from nonsense.

> Rhythm is not an ideal form to which we fit our words. It is not a musical notation to which our words submit. Rhythm is born not with the words but with the thought. Good writing exactly reproduces what we should call the contour of our thought.

I found these words in a book published nearly sixty years ago: *English Prose Style*, by Herbert Read.

The *contour of our thought* is a magical phrase for me. It has helped me in times of trouble in the way that phrases from the Bible or from Karl Marx probably help other people.

You will not be surprised to know that Virginia Woolf had a deep insight into this matter of the rightness of sentences. Here is something she wrote about it.

> Style is a very simple matter, it is all rhythm. Once you get that, you can't use the wrong words ... This is very profound, what rhythm is, and goes far deeper than words. A sight, an emotion, creates this wave in the mind, long before it makes words to fit it, and in writing one has to recapture this, and set this working, (which has nothing apparently to do with words) and then, as it breaks and tumbles in the mind, it makes words to fit in.

Something else I listen for when I read aloud ... I listen to make sure that the voice I'm hearing is my own voice and not someone else's voice. I don't always succeed in this, of course. Sometimes when I read my writing of a few years ago I recognise that I've imitated in a few places the voices of others.

I listen for the sound of my own voice because I remember something the Irish poet Patrick Kavanagh once said: 'This is genius—a man being simply and sincerely himself.'

And still another thing I hope to hear in my sentences is the note of authority. John Gardner said authority is the sound of a writer who knows what he's doing. He cited as his favourite example of prose ringing with authority this opening passage from a famous novel.

> Call me Ishmael. Some years ago—never mind how long precisely—having little or no money in my purse, and nothing particular to interest me on shore, I thought I would sail about a little and see the watery part of the world.

I've said I write sentences, but you probably expect me to say what the sentences are about.

My sentences arise out of images and feelings that haunt me—not always painfully; sometimes quite pleasantly. These images and feelings haunt me until I find the sentences to bring them into this world.

Note that I didn't say 'to bring them to life'. The person who reads my sentences may think that he or she is looking at something newly alive. But the images and feelings behind my words have been alive for a long time beforehand.

This has been a very simple account of something that begins to make me dizzy if I think about it for too long. The only detail I can add is to say that as I write, the images and feelings haunting me become linked in ways that surprise and amaze me. Often if I write one sentence to put into a form of words a certain image or feeling, I find as soon as I've written the sentence that a new throng of images and feelings have gathered to form a pattern where I had not known a pattern existed.

Writing never explains anything for me—it only shows me how stupendously complicated everything is.

But why do I write what I write?

Why do I write sentences? Why does anyone write sentences? What are sentences? What are subjects and predicates, verbs and nouns? What are words themselves?

I ask myself these questions often. I think about these matters every day in one way or another. For me these questions are as profound as the questions why do we get ourselves born, why do we fall in love, why do we die?

If I pretended I could answer any of these questions, I'd be a fool.

In 1986, **Gerald Murnane** wrote this piece for *Meanjin* after appearing on a panel of the same name at that year's Melbourne Writers' Festival. This essay was then first published in book form in his *Invisible Yet Enduring Lilacs* (Giramondo, 2005). Today Gerald Murnane is widely recognised as one of Australia's greatest literary voices. A writer of deep emotional conviction and lyrical intensity, Murnane is the author of eleven works of fiction, beginning with 1974's *Tamarisk Row*, and including *The Plains*, *Inland*, *Barley Patch*, *A History of Books*, *A Million Windows*, and *Border Districts*, as well as his essay collection *Invisible Yet Enduring Lilacs*. He is a recipient of an Emeritus Fellowship from the Australia Council, the Patrick White Literary Award, the Melbourne Prize for Literature, the Adelaide Festival Literature Award for Innovation, and the Victorian Premier's Literary Award.

Marngrook, Tom Wills and the continuing denial of Indigenous history

On the origins of Australian football

Jenny Hocking and Nell Reidy

Meanjin 75.2 Winter 2016

THE INDIGENOUS GAME of marngrook and its claimed connection to Australian rules football has provoked unusually intense debate.[1] Dismissed as 'an emotional belief', 'falsifying history', 'lacking any intellectual credibility'—who could have imagined that the seemingly innocuous matter of an Indigenous game of football would meet with such invective.

Several accounts of Indigenous football reveal a striking similarity with key features of the Australian game, suggesting an unarticulated link between the two games. In the insistent denial of such a link, a critical factor has been that none of these historic accounts of Indigenous football has placed the game directly in the Western District of Victoria, in the area where Tom Wills lived. 'Were there any reports of Aboriginal football in the Western District where Wills lived?' Hibbins asks.[2] The short answer is, yes.

1. The Indigenous game is now widely referred to as the generic 'marngrook', although each Indigenous group played its own variant and with its own name.
2. G Hibbins, 'Wills and the Aboriginal Game: A Seductive Myth', in G Slattery (ed.), *The Australian Game of Football since 1858*, GSP Books, Melbourne, 2008, p. 45.

A personal recollection by Mukjarrawaint man Johnny Connolly is the clearest and most detailed eye-witness account yet found of an Indigenous game of football. Most significantly this remarkable account, found among the personal papers of the ethnographer AW Howitt in the State Library of Victoria, is the only account by someone who actually played the game.[3] And he played it in the Grampians region in the Western District of Victoria, precisely where Tom Wills lived. In the search for the elusive Indigenous game of 'marngrook' and its contested links to Australian rules football, Johnny Connolly's firsthand account changes everything:

> In playing a game at ball which they kicked about[,] the different totems present two different sides and there were men and women in each side … Johnny remembers that he, his mother, and her mother all played on the same side at ball. His cousin George played with the Wurant in the other side.

Connolly was from the Mukjarrawaint people, a subgroup of the Wotjobaluk, and part of the complex network of intricately interconnected Indigenous communities of the Gariwerd (Grampians) region in what is now north-western Victoria. The land of the Mukjarrawaint covered the area between Ararat, Carr's Plains, the Richardson River, Horsham, Rosebrook, and extending back to the Grampians. As Johnny Connolly described it, 'Each man and each woman living in that country was Mukjarrawaint. His name is also that of a place now called Mockpilli.'[4]

When he told his story to Howitt, Connolly was living at the Ramahyuck mission, where he and many others had been relocated from Lake Condah and Framlingham missions in the west, their

---

3. Alfred William Howitt Papers, 1830–1908, MS 9356, State Library of Victoria. This section of the Howitt papers has been discussed by Ian Clark in relation to the Mukjarrawaint people in 'Land Succession and Fission in Nineteenth-century Western Victoria: The Case of Knenknenwurrung', *Australian Journal of Anthropology*, vol. 17, no. 1 (2006).
4. AW Howitt, *The Native Tribes of South-East Australia*, Macmillan, London, 1904, p. 55.

lands, families, totems and culture already irretrievably damaged by the incursions of European settlers, their stock and the ravages of dispossession.[5] In the Western District this impact was violent, immediate and utterly devastating. Within 20 years of the arrival of the first squatters in the late 1830s, less than 700 members remained of this once diverse and complex community of more than 6000 people from several distinct language groupings.[6]

In the histories of that region the Mukjarrawaint rarely feature. Howitt's notes point to an important matrilineal focus common to the area, particularly regarding totems and the complex social rules governing interrelationships. Connolly's description of the two sides in Indigenous football as replicating these totemic divisions suggests that the game was important not only as amusement and skill development, but also as a means of reinforcing these political kin relationships. With the incursions of European settlers the Mukjarrawaint and their patterns of life, land and community developed over centuries were shattered and, just as quickly, became lost to history.

In the 1980s Poulter reprised marngrook from this cultural and historical vacuum and, more dramatically, posited a clear connection between it and Australian rules football.[7] He could not have foreseen the furore that greeted this impertinence. Indigenous football had been played along the entire southern area of the continent and yet in the aftermath of Poulter's invocation of its 'previously unsuspected links' to Australian football, its nature, extent and influence, became fiercely contested in what has been called 'football's history wars'.[8]

---

5. P Pepper and T de Araugo, *You are what you make yourself to be: The story of a Victorian Aboriginal family 1842–1980*, Hyland House, Melbourne, 1980.
6. P Corris, *Aborigines and Europeans in Western Victoria*, Australian Institute of Aboriginal Studies, Canberra, 1968, pp. 2–5.
7. J Poulter, 'An old, old, ball game', *Australasian Post*, 4 August 1983; J Poulter, 'Mark-Grook—Original Australian Rules', in P Bourke and L Grogan (eds), *This Game of Ours: Supporters' Tales of the People's Game*, EATWARFLEMSD, St Andrews, Vic., 1993, pp. 64–7.
8. C Cazaly, 'Off the Ball: Football's History Wars', *Meanjin* 67.4 Summer 2008, pp. 82–7.

In recent years these arguments have become so insistent, and their impact on contemporary perceptions of Australian rules football so unsettling, that the game's own commissioned history has been called into question, and rightly so. In the AFL's official history *The Australian Game of Football since 1858*, Hibbins proclaimed in a short and provocative piece that marngrook had no connection to, and not even any influence on, Australian football. In this unusually strident piece, Hibbins dismissed the suggestion of such an Indigenous influence as 'a seductive myth', writing that 'Understandably, the appealing idea that Australian football is a truly Australian native game recognizing the Indigenous people, rather than deriving solely from a colonial dependence upon the British background, has been uncritically embraced and accepted in some places'.[9]

The emphatic rejection of 'this appealing idea' left no space even for the possibility of a link between marngrook and Australian football, much less a causal relationship between them. In this, the historiographic response is as interesting as the history itself. Such singularity reflects a conceptual position in which the settler colonial experience is the only perspective from which history is, and can be, told. The prospect of Indigenous engagement with that colonial settler experience, even through the apparently unremarkable medium of Indigenous football, has been peremptorily rejected. Hibbins' definitive view of Australian football as 'derived solely from a colonial dependence' links it irrevocably and absolutely to British football, despite the marked differences between them in which the influence of marngrook might be found.

Hibbins' claims attracted ardent supporters and critics alike and two opposing positions took shape around this question of the role of marngrook in the development of Australian football, each tightly held and neither yet conclusive.[10] The arguments coalesced around three main elements in this still evolving story: the

---

9. Hibbins, 'A Seductive Myth', p. 45.
10. Cazaly, 'Off the Ball', p. 82.

nature and extent of marngrook; the establishment of Australian football; and the equally contested role of the brilliant sportsman Tom Wills in the interface between both. Wills is widely seen as central to these debates, having lived in the Western District as a child and his famous letter to *Bell's Life Victoria* in 1858 calling for the formation of football clubs as a means of keeping cricketers fit between seasons having precipitated the development of the first football clubs.

Hibbins and those to follow argue a negative, that the absence of documentary evidence of a connection between marngrook and Australian rules means that there is none. Specifically, there is 'no evidence' in three key respects: first, that marngrook was even played in the region where Wills lived; second, that Tom Wills saw or played marngrook; and finally, that elements from marngrook were incorporated into Australian football.[11] Overarching this position is an approach to research that Cazaly termed 'myopic', marked by demands for 'evidence' narrowly focused on the time of codification of the rules.[12]

By these repeated calls for 'evidence' are meant documentary, text-based evidence, a notion and a form familiar to the British colonisers whose documentation of the penal settlement was superlative, but not one that would readily engage with Indigenous history. For a society whose cultural memory inhered in song, in dance, in stories and art, and which had so quickly been devastated, this constructs an evidentiary near impossibility.

In its landmark 1992 Mabo decision, the High Court of Australia recognised the limited utility of text-based documentary evidence alone for establishing historical patterns of life, land and ownership in Indigenous communities that had no such written tradition. Not only did that transformative judgment acknowledge the significance of ethnographic and oral history to historical

11. G de Moore, 'Tom Wills, Marngrook and the Evolution of Australian Rules Football', in R Hess, M Nicholson and B Stewart (eds), *Football Fever: Crossing Boundaries*, Maribyrnong Press, Hawthorn, 2005, p. 5.
12. Cazaly, 'Off the Ball'; G Hibbins, 'Myth and History in Australian Rules Football', *Sporting Traditions*, vol. 25, no. 2 (2008), pp. 41–53.

understanding of Indigenous communities, the court admitted such material as 'traditional evidence' of ownership.[13] If even that bastion of theoretical high conservatism, grounded as it is in notions of precedence, can accept such a radical repositioning as this, surely football's historians cannot be too far behind.

These demands for documentation and evidence also preclude the possibility that these accounts are there, to be found among the papers, reports and records of the colonial authorities and early settlers. 'Pioneer' records, diaries, correspondence, personal papers, and the exhaustive reports from the Aboriginal Protectorate in Port Phillip, reveal far more than this demand for documents suggests. The assertion that these records do not support a link between marngrook and Australian football has been too readily accepted as correct. The problem is not with the original records, but with those who continue to dismiss their significance.

There is no shortage of descriptions of Indigenous football games before the depredations of European occupation. Of these, the account given by the assistant protector of Aborigines, William Thomas, in 1858 is one of the best known: 'The Marngrook (or the Ball) is a favourite game with boys and men ... the ball is kicked into the air not along the ground, there is a general scramble at the ball, the tall black fellows stand the best chance. When caught it is again kicked up in the air with great force and ascends as straight up and as high as when thrown by the hand.'[14]

Dawson also described Indigenous football as 'one of the favourite games ... in which fifty, or as many as one hundred players engage at a time'. The local game he observed was played with two sides formed according to their totem: 'white cockatoo against black cockatoo, quail against snake', matching the totemic formations recalled by Johnny Connolly.[15] Howitt recognised

---

13. N Sharp, *No Ordinary Judgment: Mabo, the Murray Islanders' Land Case*, Aboriginal Studies Press, Canberra, 1996.
14. W Thomas, 'Vol 24 Amusements and War Implements', Papers 1842–1858, ML MSS214, Mitchell Library, State Library of New South Wales.
15. J Dawson, *Australian Aborigines: The Languages and Customs of Several Tribes of Aborigines in the Western District of Victoria, Australia*, George Robertson, Melbourne, 1881, p. 85.

in the game an additional social and cultural significance in regulating relations between these totemic divisions, through the ball itself: 'The "mangurt" or ball was sent as a token of friendship from one to the other.'[16]

A more recently discovered etching based on the observations of William Blandowski in 1857 depicts a game of football being played by the Nyeri Nyeri people of northern Victoria in which the ball 'is not thrown or hit with a bat, but it is kicked in the air with the foot ... The aim of the game: never let the ball touch the ground.'[17]

While Blandowski's observations have provided the earliest image of a football game, the papers of the artist WA Cawthorne provide the earliest image of an Indigenous football. Cawthorne's papers in the Mitchell Library include a sketch from the early 1840s of the 'pando', the oval ball used by the Kaurna people of the southern region between what is now Victoria and South Australia. The pando was sketched from Cawthorne's own observation and it formed the basis for one of his colour plates on 'the manners and customs of the natives'. It included a brief description of the pando, as 'universally used by the young and old'.[18] Cawthorne subsequently gave a more detailed description of the game of 'pando': 'The players stand together in a ring or a line. One of them kicks the ball in the air, sometimes to the height of fifty feet ... The merit of the game is to kick the ball perpendicularly and to keep it in the air as long as possible.'[19]

---

16. AW Howitt, 'Notes on Australian Message Sticks and Messengers', 1889, http://nla.gov.au/nla.obj-26171094/view; see also the discussion in B Judd, 'Australian Rules Football as Aboriginal Cultural Artifact', *Canadian Journal of Native Studies*, vol. 25, no. 1 (2005), pp. 215–37, at p. 223.
17. The etching was created in 1862 by Gustave Mutzel as instructed by Blandowski. S Farnsworth, 'Kids play kick to kick—1850s style', *ABC News*, 21 September 2005, http://www.abc.net.au/news/2007-09-21/kids-play-kick-to-kick–1850s-style/676704
18. WA Cawthorne Papers (1843), ML A105 Item 24, Mitchell Library, State Library of New South Wales.
19. WA Cawthorne, 'Rough Notes on the Manners and Customs of the Natives', 1844.

Like most other firsthand accounts, Cawthorne drew no distinction between men and women, old and young, as participants in this game. The accounts of Connolly, Howitt and Beveridge all detail female involvement in these games, with women playing as equals. 'The women participate in this game as well as the men. We have seen as many as two hundred—including sexes—engaged in it at one time.'[20] Yet in much of the recent discourse regarding Indigenous football drawing on these sources, the integral part played by women has been almost entirely disregarded. Beveridge gives this powerful observation of the start of the game:

> When all is in order, a Lyoore [woman] starts off with the ball in her hand. She walks a little way out from her own side, and towards that of her opponents, drops the ball with seeming carelessness, but 'ere it has time to reach the ground, she gives it a dexterous, and by no means gentle kick, which being correctly aimed, sends the ball spinning high into the air.[21]

In a remarkable transposition, this description of a game in which a woman starts the game by kicking the ball up and then plays with 'her side' against 'her opponents', has been re-presented and cast instead as a game that begins 'with a woman kicking the ball up *for the men to play*'.[22] This transposition means that marngrook has been presented as a game played by men when Beveridge described a game in which women played alongside men—'women participate in this game as well as the men'. In a final indignity, those women have been depicted as merely providing support for the male players. It would be difficult to find a clearer example of the process through which evidence provided by the historical record is filtered through unconscious presentiment and recast in that image.

20. P Beveridge, *The Aborigines of Victoria and Riverina as Seen by Peter Beveridge*, ML Hutchinson, Melbourne, 1889, p. 45.
21. P Beveridge, *The Aborigines of Victoria and Riverina as Seen by Peter Beveridge*, ML Hutchinson, Melbourne, 1889, p. 46.
22. R Gooch, 'Another Look at Marn Grook', *Sporting Tradition*, vol. 32, no. 1 (2015), p. 43 (our emphasis).

The contestation over marngrook and its relationship with Australian football has crystallised around three key elements: marngrook, Australian football, and between them the figure of Tom Wills, seen as the pivot between two communities, two cultures and two games. Wills was an exceptional athlete, possessed of 'transcendent sporting achievements'.[23] He had excelled at rugby, which he had played as a pupil at Rugby School, and equally at cricket, which he played again at Rugby School and then for Cambridge University, where he enrolled simply in order to play for the university team. Wills had also, most unusually, grown up in the Gariwerd (Grampians) region where the Mukjarrawaint people lived and where marngrook was also played. Wills occupied what Judd terms 'a position of cultural hybridity' between 'settler' and Indigenous peoples in the Western District—a position that, while not uncommon, is rarely acknowledged.[24] Tom Wills is not only the bridge between two cultures and two games, he is the bridge between the opposing views in this debate. For it is a rare point of agreement that if the argued link between marngrook and Australian football is to be found, it will be found in the story of Tom Wills.

Tom Wills had arrived in the region when his father Horatio Wills, the excitable mercurial son of a convict, followed the tracks of Major Mitchell to the newly opened Port Phillip district in search of his idealised 'Australia Felix'. Horatio, his wife Elizabeth and four-year-old son Tom, with 500 sheep, 500 cattle, drovers, stockmen, shepherds and their families, travelled south across the Murray to the eastern end of the Grampians mountain range. In 1840 Horatio, in the passive language of a land presumed terra nullius, 'took up' an immense tract of land called Ledcourt, 200,000 acres from Mount William, north-east towards

23. G de Moore, 'The suicide of Thomas Wentworth Wills', *Medical Journal of Australia*, vol. 171 (1999), pp. 656–8.
24. B Judd, *On the Boundary Line: The colonial identity in football*, Australian Scholarly Publishing, Melbourne, 2008, p. 65 and throughout.

the Wimmera and back towards Mount Dryden, just beyond the limits of established European settlement.[25]

The two stations on which Tom Wills spent most of his childhood, Lexington and La Rose-Mokepilli, were taken up the following year.[26] Mokepilli is the Indigenous name recalled by Johnny Connolly for the traditional lands of the Mukjarrawaint people: 'His name is also that of a place now called Mockpilli.' In its transliteration this has been variously presented as Mokpilli, Mokepilli and Noke Pillee. Lexington alone ran to 120,000 acres, its boundaries marked by the landscape itself, 'on the south from the Three Corner Waterhole … on the east by Ararat'. From there it stretched on to the junction of Mt Dryden Ridge, to Fyans Creek on the Wimmera River, on to 'Noke Pillee' and the Long Waterhole.[27]

Each of the three runs occupied by Wills—Ledcourt in 1840 for a year, Lexington and La Rose-Mokepilli for ten years—were in the country of the Mukjarrawaint people. Horatio Wills had led the first group of European settlers into that immediate region, he had named the area now known as Ararat for its biblical referents—'for here, like the Ark, we rested', he wrote in his journal.[28] As a squatter Horatio Wills was both typical and unusual in his attitude to the Indigenous people whose land he had so easily 'taken up'. He developed an unusually syncretic relationship with the local communities—a mix of brutality, paternalism and personal connection. Horatio spoke their language and worked with Indigenous people on his stations, yet the records show that

---

25. 'Claims to leases of Crown lands', No. 6 Ledcourt, Supplement to the *New South Wales Government Gazette*, 25 August 1848, p. 1078; *Crown Land Leases*, Victoria, Government Printer, Melbourne, 1856, p. 33.
26. *Crown Land Leases*, Victoria, p. 33.
27. 'Claims to leases of Crown lands', No. 62 Lexington, Supplement to the *New South Wales Government Gazette*, 25 August 1848, p. 1088.
28. Quoted in L Banfield, *Like the Ark: The Story of Ararat*, FW Cheshire, Melbourne, 1955.

he was also guilty of murder and the violent dispossession of those same communities.[29]

Most unusually, Horatio Wills acknowledged the Indigenous peoples as 'the original possessors' of his land and proposed to Governor Gipps that they should not be placed in reserves but should be given 'the right of their hunting grounds': 'Let the Blacks have the country unmolested to range upon.'[30] The local Indigenous people were always present on the Wills' properties—he encouraged it and recognised their need to be on their country—which he considered nevertheless now to be his. The chief protector of Aborigines in Port Phillip, GA Robinson, visiting the Wills property at Ledcourt in 1849, noted several 'natives' engaged as shepherds and workers there.[31] Horatio also described this land as having been 'for some considerable time back an area of general rendezvous' for the local Indigenous peoples, a place where corroborees, games and other entertainments were traditionally held including football. Cawthorne described the 'korrobery' as 'connected to these games' and considered them as part of the same group of activities.[32]

Like his father, Tom Wills spoke the local Indigenous language and there is no doubt he formed close relationships with the Mukjarrawait people, as his cousin Colden Harrison recalled.[33] For six years, until he left Lexington to attend Brickwoods Academy in Melbourne, Tom Wills was the only European child there and his friends were the Indigenous children on that land.

---

29. ID Clark (ed.), *The Journals of George Augustus Robinson, Chief Protector, Port Phillip Aboriginal Protectorate, Volume Two: 1 October 1840 – 31 August 1841*, Heritage Matters, Melbourne, 2000, p. 309.
30. HS Wills to Governor Gipps, Mount William, March 1842, Collection of Terry Wills Cooke.
31. Clark, *The Journals of George Augustus Robinson, Volume Four: Annual and Occasional Reports 1841–1849*, p. 147.
32. WA Cawthorne Papers (1843), ML A105 Item 24, Mitchell Library, State Library of New South Wales.
33. A Mancini and GM Hibbins (eds), *Running with the Ball: Football's Foster Father*, Lynedoch Publications, Melbourne, 2000, p. 79.

A letter Horatio wrote to Tom soon after Tom had left Lexington for Rugby School highlights this connection:

> 'Pussy cat' (black boy) went off to Mt. William with teams a few days ago. The day before he left he said to your Mother 'Where Tom? Tom no quambie here: when quambie Tom?' Evidently much surprised at not meeting you he continued 'You show me Tom' meaning the daguerreotype likeness, he gazed upon it a long time. The old blacks, your friends, were fond of seeing it. They told me to send you up to them as soon as you came back.[34]

While these basic facts about Tom Wills' life might appear incontrovertible, they are contested, caught up in the dispute over the role of marngrook in Australian football. Hibbins claims that Wills could not have seen marngrook played in the Grampians because he was not there long enough before leaving for school in Melbourne: 'The Lexington station house with its window, which still exists, was not built when Tom was a boy and he never lived in the house'.[35] This confuses Lexington the homestead with Lexington the sheep run. It was there, on that run also called Lexington, that Wills lived between the ages of four and ten, of this there is no dispute. The still existing homestead was built in 1851 and Tom was by then at school, but what Hibbins does not say is that Lexington homestead had replaced an earlier slab house built ten years earlier and in which Tom Wills lived with his family as a child. The slab house had in turn replaced the rudimentary tents that the family lived in for much of their first year in the district.[36] In 1841 Robinson recorded that he had ridden to the Wills' home station nine miles from Mt William and described Mrs Wills 'living with her child (boy) in a small tent'.[37]

---

34. HS Wills to TW Wills, 1 May 1853, Collection of Terry Wills Cooke.
35. Hibbins, 'Myth and History', p. 50.
36. Diary of Horatio Spencer Howe Wills from April 1843 to August 1851, Lexington, Ararat, Collection of Terry Wills Cooke; Heritage Victoria, 'Lexington'.
37. Clark, *The Journals of George Augustus Robinson*, p. 311.

The basic biographical material clearly shows that not only did Tom Wills live in this area from the age of four, he lived in the very area in which the Indigenous football game played by and described by Johnny Connolly was played. Johnny Connolly's is the only firsthand description of marngrook from someone who had played the game before the reach of settlement. Connolly was later engaged as a stockman on the stations in that same area, one of which was Ledcourt, the first run 'taken up' by Horatio Wills.[38]

While the testimony of Connolly has not previously been acknowledged, the reports of Howitt and Thomas have been key sites in the contention over marngrook and its influence on Australian football. In the debates over the marngrook connection, these reports of Indigenous football in the western region have been disputed, at times on the slightest, almost whimsical, grounds. Thomas provides one of the most important descriptions. In his 1844 journal he writes of a 'great body' of people coming into the settlement of Melbourne from the north-west. Thomas writes that after a day corroboree 'about 35 fine young men of various tribes have a fine game of ball'. This is a significant firsthand reference to the Indigenous game since it is one of the earliest contemporaneous records of it, yet it too has been disputed.

Indeed Gooch dismisses the observations of both Thomas and Howitt, suggesting that their descriptions of Indigenous football refer only to 'ball', not specifically to 'football', and could therefore be referring to a different game altogether.[39] This is a strained interpretation at best. Thomas elsewhere uses the same construction of 'ball' as meaning 'marngrook': 'The Marngrook (or the Ball) is a favourite game with boys and men.'[40] Similarly, it is suggested that Howitt 'only ever mention[s] a ball game, apparently not football ... those who support *Marn grook* have usually turned this game into football, but that is not actually what

38. FA Hagenauer Papers, c. 1870–1908, MS 9556, State Library of Victoria.
39. Gooch, 'Another Look at Marn Grook', p. 42.
40. W Thomas, *Brief Remarks on the Aborigines of Victoria, 1838–1839*, MS 7838, State Library of Victoria, p. 28.

the Howitt records say.'[41] In fact it is—the Howitt records include Connolly's account of 'a game at ball which *they kicked about*'.[42]

Thomas, Howitt and Cawthorne all noted the meanings of Indigenous words and it is clear from those and other contemporaneous reports that 'marngrook', 'mangurt' and 'pando' for instance each signified 'ball' as well as 'football'.[43] Several of the sources discussed here do not use the term 'football' at all when describing an Indigenous game of football. Connolly refers to 'a game at ball' and Howitt similarly writes of a 'game of ball-playing'.[44] By expecting 'evidence' of Indigenous football to take a contemporary form—namely the word 'football' itself—this historical evidence has been overlooked and seen as irrelevant.

What these repeated attempts to dispel the earliest reports of marngrook ineluctably lead to is the suggestion that Indigenous football did not exist until after European colonial expansion into the region. Gooch claims that Dawson's account of the Indigenous game is undated and 'unsourced' and could therefore refer to a game witnessed later than the 1850s, after the development of Australian football.[45] What follows is a dramatic claim, given the reports of the existence of marngrook throughout south-eastern Australia, for Gooch suggests that marngrook was not a genuine Indigenous game but mere mimicry of European football: 'If, in this instance, it was Aborigines who did the copying, they were known everywhere as brilliant mimics, a facility which included their ability to imitate the British, right down to every lisp and limp.'

In this way a unique Indigenous game has been expropriated by and into the colonial present as nothing more than a mimic of the European game, in a modern variant of the silencing of Indigenous history. Here is the ultimate logic of the denials

41. Gooch, 'Another Look at Marn Grook', pp. 47–8.
42. Howitt Papers, MS 9356 (our emphasis).
43. WA Cawthorne Papers, 1843.
44. Howitt, 'Notes on Australian Message Sticks and Messengers', 1889, p. 316, n. 4.
45. Gooch, 'Another Look at Marn Grook', p. 45.

of marngrook, the rejection of the essence of indigeneity—its agency, history, identity and memory.

Three features of marngrook are common to all descriptions: the ball is kicked directly up and high; the ball is kept off the ground; and from these comes its third and most visually arresting aspect, its high leaping and catching—the 'high mark'. These are well captured by Thomas: 'The ball is kicked up in the air ... when the ball is caught it is kicked up in the air again by the one who caught it, it is sent up with great force and ascends as straight up and as high as when thrown by the hand'.[46] The final contention revolves around whether any of these elements of marngrook were incorporated into Australian football and its early rules.[47]

De Moore argues that, for the first 20 years, 'the game was characterised by play that was, for the most part, close to the ground', precluding any influence of the above ground style of play characteristic of marngrook. An unpublished letter by Tom Wills to his brother Horace shows that this was far from the case. Keeping the play and the players off the ground had been the intention of its founders from the outset. This letter, which Tom wrote to Horace in Queensland, was among the extensive papers, letters and original documents held by Terry Wills Cooke. Wills Cooke is a Wills family descendant, and although he is far from convinced of a connection between marngrook and Australian football, his own material suggests otherwise.

In this letter, according to Wills Cooke, Tom Wills indicates that the critical factor in the adaptations made in the new game of Australian football was a matter of geography—that the grounds were too hard for rugby, in which players were routinely thrown to the ground. The game then had to be adapted to keep the players and the play off the ground. Wills had proposed the new game in these terms in 1858 to the Melbourne Cricket Club and the early

46. Thomas, *Brief Remarks on the Aborigines of Victoria*.
47. The first written rules were codified in 1859 by Tom Wills, WJ Hammersley, JB Thompson and TH Smith as a sub-committee of the Melbourne Football Club. *The Yorker* no. 39 Autumn 2009.

unwritten rules of Australian football were devised to ensure that players were not thrown to the ground and 'kept the ball in the air'.[48] Wills' cousin Colden Harrison also recalled this potential for injury as central to the game's early form, that Wills considered rugby 'unsuitable' for working men who needed to stay fit for work as well as for cricket.[49] The context in which football had been established is the key to understanding these changes. Australian football had been developed in order to keep cricketers fit and healthy between seasons, and not as the primary focus of the sporting calendar that it quickly became.

Tom Wills' letter crystallises some key points of contention in the debate over marngrook and its influence on modern Australian football. First, it confirms the view, already widely acknowledged, that football had derived primarily from rugby, in keeping with Tom Wills' schooling and experience and his undoubted expertise at that game. Second, and in terms of the arguments over the influence of marngrook most significantly, rugby was not simply adopted wholesale. Instead, changes were made in order to address local conditions in its Australian adaptation, specifically the hardness of the ground. The key changes described by Wills and others were made in order to keep the players and the game off the ground and the ball in the air—there would be no 'hacking' or kicking of shins, no tripping and the ball could be kicked from player to player, not thrown.

It is here, in the interstices between rugby and Australian football, that the influence of marngrook can be seen most clearly. The distinguishing features of marngrook, the high kicking, leaping and marking, all advanced its central aim of keeping the ball off the ground. The early accounts of marngrook described the aim of the game in precisely those terms: Beveridge writes that 'the whole of the play is merely to keep the ball in motion,

48. L Sandercock and I Turner, *Up where, Cazaly? The Great Australian Game*, Granada, Sydney, 1981, p. 19.
49. HCA Harrison, *Story of an Athlete: a picture of the past*, Alexander McCubbin, Melbourne, 1923, p. 89.

and to *prevent its coming to the ground*'; Cawthorne that 'the merit of the game is to kick the ball perpendicularly and to *keep it in the air as long as possible*'; and Blandowski identifies 'The aim of the game—*never let the ball touch the ground.*'[50]

As a reconstruction of the past, history is always a narrative formed from imperfect knowledge, drawing on sources of vastly differing forms, veracity and relevance. As more and more material is uncovered about marngrook, Tom Wills and Australian football, the accumulating evidence all points in the same direction—the inescapable link between marngrook and Australian football. With Johnny Connolly's testimony, a critical component in the denial of that link has crumbled.

Marngrook was played across the Western District, including the area Tom Wills lived in as a child from the age of four. That land was the land of the Mukjarrawaint people and a meeting place for local communities where corroborees were held and games were played. The local Indigenous people were Tom Wills' childhood friends, he spoke their language, knew their customs, and he was close enough to them for young and old to pine for him when he went away to school. Instead of asking 'where is the evidence he saw or played marngrook?', we might ask, why would he not? Are we really to accept that Wills did everything but play football with the Mukjarrawaint people, that football was a hermetically sealed part of their relationship such that whenever a game began, Tom Wills—who arrived at school at the age of ten already highly skilled at sport—neither watched nor played?

The intense debate over marngrook and Australian football reflects something beyond just football. It reflects what Stanner called 'the other side of a story over which the great Australian silence reigns ... the story, in short, of unacknowledged relations between two racial groups within a single field of life'.[51] At the heart

50. Beveridge, *The Aborigines of Victoria and Riverina*, pp. 46–7; Cawthorne, 'Rough Notes'; Farnsworth, 'Kids play kick to kick'.
51. WEH Stanner, The Boyer Lectures 1968, published as *After the Dreaming*, ABC, Sydney, 1969, p. 25.

of any connection between marngrook and Australian football is precisely this acknowledgement of relations between two cultures, the recognition of a shared history 'within this single field of life'. Australian football has an Indigenous history.

Professor **Jenny Hocking** is an award-winning author, biographer and film script writer. She is Emeritus Professor at Monash University, a Fellow of the Academy of the Social Sciences in Australia, and a highly regarded scholar and commentator on Australian politics and history, political biography, counter-terrorism and security matters. After a circuitous legal battle initiated by Hocking in 2016, in 2020 the High Court of Australia compelled the National Archives of Australia to release all official correspondence between Sir John Kerr and the Queen over the dismissal of the Whitlam Government.

Nell Reidy is a Research Fellow with the Fire to Flourish program at Monash University. She engages in collaborative research with First Nations communities across Australia, with a focus on building and maintaining trusting and respectful relationships to develop research priorities and positive outcomes for communities. Reidy has also worked in State Government leading community engagement and policymaking, including supporting First Nations communities to work towards their collective aspirations such as Treaties with the Victorian Government.

The act of disappearing

On the silences that shroud the disappearances of Aboriginal women and girls

Amy McQuire

Meanjin 81.4 Summer 2022

> This woman is Black
> So her blood is shed in silence
> This woman is Black
> So her death falls to earth
> To be washed away with silence and rain
>
> … I do not even know all their names
> My sisters' deaths are not noteworthy
> Nor threatening enough to decorate the evening news
> Not important enough to be fossilised
>
> —Audre Lorde, *Need: A Choral of Black Women's Voices*

WE DO NOT know how many Aboriginal women have gone 'missing' in this country. The archives are filled with the 'missing': the Aboriginal women who are no longer here to speak; the Aboriginal women who do not have names; the Aboriginal women who do not have graves or places where their families can remember them. There is a comfort that comes with the word 'missing', because to be 'missing' implies that perhaps they have left on their own accord; that there are no perpetrators or violence enacted against them. As Canadian First Nations lawyer and activist Pam Palmater says, the term 'missing' is a misnomer:

'It seems to imply that these women or girls are just lost or ran away for a few days.' 'Missing' also comes with the assumption that the case is still active. When the police speak of 'missing persons', there is an implication that the police are still searching for them, and that they will never tire in their search until those who are 'missing' are found or come back. Because they are still 'missing', the police do not see themselves as responsible for failing to find them; but instead, see the women themselves as 'responsible' for going missing in the first place. There is a term specific to this place, in that women are accused of going 'walkabout', which serves to naturalise their disappearances as innate to Aboriginal culture, and not a distinctly settler-colonial phenomenon.

We don't know how many Aboriginal women have gone 'missing' in this country because until recently no-one was really counting, and even when there are attempts to gather numbers, it remains limited to police datasets. As First Nations journalists Isabella Higgins and Sarah Collard wrote in 2019, police will often categorise a 'missing' person into three categories: 'lost, missing, or murdered'. The definition of 'missing' is 'willingly left, or were forced to leave'. But there is no category for those who have 'vanished' into a state of ambiguity between life and death, who are seen as not 'missing' or 'murdered' or 'lost'. By relying on police categorisation of 'missing persons', the racial violence that obliterates women and their ties to country and community is left shrouded in silence. And because this racial violence is unspeakable through this erasure, the role of the police in these disappearances is left uninterrogated. In a *Four Corners* investigation that aired in October 2022, First Nations journalists Bridget Brennan, Suzanne Dredge and Brooke Fryer found that there have been 315 Aboriginal women who have been murdered, disappeared or died in suspicious circumstances since 2000.

In 2010 the National Women's Association of Canada announced its own research into the number of Indigenous girls deemed missing or murdered over two decades. They found 582 cases, and that number rose to 1181 when the Royal Canadian Mounted Police announced its own statistics into cases of 'police-recorded incidents of Aboriginal female homicides and unresolved missing Aboriginal females' between 1980 and 2012. Until the *Four Corners* investigation, we did not have the same dataset, and the issue is complicated by the fact that across Australia there are Aboriginal women whose deaths or disappearances have never been investigated.

Nearly three decades ago, Professor Judy Atkinson wrote on how the deaths of Aboriginal women by violence were being determined as 'natural causes', prior to any investigation. There are cases of Aboriginal women whose deaths are quickly determined as 'suicides' and sent to coronial courts. For example, in 2020 the NT coroner referred the case of three Aboriginal girls who had died by suicide to the DPP due to the highly suspicious nature of their deaths. In one of these cases—Keturah Mamarika, who was known as Cheralyn—counsel assisting at the inquest suggested the potential of foul play. The two other girls, Layla Leering and Fionica James, had also suffered tremendous trauma and sexual violence prior to their deaths, and were referred to the DPP with the coroner stating it was possible that crimes had been committed against them. This means that the data is always limited, always predicated on police investigations that are so often ineffective.

We know that it is relatively rare for homicides or cases of missing persons not to be solved or resolved in this country. Every year in Australia, nearly 40,000 people are reported 'missing', and most of these people are found within a day, with only about 2 per cent remaining unsolved 'missing persons' cases. In my home state of Queensland, it is extremely rare for those who die by homicide not to be found.

By relying on police categorisation and protocol on 'missing persons', or on homicide, the racial violence that disappears the women and their ties to country and community is left shrouded in silence. The focus on data also foregrounds the police in the analysis even though police are those who are making it possible for the women to disappear in the first place. The numbers can never reveal what made it possible for the disappearances to occur. Because it is not just the cases in which the bodies of Aboriginal women have disappeared, but also those who are found, and whose deaths are never properly investigated, whose families are left with the continuing trauma of not knowing, and whose names go unheard and are never written of, are never aired or never broadcast in ways that could lead to national displays of mourning, like in the cases of other deaths.

The 'real' silence

For so long, Aboriginal women have been accused of being complicit in a 'silence' surrounding violence against Aboriginal women, while simultaneously being tasked with the responsibility of 'breaking' it. This is shown in the ways the bodies of black women are spoken of. During the days of the frontier, violent tropes were circulated and reproduced without evidence in order to claim 'savagery' by Aboriginal men, in contrast with the discourse of 'settler gallantry', as historian Liz Conor has written in her book *Skin Deep*: 'In hundreds of printed accounts that reflected on gender relations in Aboriginal society, settlers routinely believed women were utterly subjugated by their "tyrannical men", whom they pilloried as "lords and masters".' These accounts were unsubstantiated but reproduced to support the lie that Aboriginal men were a 'threat', to be intensely policed and placed under surveillance.

These tropes and representations have continued into the present and are used to enact brutal forms of state-sanctioned violence against not just Aboriginal women, but also men and children. The key example is that of Crown Prosecutor Nanette Rogers, who painted Aboriginal culture as 'punitive' and violent in 2006, and laid the groundwork for the NT intervention. It resurfaced in the words of NT Supreme Court judge Judith Kelly who claimed in 2022 that Aboriginal communities 'prioritised male perpetrators' over that of female victims and claimed again as a problem of Aboriginal culture that 'tolerates violence against women'. According to Kelly, the courts were doing a 'good job', but instead were scared to speak out for being branded 'racists'. Through the voices of white witnesses such as Kelly and Rogers, who are painted as courageous crusaders and breakers of the silence, the real silence is maintained, in which Aboriginal women can speak but only in the limits prescribed by these witnesses; limits in which the role of racial violence as a tool of the settler colony is deemed unspeakable. Silencing works not through a lack of speaking, but through one discourse replacing the other, less palatable discourse.

Aboriginal women have never been silent about violence, but have been writing and producing reports, and speaking out at the grassroots level for decades. And yet, because this silence has been constructed, ironically around the artificial 'silence', our voices have been in turn silenced so that we are yelling into a deep abyss. Violence against Aboriginal women has always been seen in the context of 'black on black crime', in ways that obscure the role of the police and courts in not only sanctioning but providing the conditions for violence to occur. Because of this silencing, it is Aboriginal women who are not just seen as 'victims' when voiceless, but are also painted in turn as perpetrators and criminals, devastatingly demonstrated in the fact that over the years, Aboriginal women have been locked up at higher and higher rates, with most of them being victims of violence.

Aboriginal women, when killed or have disappeared, are still painted as criminals; seen as 'drug addicts' or uncaring mothers. They are not just viewed as unworthy of love, but incapable of loving; even though in their absence it is their families who gather to resist the colonial versions of their loved ones with their own grieving practices, grounded in relationality, love and care. Whether inside or outside, the deaths of Aboriginal women are not seen as notable or grievable deaths. This is because the stories we tell of this violence is not the story that the mainstream media or the courts want to tell, and in order to break through the silence we are told we must privilege their accounts.

What I began to understand was that the framework was not one of 'violence against Aboriginal women', but rather of the disappearance of Aboriginal women in this colony. I use 'disappearance' deliberately because it ties the deaths and disappearances of black women to an ongoing settler-colonial project that actively targets black women. It is linked to a genocidal practice rather than Aboriginal women existing in spaces of violence, as bodies to which violence is done. 'Genocide' was a key determination of the National Inquiry into Missing and Murdered Indigenous Women and Girls in Canada, which sought to clarify how it operates distinctively in settler colonies. The inquiry found that genocide encompasses a variety of lethal and non-lethal acts, including acts of 'slow death', all of which have very specific impacts on women and girls: 'The reality must be acknowledged as a precursor to understanding genocide as a root cause of violence against Indigenous women and girls in Canada.'

'Disappearance' and 'disappearing' are political acts; they are projects that have not ended and so we must speak of it in order to understand how they have been silenced for so long. By speaking of disappearance, we can see how the deaths and disappearances of Aboriginal women are a part of a practice that defines the country, one in which 'disappearance' is the inevitable goal in order to sustain, maintain and assert a 'truth' built upon Indigenous absence from Indigenous lands. In the context of Canada, Mohawk scholar Audra Simpson shows clearly how this is a political project, how these disappearances and deaths of Aboriginal women are a requirement of the state 'in order to secure its sovereignty'.

She speaks of how Native women have been 'rendered unrapeable (or highly rapeable), because she was just like the land, matter to be extracted from, used, sullied, taken from, over and over again, something that is already violated and violable'. It is through this prism that she sees the crisis of missing and murdered Indigenous women and girls in the country: 'When we account for this way of looking at Indian women it is not a mystery, nor is it without explanation, their so-called disappearances are consistence with this ongoing project of dispossession.'

The act of disappearing

In the 1970s, a term emerged to describe the tens of thousands of people who had disappeared under the dictatorial regimes of several Latin American countries. The term used was 'enforced disappearance'. It was a practice that involved the kidnapping of thousands of people in a move to wipe from society those whom governments deemed as an affront. The use of 'disappearing' was deliberate, as Argentina's first commander in chief Jorge Rafael Videla said: 'The disappeared are just that: Disappeared; they are neither alive or dead.' In Argentina an estimated 30,000 people disappeared by force during its dictatorial regime. In the acts of disappearing, those who are made to disappear are confined to spaces of disappearance; not just in the places in which they are disposed, in which they are buried, but in the spaces set up to ensure that they are never found; in the apathy of the police, and in the refusals of the courts to prosecute, to the silence of the media and the acquiescence of the state and in turn society. Disappearance on such a scale means that there are many actors involved beyond the original perpetrators.

In the context of Argentina, the practice of 'disappearing' only became widely known when the *madres* and *abuelas* began protesting for their children and grandchildren. Secrecy had characterised and sustained the practice. The tactics involved not only the removal of 'undesirable elements' to clandestine detention centres, but also the methods of disposal, which included the notorious 'death flights', where people would be thrown from planes in the middle of the night into oceans and rivers, only to be discovered when their bodies washed upon the shores. When relatives of the disappeared went to authorities for help in finding their loved ones, they were often turned away, or told that their loved ones had simply run off. As Jacqueline Adams writes:

> the relatives were met with 'nos' at every turn. Government officials told them that the disappeared person was not in their records, some said they had probably run away with another woman. Even the judicial system responded negatively, not presenting the disappeared persons in court ... moreover, government officials, the courts and the media denied or expressed doubt that the disappearances had occurred. The media at first called the disappeared the 'allegedly disappeared' or 'presumed disappeared'.

The families were confronted with the fight not just to find their loved ones and discover what happened to them, but also to have the issue acknowledged. There was a keen psychological impact on those who were still there, the way they felt marginalised by the denial and pained by the ambiguity associated with not knowing. The vast scale of the pain associated with disappearing was difficult to grasp, because once a person has disappeared, it is not only that person who becomes a victim, but also those who have been harmed by the disappearance. Because those who disappear are absent, it is their absence that comes to define them, as Gatti writes. This is the violence inherent in the act, because it is a way of exerting a violence that never ends, acting as a continuum to those who are closest to those who are not here. As Gatti writes: 'The condition of the "disappeared" is determined by what we do not know about them (their captivity, their death, the whereabouts of their remains ... What we don't know, negation is what defines them.' To have disappeared, he writes, represents a new state of being, one in which the disappeared 'exist as present absence' and this is an act for which we do not have any form of representation, or way of making meaning of it. 'It is a space that is unresolvable: there is no resolution even with the likely certainty of death.'

The United Nations Convention for the Protection of all Persons from Enforced Disappearance defines the practice as

> considered to be the arrest, detention, abduction or any form of deprivation of liberty by agents of the State or by persons or groups acting with the authorisation, support or acquiescence of the State, followed by the refusal to acknowledge the deprivation of liberty or by concealment of the fate or whereabouts of the disappeared person, which place such a person outside the protection of the law.

It is the second part of the definition that I am interested in; the idea that 'groups acting with the authorisation, support or acquiescence of the state' make this a form of 'enforced disappearance'. The inquests into the disappearances of Aboriginal women in Queensland have shown me that there is a general apathy when

Aboriginal women are deemed 'missing', and their cases are not properly investigated. For example, in the case of Monique Clubb, a police officer from the Missing Persons Unit had said that the coronial report had been prepared within a month of her disappearance, which largely signals the end of an investigation. He said the report had been compiled after the 'dust had settled'. The term struck me as so casual in its callousness, because even as the dust was still in the air, the police had begun burying her story. The dust could never settle for her family until she was found and brought home.

This apathy is shown even in cases where Aboriginal women are found, and where there is evidence of injury. The state is then complicit in the disappearance due to its failure to search or penalise and prevent. The responsibility for finding the missing person or delivering justice is obscured by placing responsibility upon the women and their families and communities; or through the continual colonial representations that Aboriginal culture is 'violent'. The state, the nation, becomes an active participant and conspirator in these acts of disappearing.

The failure to situate these deaths and disappearances in a framework of disappearance in which the state is complicit means that the mainstream media also becomes part of this wider apparatus. In relation to the shocking feminicides in the border city of Ciudad Juárez, in Mexico, Ignacio Corona critiques the role of the media in perpetuating representational violence on women who have been killed and disposed of. He labels this 'violent journalism', which 'depicts (in both fact and opinion) and produces (in its discursive formalisation) a more violent reality'. He shows that there is a double editorial strategy in which the media 'reap the benefits of the sensationalist appeal' of the women's deaths, and then, by hiding them again when their stories immediately fall out of the news cycle. 'This symbolic transfer of information to the black box of the authorities' desks for their supposed investigation amounts to a second disappearance of the bodies, given the endemic corruption in the country's criminal justice system.' He writes that the 'news media's treatment of the murdered women further disappears them'; their anonymity based on the descriptions of their bodies confines them to the 'unknown'. When these individual deaths are reported, they become simply fragments of a wider puzzle, allowing for speculation as to unnamed perpetrators while making absent the underlying conditions of violence that lead to these murders.

'Feminicide' is a term that became widely used to describe the shocking levels of violence perpetrated against women throughout Latin America but characterised specifically the violence in Ciudad Juárez. One definition is provided by Julia Estela Monárrez Fragoso, who says 'feminicide is the assassination of a woman committed by a man, where one finds all of the elements of the relationship of inequality between the sexes ... *not only is the woman's biological body assassinated, but what the cultural construction of her body has signified*'. This is where I see the phenomenon of disappearance as being not only the physical disappearing of Aboriginal women, but also the disappearing of their personhood in the ways that they are represented, which so often is based not on who they were but rather how a violent settler colony has imagined them to be.

Aboriginal women have throughout history been labelled promiscuous, highly sexualised, and their bodies open and available for violation. When Aboriginal women are reported on in the media, they are immediately seen as disposable, so their deaths are not inherently newsworthy, but in fact a continuation of the norm. This is where the media is complicit: in not presencing them in their absence, in not allowing for a discourse in which they can be mourned and seen as grievable deaths. By disappearing them, they are disappeared from a nation founded on the notion of the inevitable disappearance of Indigenous peoples, for which the targeting of Aboriginal women was essential.

Just like the madres and abuelas in Argentina who gathered in public spaces weekly to find their loved ones, to protest against the lies they were being told, so do the families of the Aboriginal women who have disappeared, who fight in their own way even when told that their loved ones' deaths are the result of issues such as 'addiction', 'family violence' and 'black on black crime'. Aboriginal families must go to greater lengths to get media attention, and their testimonies are still only validated when first backed by 'authoritative accounts' of white witnesses who are seen as 'reliable'. I know of many Aboriginal families who, when faced with police apathy and inadequate searches, conduct their own searches, contact the media and fight in their own way, because just like the madres and abuelas, they are told that these disappearances or deaths are perhaps just cases in which they have gone 'walkabout', or have caused their own deaths.

When we speak of disappearing Aboriginal women, the focus is never on 'justice'. Instead, there is a focus on the coronial inquiry, which is framed around police protocols, entrenching the notion of disappearance in the way it is orientated not towards justice or repatriation but towards absolution. In their absence, sometimes the physical absence, but certainly the symbolic and representational absence, it is easy to begin absolving police of their failures to search and provide answers to families. This is key to coronial processes in settler-colonial societies. As American scholar Lisa Stevensen has critiqued, in the coronial process there is an expectation of death, and a benevolent display in which Indigenous peoples are 'exhorted to live … while simultaneously expect(ed) to die'. Similarly, Canadian scholar Sherene Razack critiques the coronial process as one in which 'state accountability receded the more that details about physically and emotionally ravaged Indigenous people came into view'. Justice cannot be found in these processes, because the stories that emerge always rest on Indigenous dysfunction rather than the acts of disappearing, and define 'violence' as existing only in Indigenous spaces.

Indigenous resistance to violence is always told through these frameworks, which only makes this resistance seem 'violent' when told through the limited prism of a place designed to deny us the power to speak our own truths and realities. Michi Saagiig Nishnaabeg theorist Leanne Betasamosake Simpson says that this is always about 'justice' defined through a Western lens: 'A lot of the time state justice is about white people feeling better about themselves. State narratives of justice are processes that are about injustice for us'. Justice is so often a foreign concept, to be found and defined in the very places that enact the most brutal violence, that are set up for the 'disappearance' of Indigenous peoples again.

Not only does this framework of disappearance show how Aboriginal women are victims, but it also speaks to the use of the justice system as one that contains and causes Aboriginal women to disappear from public space and sight. In all the cases I attended in Queensland, the women had been criminalised throughout their whole lives. While living they were always highly visible to police, when they were 'missing' they were treated more like 'wanted persons'. The photos on their 'missing persons' posters didn't show how they lived and how they were loved, but rather were the mugshots held in police archives, which showed them as criminalised people, in spaces of containment that meant they had disappeared from their families, communities and children. When 'missing' or 'murdered' Aboriginal women are seen as 'criminals', they are made invisible in public consciousness, and the urgency to find them or deliver 'justice' wanes.

The failure to see police as perpetrators of violence is another example of the silence. In the year the report of the Royal Commission into Aboriginal Deaths in Custody was handed down (1991), the Human Rights Commission released its landmark report into racial violence across the country. The report dedicated an entire chapter to racial violence perpetrated on Aboriginal people by police. While the royal commission had failed to identify police as perpetrators, stating that the issue of 'black deaths in custody' was instead largely due to over-incarceration, and notably erased the unique experiences of Aboriginal women in custody, the Human Rights Commission report revealed shocking accounts of police officers as perpetrators of sexual violence. For example, the report said 'in Mossman, an Aboriginal woman alleged that she had been raped by a police officer while in custody'.

There were also complaints from Alice Springs that Aboriginal teenage girls had been assaulted and raped by police officers and other white males. There were reports from Burketown of police offering young women to white male patrons for sex. There were reports heard from Townsville of Aboriginal women being assaulted in the watch house, as well as threats of rape. There was evidence presented from New South Wales, Western Australia and Queensland of Aboriginal girls being 'abused with sexist and racist language by being referred to as "black sluts", "black molls" etc., and evidence of them being assaulted'. In the silences that shroud the disappearance of Aboriginal women from national discourse, there are also silences that emerge to protect perpetrators, especially those in uniform.

The act of disappearing works to conceal, to barricade the silence already enforced through representation, and to minimise the issue of the disappearance of Aboriginal women and girls. It keeps the cries of families out of sight and refocuses the violence from the state and its processes on the communities themselves. In the case of Lynette Daley, whose two killers were only charged after a *Four Corners* report and public outrage, Professor Marcia Langton wrote: 'I fear the message that this case sends: that there may be no repercussions for assaulting us. Some will think it is "open season".' This is not a hyperbolic claim. The failure by police, the courts and the state to acknowledge that racial violence is occurring, that Aboriginal women are specifically targeted, and that the processes of 'justice' are set up against families, shows us that Aboriginal women are not protected by a state that has enacted the most brutal harms upon us. It suggests that there is something more sinister at play in the act of disappearing: how it provides conditions for impunity.

Black justice

I do not know how to define a concept of 'justice' in cases of disappeared Aboriginal women. So often the focus is carceral, and yet we know that the carceral systems are set up on disappearance, and specifically Indigenous disappearance. Instead of reproducing the same colonial logics of those conspiring in these acts of disappearance, we must formulate different methods of writing that can be used as weapons for families in the ongoing fight and as tools for repatriation, not just in fighting to repatriate the women physically, but also their memories, buried under the weight of 200 years of stereotyping.

I find a concept of 'black justice' in the fight of the families. Disappearance is predicated on the idea of disconnection. By rupturing connection, you rupture ties to community and place, but so often I see this as a failed project because even though the women may not be here physically, there are ways the family brings them back, and brings them closer, through acts of presencing. It can be the photos on display in the court room, or in the hands of the mother in the first row. It can be the way they are grieved for, how they are mourned. I see black justice as the chanting of spirit; the spirit that has never disappeared, still exists and is felt across the waters and caught on the wind. Black justice is the families who bring their loved ones back from those spaces of disappearance, who say that these women do not 'cease to exist' but are always present.

To understand the violence of silence and silencing, we must first understand what has been silenced. And to understand, we must first listen to the families of women who have disappeared and, most critically, listen to Aboriginal women. We must do so by remembering that the acts perpetrated against them do not define them. What defines them is not their absence but their presence, which is never lost, despite continuing attempts, but lives on in the memories they leave behind, and those who continue to fight for their return.

Amy McQuire is a Darumbal and South Sea Islander writer and journalist. She is a postdoctoral Indigenous fellow at the Queensland University of Technology, and recently submitted her PhD in media representations of violence against Aboriginal women at the University of Queensland. She is the co-host of the investigative podcast Curtain the Podcast, and has been working in Aboriginal and independent media over the past 16 years. She has written for *New Matilda*, *BuzzFeed*, *Meanjin*, *Griffith Review*, *Saturday Paper*, *Vogue*, *Marie Claire*, the *New York Times* and *Washington Post* among others. Her first book *Black Witness* is due to be published by UQP in the near future. For this piece, McQuire won the Hilary McPhee Award for essay writing that makes a fearless contribution to the national debate.

The temperament of generations:

The monstrous accent on youth

Thea Astley

Meanjin 27.1 Autumn 1968

TWO YEARS AGO at a middle-class girls' high school in Sydney, I set the top-level stream of students the task of writing about their attitudes to conscription for Vietnam. Seventy per cent favoured conscription for boys. They used anachronistic phrases like 'question of courage', 'man's duty to defend his family', 'making the world safe for democracy'. As the mother of a son I was perturbed and interested. After an interval of two months I suggested they write on conscription for girls, conscription to national service which would use them for nursing (perhaps in Vietnam), relief work for two years overseas, and so on. This time less than ten per cent favoured conscription. Girls, like female spiders, want to have their men and eat them, too. I was appalled by the selfishness of their reactions and wondered if this were merely a by-product of thinking in a Liberal Party voting area.

I cite this incident merely as an introduction to the attitudes of this generation which, despite engaging frankness on matters like sex and drug-taking, still has a hard conservative core. Perhaps they are only hard and conservative when it is a question of unselfishness. Perhaps they are tolerant merely in matters that concern self-indulgence.

In my evening tutorial classes at Macquarie University, I found more liberal discussion standards prevailed, a trait particularly noticeable in the nuns (I speak as one who recalls with some anguish the narrow dogmatism of the Irish teachers of my youth). General reading standards were low—again except for the nuns. This is an interesting point! Writers such as Compton-Burnett, Cheever, Edmund Wilson, Nabokov, Gordimer (even funny men like de Vries) were literally unknown as names. (I clutch a handful at random.) Discussing DH Lawrence and the war between men and women, only one in sixty had read Thurber's *The Unicorn in the Garden*.

Maybe the average of this generation have not the time for reading or perhaps not the interest. They drink much more. (I went through university on four sweet sherries.) And they have more money to do it with. Where my generation enjoyed faculty picnics up the Brisbane River with bottles of lemonade and a lot of earnest conversation, final year students at leading Sydney private schools prefer pub crawls and regard a party where the drink runs out early as a wash-out. I don't know what this proves. I feel their livers are in more danger than their morals. But I do deplore the jaded attitude that can only get its kicks in a semi-inebriated state.

The generation before mine was probably sour-puss because the Depression made every personal achievement heroic. We still tend to think the young should fend for themselves when, as everyone is aware, nepotism and privilege, the unsubtle play of 'influence', are at work all the time. One is sorry life is so easy for the young and, because of this, so difficult.

The permissiveness of our generation to the younger has created the monstrous over-rated importance of youth. Oldies—pregnant, sick, reeling—can tremble vertical upon trains and buses while thick-thighed youngsters cling to their seats. There is no reverence for age as such and while this is understandable and not expected, one longs for a little sympathy such as might be meted out to the under-privileged.

Recently I said to a colleague and his wife after we had been discussing youth, 'Oh God, sometimes I loathe the young!'

Instantly and together they cried, 'Yes, so do we!' But of course they don't. And I don't. They adore their children and students as I do mine. It's only that at times we grow a little fearful of the Frankenstein we have created.

In 1968, **Thea Astley** (1925–2004) was already an internationally renowned writer, and had won two Miles Franklin Awards. Thea published more than a dozen novels and short story collections across five decades, including *The Acolyte*, *The Slow Natives*, *Drylands*. Astley was the first person to win multiple Miles Franklins, winning four across her career; in her lifetime she held the record for Miles Franklin wins. With many of her works published internationally, Astley was a trailblazer for women writers. In her personal life, she was renowned for her dry wit, eccentricity and compassion.

Battle

Vance Palmer

Meanjin No. 8 March 1942

THE NEXT FEW months may decide not only whether we are to survive as a nation, but whether we deserve to survive. As yet none of our achievements prove it, at any rate in the sight of the outer world.

We have no monuments to speak of, no dreams in stone, no Guernicas, no sacred places. We could vanish and leave singularly few signs that, for some generations, there had lived a people who had made a homeland of this Australian Earth. A homeland? To how many people was it primarily that? How many penetrated the soil with their love and imagination? We have had no peasant population to cling passionately to their few acres, throw down tenacious roots, and weave a natural poetry into their lives by invoking the little gods of creek and mountain. The land has been something to exploit, to tear out a living from and then sell at a profit. Our settlements have always had a fugitive look, with their tin roofs and rubbish-heaps. Even our towns … the main street cluttered with shops, the million-dollar town hall, the droves of men and women intent on nothing but buying or selling, the suburban retreats of rich drapers! Very little to show the presence of a people with a common purpose or a rich sense of life.

If Australia had no more character than could be seen on its surface, it would be annihilated as surely and swiftly as those colonial outposts white men built for their commercial profit in the East—pretentious façades of stucco that looked imposing as long as the wind kept from blowing. But there is an Australia of the spirit, submerged and not very articulate, that is quite different from these bubbles of old-world imperialism. Born of the lean loins of the country itself, of the dreams of men who came here to form a new society, of hard conflicts in many fields, it has developed a toughness all its own. Sardonic, idealist, tongue-tied perhaps, it is the Australia of all who truly belong here. When you are away, it takes on a human image, an image that emerges, brown and steady-eyed from the background of dun cliffs, treed bushlands, and tawny plains. More than a generation ago, it found voice in the writings of Lawson, O'Dowd, Bedford, and Tom Collins: it has become even more aware of itself since. And it has something to contribute to the world. Not emphatically in the arts as yet, but in arenas of action, and in ideas for the creation of that egalitarian democracy that will have to be the basis of all civilised societies in the future.

This is the Australia we are called upon to save. Not merely the mills and mines, and the higgledy-piggledy towns that have grown up along the coast: not the assets we hold or the debts we owe. For even if we were conquered by the Japanese, some sort of normal life would still go on. You cannot wipe out a nation of seven million people, or turn them all into wood-and-water joeys. Sheep would continue to be bred, wheat raised; there would be work for the shopkeeper, the clerk, the baker, the butcher. Not everyone could be employed pulling Japanese gentlemen about in rickshaws. Some sort of comfort might even be achieved by the average man under Japanese dominance; but if anyone believes life would be worth living under the terms offered, he is not worth saving. There is no hope for him unless a breath of the heroic will around him stirs him to come out of the body of this death. Undoubtedly we have a share of the decadent elements that have proved a deadly weakness in other countries—whisperers, fainthearts, near-fascists, people who have grown rotten through easy living; and these are often people who have had power in the past and now feel it falling away from them. We will survive according to our swiftness in pushing them into the background and liberating the people of will, purpose, and intensity; those who are at one with Australia's spirit and are capable of moulding the future.

I believe we will survive; that what is significant in us will survive; that we will come out of this struggle battered, stripped to the bone, but spiritually sounder than we went in, surer of our essential character, adults in a wider world than the one we lived in hitherto. These are great, tragic days. Let us accept them stoically, and make every yard of Australian earth a battle-station.

By 1942 **Vance Palmer** (1885–1959) was a well-established writer of poetry, short stories, criticism and journalism, and the author of several novels. With his partner and collaborator Nettie, Palmer was an ardent advocate of Australian literature throughout his career, as well as a strong voice against the rise of fascism. His most renowned works include the novels *The Passage* (1930) and the political trilogy *Golconda* (1948) *Seedtime* (1957) and *The Big Fellow* (1959); short story collections *Separate Lives* (1931), *Sea and Spinifex* (1934), *Let the Birds Fly* (1955) and *The Rainbow Bird and Other Stories* (1957); and poetry collection *The Forerunners* (1915). The Victorian Government's highest honour for fiction was named the Vance Palmer Prize, and the prize for non-fiction the Nettie Palmer Prize, from 1985 until 2010 when they were renamed as the Victorian Premier's Literary Prizes.

Gaza and the twenty-year War on Terror

Nahed Elrayes

Meanjin Daily: 7 June 2021

As new enemies replace 'terrorists', Westerners will reflect on how one word justified colonial massacres in Gaza—and what, in truth, that word was good for.

MAY 27's *Q&A* farce did not surprise me in the way it could have. I was not surprised by the difficulty of Palestinians to get one voice on the panel, or that the two handpicked questions[1] were from Zionists. I was not even surprised by the lobbyist who described the 'distress' of an IDF captain's[2] dog in a room safe from potential Hamas fire.

I was somehow surprised that, when Randa Abdel-Fattah responded to this dog anecdote—with a reminder that dozens of our children were being massacred with nowhere to hide—the audience member fell silent and nodded, and the audience applauded. I am somehow surprised every time that Palestinian life is recognised—but in retrospect, I am surprised at our surprise. As great power politics return and the Western gaze pivots to Asia, things feel different than they did five years ago.

---

1. See the ABC's archived recording at www.abc.net.au/qanda/2021-27-06/13352714
2. See Israel Defense Forces spokesman Capt. Benjamin Rutland's video log at https://www.youtube.com/watch?app=desktop&v=B5xio6OE5Co&ab_channel=IsraelDefenseForces

'It's very good,' Netanyahu said in his first reaction[3] to 9/11. 'Well, not very good, but it will generate immediate sympathy.' Israel has long enjoyed a claim to identity with a Western Self, against Palestinians in an undifferentiated Islamic Other.

What Netanyahu anticipated was not precisely 'sympathy' for Israel, but a means to dehumanise the population it kept under occupation. To be human is a twofold experience[4]: it is about one's life and one's death. We see the human as living vulnerably, rationally, uniquely and with agency. Having lived meaningfully, their death is then bestowed with meaning. Nobody at the funeral subjects it to utilitarian rationalisation—certainly not the person's murderer.

But what if some array of words could preserve the coloniser's ability to be mourned, and not the colonised? What if those words, by definition, only evoked the vulnerability of those with state power, against the violence of those without? Highlighting existential threats to the state, rather than to certain people in it? What if all of those people's subjugations and human aspirations were obscured, replaced with immaterial, 'irrational' religious motives neatly positioned against a 'civilised' Western protagonist?

What if this alien irrationality foreclosed the possibility of negotiation, enabling violent discipline as a first resort? What if it also meant the people and their culture were in some perpetual state of 'deadness', and so could not really be killed? What if it created a double standard of recognition, where only existing statehood had to be defended, maintained and recognised without question?

What if it helped us forget one very important fact—that all violence is intended to terrorise, especially the urban bombardment

3. James Bennet (2011) 'On 9/11/11', *The Atlantic* https://www.theatlantic.com/magazine/archive/2011/09/on-91111/308594/ accessed 06.05.2024
4. See Judith Butler (2006) *Precarious Life: The Powers of Mourning and Violence*, Verso Books, available at https://www.versobooks.com/books/112-precarious-life

of civilians, which has been a state tactic since World War II? That to 'evacuate' civilians before obliterating their homes, schools, hospitals and every space that could remind them of their humanity, is in fact to terrorise? Or that to give people no option to 'evacuate' a 12-kilometre-wide open-air prison, is to terrorise?

What if the stateless other—without legitimised, non-'terrorist' leadership—became an undifferentiable mass, whose lives were thus disposable as statistics? What if they were collectively responsible, and thus all punishable? Part of a global mass, in fact, so that two unrelated militias at war with each other were 'branches of the same poisonous tree'?

What if the juxtaposition of enlightened democracy with oppressive 'terrorist' rule eradicated the agency of the colonised, muting their political and linguistic existence? Wouldn't that mean they were both unaccountable for the violence and collectively punishable for it?

Well … they're irrational, remember, so their preferences are indeed violent, but self-defeating. We just need to liberate their true preferences, those which coincide with the interests of the colonising state. So what if they only 'lived' as undignified objects of their own backwardness, as 'cattle' women and human shields, sent by the agents of terror to protest and be shot by us in the thousands? What if we needed to trap them in order to free them from … themselves?

What if these deaths were tragic—truly tragic—but also the cost we pay to fight terrorists? The same terrorists who kill our people in the disgusting belief that a murder could ever be justified for any political end? What if we glorified our fallen fighters against terror, in televised national funerals, while denying any family the right to bury a terrorist child? Wouldn't grieving only prove that there was a human life, worthy of grief?

What if this word and its discourse were so self-hegemonising that for decades, anyone of the colonised race would be nervous to openly unpack how meaningless, sinister and racist they were, for the very fear of being swept under its implicit categorisations and targeted by the public, the media and the state as a sympathiser?

What if the War on Terror's binaries, while legitimising all of the atrocities necessary to maintain a settler-colonial state, actively silenced those with the greatest incentive to oppose it?

Well, that would have been 'very good'.

Nahed Elrayes is a Palestinian-Australian composer, writer, and Arab America 30 Under 30 awardee. His Mahmoud Darwish-inspired music composition 'A Lover from Palestine' sparked a global video project involving 45 other Palestinians, earning accolades from SBS, Palestine News Network, and 24FM. In the academic realm, he is a recipient of both the Margaret Schofield Scholarship in Music Composition, and the University of Melbourne's WM Ball Prize for Best Essay in International Relations (2020), for his Master's thesis on the self-reproducing notion of Arab 'sectarianism'. His literature efforts have been recognised through the Ghassan Kanafani Resistance Arts Scholarship (2021) earned for his 'Letter from Sacramento', a fictional reflection on the role of Palestinians in the diaspora. Elrayes has challenged Arabophobic discourses in his articles for *Meanjin* and *The New Arab*, and following a visit in summer 2023, Elrayes now aims to present an unseen side of Gaza through his 12-part short video series, 'Why I Love Gaza'.

Heaven and a Hills Hoist

Australian critics on suburbia

Tim Rowse

Meanjin 37.1 Autumn 1978

'IT IS NEVER a waste of time to study the history of a word', Lucien Febvre tells us. Many images of Australia's social history have been garnered from a study of the colloquialisms that are Australia's and nobody else's. At first sight 'suburbia' does not seem to be one of those words, since it is manifestly part of a wider intellectual culture common to Britain and North America. Among social critics of these countries, 'suburbia', 'suburban' and 'suburb' have been used to describe a certain form of social life which emerged in the metropolises of Europe at the beginning of the era of Imperialist and monopoly capitalism. With the expansion of the middle strata occupations of modern financial and commercial capitalism, and with the gradual improvement in the economic security of the industrial working class, the suburb became the typical mode of domestic living for the majority of people in these countries. As early as 1883, the suburban life style was sought and fostered by the British government in order to reduce the social tensions of the overcrowded inner areas of London. That year saw the passage of the Cheap Trains Act, which compelled the private railways to offer low commuting fares for workmen who chose to live away from the inner city. Since then, according to most observers, the suburban way of life has indeed been a peaceful domicile. A recent overview of studies in the USA and Britain listed the following as being the qualities most frequently attributed to suburbia: a preoccupation with family life; an active social life; a homogeneous population; a 'middle class' style of life; and political conservatism.[1]

Australian writers on suburbia are dearly part of this tradition of observation: they have been commenting on a nation which has been suburban since the 1870s and 1880s. Birch and Macmillan indicate the following changes in the distribution of Sydney's population:[2]

YEAR	CITY	SUBURBS
1871	74 566	63 210
1881	100 152	124 787
1891	107 652	275 631

In Melbourne, the suburbs expanded in the same decades with the extension of the railways. It is commonplace now to remark on the urban nature of Australian society, to which many commentators have added 'suburban'. In 1964 Donald Horne evoked Australia's typicality:

> Australia may have been the first *suburban* nation: for several generations most of its men have been catching the 8.2, and messing about with their houses and gardens at the weekends. Australians have been getting used to the conformities of living in suburban streets longer than most people: mass secular education arrived in Australia before most other countries; Australia was one of the first nations to find part of the meaning of life in the purchase of consumer goods; the whole business of large-scale organised distribution of human beings in a modern suburban society is not new to Australians.[3]

1. David Thorns, *Suburbia*, (Paladin, London 1973) pp. 149–150.
2. A Birch and DS Macmillan (eds.) *The Sydney Scene 1788–1960*, (Melbourne University Press 1962) p. 166.
3. Donald Horne, *The Lucky Country* (Penguin, Ringwood, 1971 edition) p. 26.

It is precisely because Australian intellectuals have made this equation between suburbia and Australia's 'civilisation' that the word's uses are so rewarding to study. For the history of its uses condenses a number of themes in the history of our ideologies; in particular the question of an Australian experience as evident in the rural-urban conflict, and the fate of working class radicalism. There is no doubt that Australia is a profoundly conservative country, a stable place for capital investment where the basic political institutions are respected. Accordingly there is something undeniably authentic in any observation of Australia as suburbia; it probably is the most suburban nation in a strictly demographic sense. However, relying on 'suburbia' as a summary image and in part as an explanation of Australia has entailed the unquestioning acceptance of a certain ideology of society. The ideology I am referring to will be illustrated extensively below, but it can be summarised in abstract form as consisting of three related themes. Firstly, the focus on and amplification of 'suburbia' suggests a homogeneity in Australian society. Preoccupied by a search for the 'average' Australian home and its life-style, commentators ignore important ethnic and class differences that are recreated daily in the context of work and reinforced by government policies. Secondly, commentators have tended to see Australia as an ensemble of discrete individual house-holders, ignoring the less visible but more important relationships which connect individuals (in ways of which they may not be aware), relationships that make up social classes and political forces. For 'suburbia' is a society without history or politics. Thirdly, though commentators have disagreed on whether suburbia constitutes a good or bad civilisation, they have all tended to pose the question of the good life in terms of what goes on inside the 'spirit', or at least within one's suburban plot; hence apathy and isolation from politics have been idealised by some writers. In short, there has been a tendency to idealise people's apparent ability to escape the nemeses of the world 'outside' suburbia: the world of work, industrial conflict, politics and collective action.

The distance between the rather abstract language of these last few sentences and the concrete and even colloquial discussion of everyday life and character that we find in our social critics is both a yardstick and a cause of the success, or the 'convincingness' of the 'suburbia' ideology.

Three periods can be discerned in its development. In the first period suburbia is portrayed as the antithesis of the fine place that a particular writer hopes Australia will be. In the second, the memory of this antithesis persists in an ironical *acceptance* of Australia's unquestionably suburban fate. In the third, the suburban home is reborn as a crucible of a more humane civilisation.

'The Suburban Home is a Horror'

In 1945 Nettie Palmer wrote to her daughter of some mutual friends:

> She was answering one I wrote her some time ago asking her to tell me at her leisure why and how she found the life here unreal and unsatisfying ... I felt the subject was really interesting and even important. She has answered carefully: but I think part of the explanation is unexpressed—it is latent but clear that here at home she mixes mostly with people who are suburban, and satisfied to be so; I don't mean merely that they live out of town, but they have the suburban outlook. In London—didn't live in the mental suburbs—there and in the US she lived among intellectuals and cosmopolitans. There are such here, perhaps not so easy to find: or perhaps the suburbans are too easy to find.[4]

The antithesis between the cosmopolitan and the suburban was not one that existed between nations, say Britain and Australia: the struggle between them took place in every country. It was a contest between two attitudes to life: one whose intellectual horizons were broad, and which liked to look ahead and aspire

4. Nettie to Aileen Palmer, National Library of Australia MS. 1174/1/6750, a reference given me by Humphrey McQueen.

to adventurous schemes of individual and social progress; and one that was narrow, self-satisfied, materialistic and parochial. This assured dichotomy was the property of a certain generation of Australian intellectuals which included the Palmers and their friends.

Louis Esson (1879–1943), a friend of Nettie and Vance Palmer, wrote into his play *The Time is Not Yet Ripe* (1912) a visionary protagonist and alter ego, Mr Sydney Barrett. Barrett is a socialist, standing for the electorate of Wombat, whose socialism is not so much a scheme of social reconstruction but rather a provocative anti-morality, a precocious creed of nonconformist rebellion against the timid Philistines who formed the Establishment. His political failure is inevitable, for he is espousing a concept of revolution which is so much a matter for the individual spirit that it leaves the politics of mass persuasion behind. The text of the play is followed by a small essay, 'Our Institutions', which elaborates some of Barrett's aphorisms.

> The suburban home must be destroyed. It stands for all that is dull and cowardly and depressing in modern life. It endeavours to eliminate the element of danger in human affairs. But without dangers there can be no joy, no ecstasy, no spiritual adventures. The suburban home is a blasphemy. It denies life. Young men it would save from wine, and young women from love. But love and wine are eternal verities. They are moral. The suburban home is deplorably immoral.[5]

Esson's friend Vance Palmer shared similar hopes for an immanent Australian Socialism—a flowering of the best ethos of the Bush. By 1921, when it was clear that no such utopia was going to eventuate, Palmer ruminated sadly on 'Australia's Transformation'. Whereas in fact this transformation hinged largely on the defeat of working class militancy, Palmer portrayed

---

5. Louis Esson, *The Time Is Not Yet Ripe*, ed. Philip Parsons, (Currency/ Methuen, Sydney 1973) p. 73.

it as a becalming of the national spirit in a Sargasso Sea of 'economic struggle'.

> Today villadom and proletaria combine to fix the national life or cross swords in the struggle for economic power. *The Man From Snowy River* is deposed to make room for a sentimental 'bloke' from the slums, and the life of the continent is held up by a quarrel between two classes of people on the seaboard.[6]

The contrast between the Bloke and Paterson's 'Man' is conducted at a number of levels. The 'Man' was bold and fine, riding forth on a metric scheme as wide as New South Wales; the Bloke's poetic gait and personal wants were simple and conventional. The 'Man's' domain was the Bush, whereas Dennis sentimentalised the City. Palmer went on in this article to use the phrase 'the dominance of villadom', and denounced modern productive life as being nothing more than the 'supply of boots and chocolates to the suburbs'. It is true, as David Walker has recently pointed out, that the socialist ferment of the decade 1910–20 is important in reaching an understanding of Vance Palmer;[7] but it must also be pointed out that Palmer never realistically related his socialist vision to the actual contemporary struggles of the working class: instead he saw them as tainted by their obsession with the material and indifferent to the 'spiritual dimension'. Suburbia and 'villadom' for him evoked the pettiness of *all* parties to that 'quarrel on the seaboard'.

Hancock, an avowed admirer of the 'Palmer standard' of cultural criticism, repeats this trivialisation of the urban working class's defence of its economic rights. In *Australia* (1930), written in the midst of a serious crisis in the Australian economy, he expressed concern that the ruling ethos in political life had

6. Vance Palmer, 'Australia's Transformation', *Fellowship*, March 1921, pp. 119–20.
7. 'The Prophets Downcast: the Palmers and their Nationalism', *Meanjin* 35.2 Winter 1976.

permitted a soulless prosperity to grow up in the cities at the expense of primary producers' industries. The visitor to Australia

> has expected to see some evidence of the rigours and heroisms of pioneering, and such a stolid mass of commonplace urban prosperity heaped around the doors of an empty continent will appear to him unnatural, unseemly.[8]

In the late 1920s this familiar dichotomy had a new, urgent and conservative pertinence to the struggle between and within classes. In 1928 Hancock had written on 'The Australian City' in the *New Statesman*. Starting with some sardonic cameos of the aesthetic innocence of the typical Australian home and the suburban wife's alleged hunger for social status, Hancock goes on to place these piquant vulgarities in the context of the political and spiritual dominance of the City over the Country. 'Suburbia' in this article functions as a metonym in an argument (then emanating from the Country Party and representatives of British economic interests in Australia) for the scaling down of New Protection on the grounds that it gave the urban populace a standard of living which primary exporters could not afford to subsidise.[9]

But Hancock had a sense of the political ambiguity of the suburban spirit. 'Conservatives may console themselves that, even in a so-called socialist community like Australia, this vast suburban mass is inevitably opposed to subversive change. There is no fear of its pulling down the comfortable house which it inhabits.'[10] Frederic Eggleston drew the same comforting conclusion in his *State Socialism* (1932). The final chapter attempts to explain sociologically the intractable materialism that he saw as the leading trait of an electorate which voted for 'state socialism'—an affluence underpinned by economically 'unsound' government policies. The political success of Labor had integrated the proletariat into capitalism; but their self-interested materialism was a dead weight

8. WK Hancock, *Australia*, (1961 edition) p. 160.
9. 'The Australian City', *New Statesman*, 21 January 1928, pp. 454–6.
10. Hancock [1928] *ibid.* p. 456.

in the process of economic adjustment. The masses lacked the civic virtue to renounce material wants for the sake of threatened profit margins. Eggleston sketched a portrait of this stubborn 'self-contained man'.

> The home of the 'self-contained man' is in the suburbs; and in the highly developed suburbs of an Australian city, with good accommodation, a nice garden, a back yard, vegetables in his plot and fowls in the shed, a fence against intrusion, he has probably reached a higher pitch of development than anywhere else.[11]

Vance and Nettie Palmer, Esson, Hancock and Eggleston all equated 'suburbia' with a stifling materialism of outlook. But whereas the first three intellectuals saw only the obliteration of their hopes of a spiritually finer Australia, the latter two also adopted a more pragmatic and political perspective. That spiritual banality stood as a bulwark against Bolshevism. The question of just how an individual suburbanite affirmed or denied 'civilisation' had started to become more complex.

No Flies on the Nature Strip

The generation of intellectuals who came to maturity just before, during or just after the First World War inaugurated a use of the term 'suburbia' in an overwhelmingly pejorative sense that is still sometimes heard. But the seeds of a different evaluation, found in Eggleston and Hancock, have germinated since World War Two in a more ironical appreciation of its strengths, particularly in the writing of a younger generation of intellectuals who had never known at first hand the earlier optimism about Australia's potential as a 'socialist' Promised Land. By the early 1950s, when the Keynesian welfare state seemed to have set mass material contentment on a firmer economic footing than in the interwar years, suburbia came to be seen in a more positive light—as an innocent utopia. This seems to be the viewpoint controlling

11. Frederic Eggleston, *State Socialism*, (PS King, London 1932), p. 331.

Robin Boyd's classic evocation of suburbia in *Australia's Home* (1952). His point was that while 'factory, shop, office, theatre and restaurant were not radically different the world over …, in the suburb was experienced that essentially Australian part of town life which lay between work and home'.[12] Moreover, suburbia was coming to be seen not so much as an aberration of the Australian spirit, but as its abiding manifestation. The blurb on the Pelican edition of *The Australian Ugliness* stated the relevance of Boyd's concerns: 'Looking at the face of Australia, Robin Boyd goes deeper, to analyse the character that gave it the expression it wears.' As 'suburbia' became accepted as an authentic image of the way ordinary Australians lived, the critical connotations of the term began to lose their force, giving way to a gentle irony and even to an aloof benediction. No-one did more to facilitate this shift than Barry Humphries.

At the time when the humorous Australian archetypes Dad and Dave, Ginger Mick and the Sentimental Bloke were losing their appeal, undercut by demographic changes and the political failure of Labor's 'common Man' stereotype of the 1940s, Barry Humphries constructed new characters, notably Edna Everage and Sandy Stone. Neither inner urban larrikins nor bucolic yokels, they are truly 'suburban'. Everage apes but violates the conventions of taste, status and worldliness; Stone's life is a pathetic shell of would-be gentility and conformity. But the sense of their authenticity and familiarity has, over the years, come to undercut the critical edge of Humphries' satire: there has grown up an undeniable element of sentimental patriotism in the appreciation of Humphries' work. Edna and Sandy, understood as something indigenous, allow a cock-eyed pride in the uniqueness of Australian mores. That innocence was seen to be somehow admirable.

For many intellectuals in Australia, pride in its way of life and culture had always been a temptation to be resisted. The choice they faced until the Fifties was usually seen as between

12. *Australia's Home* (Pelican edition, Ringwood 1968) pp. 12–14.

a sentimental and parochial defensiveness (as embodied in the Jindyworobak aesthetic or in Australian social realism) or a disdainful cosmopolitanism. In presenting suburbia as a satirical object, the dilemma of these alternatives was partly resolved by irony. Humphries made it possible to savour an authentic Australian-ness, without having to make a strong emotional commitment to it; irony afforded intellectuals a saving distance. Satire was the most appropriate mode for living with the ambivalence of needing to identify with a national ethos which did not completely measure up to one's standards.[13] This was the ironical 'populism' which grew up in the Sixties as a counter to the Left Australianism which saw in the Australian character an immanent socialism. Thus the celebration of the social peace of the Menzies era tended to reproduce and develop the complex and ambivalent estimate of suburbia that we have already seen in Eggleston and Hancock. Donald Horne and Craig McGregor represent this complex 'structure of feeling' well.

In *The Lucky Country* Horne adamantly rejected the interwar snobbery about suburbia: it effectively dismissed the whole nation. Instead, he defended the vitality of the suburban lifestyle. 'The profusion of life doesn't wither because people live in small brick houses with red tile roofs'.[14] Moreover, it was *the* national lifestyle, a classless ethos: 'The genteel have been vulgarised, the vulgar made more gentle. People now enjoy themselves more in the same kind of ways.'[15]

But this commitment to suburbia is not sustained by Horne elsewhere. In a 1962 essay he defended Australian businessmen from their negative stereotype which he described as: '... uneducated, provincially ignorant, suburban-minded, vulgar, anti-intellectual, reactionary, materialistic ... more Babbitt than

13. I have drawn here on a paper given by Jim Davidson on Humphries, at the Australian Cultural History Seminar, Melbourne University, October 1976.
14. *The Lucky Country*, p. 27.
15. *ibid.*, p. 29.

Babbitt'.[16] More recently, in *The Australian People* (1972), the section called 'The First Suburban Nation' is part of Chapter Fourteen: 'The End of Improvement: 1919–39' which traces, in the interwar period, the extinction of Australia's vital, progressive, nationalistic impulse. He pictures a period of philistine self-satisfaction in which life was privatised and domestic rather than open and communal, and in which 'women developed the rituals of afternoon tea (dainty sandwiches and many varieties of sponge cake) into a complex art.'[17] Horne's critique of this period relies on the Palmeresque image of suburbia. But overall his work is clearly ambivalent: suburbia's domesticity is on the one hand in the spirit of Boccaccio ('the entire range of human comedy and tragedy') and on the other, a species of Babbittry. Horne's ambivalence towards suburbia is the inevitable result of an attempt to identify rhetorically with 'the people', who are sound and happy but who deserve better government, and substantively with an emergent body of technocrats—those confident they could govern more effectively than the Coalition governments of the Sixties.

Craig McGregor, presented by one publisher as a representative social critic of the young iconoclastic post-war generation, was more critical of Australian life than Horne was. But, like Horne, he also celebrated its vitality.

> There is a zestfulness about much of suburban life which is apparent in a thousand particulars from the sense of bustle and good humour in the thriving suburban shopping centres to the discotheques, sportscars, surfboards and juke boxes which help enliven the life of the younger suburbanites …

---

16. 'Businessmen', in P Coleman (ed.) *Australian Civilisation*, (Cheshire, Melbourne 1962) p. 177.
17. *The Australian People*, (Angus and Robertson, Sydney 1972) p. 193. The negative image of suburbia is often equally a negative image of women. A rough equation that seems to be employed is: women + domesticity = spiritual starvation. (Men + wide open spaces + achievement = heroism of the Australian spirit.) The female influence in the 'culture' is often taken to amount to an obsession with status and difference. Lady Macbeth has been written into this myth of mateship.

> Fairfield, probably Sydney's dullest suburb, also has the highest juvenile delinquency rate. Behind that façade, *something* is always happening.[18]

McGregor became a champion of 'Alf'—the archetypal suburban householder. Yet in a subtle way this populist affirmation undercut his critique of Australia. He was more interested in evoking a 'way of life' than in describing the structural features of Australian society which caused inequality and alienation in the first place. When he wrote approvingly that 'for most people life begins at five o'clock on Friday arvo',[19] he was spelling out a theoretical emphasis, an implicit sociology. The Australia he described existed outside the workplace: the relations of home and hearth were held to be the locus of the 'real' Australia, not the worlds of work and politics. He thus helped to support the apologetic image of Australia as an undifferentiated suburbia, composed of individual households standing free of class relations. McGregor was alert enough to see the dilemma raised by this perspective: if Australia was to change from being unequal and alienating, then each of its individual citizens would have to step away from the comfortable social anonymity of suburbia and become involved on one side or the other. Could McGregor endorse such involvement without shattering the image of suburban utopia?

> The man who becomes absorbed in his home is much less likely to become involved in public issues such as conscription or Vietnam or free enterprise, in the whole fabric of democratic activity. I think this is probably true but once again it has to be kept in perspective. There are some advantages in such a disengagement: the man who lives in a bung in Padstow is much *freer*, much less oppressed by community pressures and conformism, than Dublin terrace-dwellers or Naples proletarians; it is much easier for him to opt out of the church

---

18. *Profile of Australia*, (Hodder and Stoughton 1966; Penguin 1968.) All references to Penguin edition; see pp. 129–130.
19. *ibid.*, p. 131.

> ... mass prejudice and social authority and to choose his own allegiances. The Australian suburbanite is probably freer of the stifling pressure of social authoritarianism than any other city dweller in history.[20]

In this crucial passage, McGregor continues the ambivalent estimate of suburbia: Alf was apathetic about the Vietnam question and about poverty, but at least he was happy and free and able to escape the pressures of the world. McGregor offers to suburbanites the prospect of continuing to opt out of history, as it were—a choice less happily acknowledged by Eggleston in the Thirties. Thus McGregor's Alf is the son of Eggleston's self-contained man.

Green Thumbs Up

During the 1960s the Australian Labor Party developed a theory of reform which was quite coherent with McGregor's and Horne's emphasis on suburbia as the locus of Australian civilisation. ALP ideologues saw reform as the task of equalising different regions' access to community amenities. More equality between suburbs was to be achieved by siphoning off a greater proportion of the nation's wealth and spending it on better health services, housing, transport, sewerage. Suburbs of the major cities which had been denied these services by years of Coalition neglect were to benefit. Labor's perspective was that it represented not the aspirations of a working class constituted by its subordinate place in production, but the needs of disadvantaged householders concentrated in regions. Just as the liberal-democratic notion of suffrage fragments social classes, by treating society as an ensemble of individual voters, so Labor's view fragmented the nation into privileged or disadvantaged households and neighbourhoods. As in Horne and McGregor, its emphasis was on the social world outside the workplace, where the mobilisation of interests was much less

---

20. *People, Politics and Pop: Australians in the Sixties*, (Ure Smith, Sydney 1968) p. 52.

saliently that of a class. After all, a class-oriented conception of the ALP constituency was inadmissible to these ideals precisely because the whole program was to be financed by the continued, privately-directed expropriation of working class labour—the fundamental source of all the inequalities being dealt with.

This schema of reform produced a truly formidable theorist in Hugh Stretton. No one has formulated such an articulate economic and philosophical case for the suburban way of life as he; where the Palmers condemned and Horne and McGregor hedged their celebration, Stretton praises without reservation. His words are simple and, at first, plausible:

> You don't have to be a mindless conformist to choose suburban life. Most of the best poets and painters and inventors and protesters choose it too. It reconciles access to work and city with private, adaptable, self-expressive living space at home. Plenty of adults love that living space, and subdivide it ingeniously. For children it really has no rivals. At home it can allow them space, freedom and community with their elders; they can still reach bush and beach in one direction and in the other, schools to educate them and cities to sophisticate them. About half the lives of most of us are spent growing up then bringing others up. Suburbs are good places to do it, precisely because they let the generations coexist, with some continuing independence for each.[21]

Recently Stretton has turned his fire on a Left orthodoxy which he sees as being hostile to the development of private life and the private ownership of the things which really matter to people's daily lives. 'Seeing the masses seduced by capitalism, "hard" socialists respond by doubling their distrust of ownership. It does not occur to them that the house and garden and car turn people away from the party of equality chiefly because the party of equality officially despises the house and garden and car, and

---

21. Hugh Stretton, *Ideas For Australian Cities* (published by the author, North Adelaide 1970) pp. 2021.

the life they allow.'[22] The Left, says Stretton, forms an unholy alliance with the economic orthodoxy, which refuses to count in the National Product the useful things which people do for themselves at home, and so neglects to direct social investment into areas that will improve the domestic quality of life.

Stretton's argument is on the one hand a very eloquent plea for things which Australia needs badly: better housing, town planning and transport policies. But it is also a blueprint for the consolidation of modern capitalism's domestic annexe. Efforts daily expended in the ordinary Australian home are vital to the reproduction of labour, both biologically and in the sense of a day to day fitness to work. The payment of a family wage takes this into account, but also makes assumptions about the amount of domestic work which is done unpaid by women taught to think of this as their duty. Moreover, programs like the Victorian Government's 'Life. Be in it.' campaign attempt to confirm the domestic setting and leisure time generally as an arena of escape from the pressures of social life. For capitalism, the domestic sphere is both cheaply reproductive and privatised—a crucible of affluent quiescence. Any attempt to upgrade community life that does not challenge the relationships of capitalist production would thus cut two ways. Life would be genuinely better, for some; but at the expense of leaving unquestioned the social division of labour, between workers and owners, and between men and women. The 'ideal home' is still a gilded cage. And we need not take seriously Stretton's secondary argument that socialism could one day come through the ballot box. Stretton's conservatism lies in his defence of the separation of the 'private' world of consumption and sexual relations from the larger social processes, in work and in politics, in which this 'privacy' is ultimately articulated. His enquiry into this crucial nexus is bracing—he has made a case against the Left which it must answer firmly—but ultimately he confirms it as a necessary separation. In Stretton, we find Alf's apotheosis.

---

22. Hugh Stretton, *Capitalism, Socialism and the Environment*, (Cambridge University Press, Cambridge 1976) p. 202.

Throughout the different uses discussed here, the term 'suburbia' has developed in its idiomatic force its apparent authenticity as a description of the 'Australian way of life'. Beginning as an abstract Nietzschean dismissal, it enjoyed a career as the metonym of a half-accepted civilisation—stolid electorate or satirical object. Recently it has passed into a much more accepting sociological usage, connected to a program of reform which is sophisticated but fundamentally conservative of capitalist social relations. Inscribed in this career is the gradual acceptance by Australian intellectuals of their national civilisation as its urban and suburban self. The extent of this shift is marked strikingly at one point in Stretton's latest book:

> It is in private houses with storage space and some land around them that it is easiest to use more human energy in satisfying ways, and to manage with less powered commercial services ... Environmental policies will always be determined chiefly by peoples' values; and urban houses and gardens are the nursery of most of the best environmental values. People who live in town but grow some foliage of their own, and keep a cat to deter mice, are the mainstay of all the movements which work to protect larger landscapes and eco-systems. Private residential land is both an environmental good which ought to be fairly shared, and a vital educator: a classroom for work-skills, play-skills, nature study and environmental values which an environmentally careful society could be mad to deny to any of its people.[23]

Palmer saw an unbridgeable antithesis between 'villadom' and 'the Bush'; Stretton sees in suburbia the nursery of a sentiment organic with the eco-system.

But the continuities in the tradition of usage are stronger than this small upheaval in the geographical metaphors of Australian romanticism. All the authors mentioned have adopted a skeptical or disdainful attitude to revolutionary socialism as a movement

23. *ibid.*, p. 192.

based tenuously in an often unglamorous working class struggle. Each writer has been seduced by the relatively high degree of sameness in the lives that we Australians live outside the place of work. As Hancock said, with a playful mixture of banality and insight: 'There are no classes in Australia except in the economic sense'. He was viewing Australian society through the wrong end of a Marxist telescope. His use of the word 'except' trivialises the very processes which constitute ours as a class society, but it draws attention to the undeniably strong tendency for these divisions to be obscured in the forms of life led outside the workplace. Those who use 'suburbia' as a defining image of Australian society lend their support to this obscuring emphasis. As well they ignore the profound connections that exist between the exploitation of labour at work and in the home, a connection now being explored by Marxist feminists. Lastly, all of these social critics have defined the search for a better life in the same individualist and apolitical terms as has been recommended more brazenly in the acquisitive consumerist society which each of them would claim to criticise.

Author's note (2024)

In the (almost) half-century since writing this essay, I have shifted from its 'hard' socialist perspective (I was a member of the Communist Party of Australia 1974–76) to a position on the political spectrum that would welcome a Green–Labor coalition. This change has included (and has been informed by) a more positive assessment of the writings of Hugh Stretton (1924–2015). Better than I could in 1978, Stretton connected humane values (which were also mine) to a public policy agenda that exceeded (at that time) my comprehension. His book *Capitalism, Socialism and the Environment* (1976) should now be read for its parallel projections of Australia's late twentieth century future: the neo-liberal era strewn with mistakes that he anticipated, and the social democratic road—not taken by Australia, but advocated by Stretton.

In 1978, **Tim Rowse** had just authored a study of Australian social critics titled *Australian Liberalism and National Character*. Today Emeritus Professor Rowse is an Editorial Fellow at the ANU National Centre for Biography. Rowse has held research and teaching positions at Macquarie University, the University of Western Sydney, the University of Sydney, the University of Melbourne, the University of Queensland and Harvard University, where he held the Australian Studies chair. With formal training in sociology and anthropology, Rowse's research has focused on the relationships between Indigenous and non-indigenous Australians, and on the national political sphere, including the constitutional recognition debate.

The table in space

A planning perspective

Susan Parham

Meanjin 49.2 Winter 1990

OUR PLEASURES OF the table are crabbed and constrained by the design of our cities—not only by the physical nature of the city, although that's crucial, but also by the attitudes that shape our perceptions of what is appropriate in urban life, and incidentally limit the location and manner of dining. If the destruction of language can teach us to unknow or unsay, the constraints of city design can reduce our chances of enjoying the range of experiences, conversations and ideas excited by the process of sharing food.

When I first became interested in this subject, I was looking for answers to a number of questions. Why don't we habitually take over the streets for meals together? Why, for example, have planners designed corner-shops and cafés away from residential areas? Why do we allow our best viticultural and horticultural land to be subsumed by housing development? Why has Australia never had much of a culture of outdoor cafés, arcaded streets, the promenade—all things that seem to be adjuncts to a rich intellectual life centred around the sociable and socialising act of public dining?

The short answer, I was told by a number of people, is very simple: flies. But I don't think this is good enough; the explanation runs much deeper. There is a long tradition of dualist conceptions of the city in which dining has been firmly situated as central to the private domestic sphere. The construction of the physical city has reflected a symbolic dichotomy in urban life. The city has been framed by a series of oppositions—public/private, urban/suburban, work/home, production/consumption, market/domestic economy, labour/reproduction of labour—and the roles assigned to men and women have reflected and perpetuated this duality.

Women have represented the domestic sphere. Kitchens have been seen as their natural home, and the role of physically nurturing their families has been regarded as a primary source of fulfilment, and simultaneously of self-abnegation. Kitchens and cooking occupy a contradictory position in many women's lives. On the one hand, the kitchen is the centre of never-ending consumption, mystified as love rather than labour; on the other, this very private space is one that women control as they do no other.

While cooking remains one of the more pleasant creative parts of the domestic routine, kitchens have very often been badly designed, ill-lit, cramped and poorly oriented. There have been many attempts to exercise social control through kitchen design. Some modern English architects expressly designed houses with small kitchens to eliminate the 'working-class' habit of dining and receiving visitors in the kitchen. Others have simply arranged kitchens to be efficient 'work spaces' without much overt concern with ideology—or with the social aspects of eating and preparing food.

In the early nineteenth century, European social theorists, mostly of Utopian socialist persuasion, argued that domestic labour was unnecessarily duplicated in private houses and should be socialised to cut down the needless work that sapped women's time and energy. To this end they produced housing schemes arranged around communal facilities for dining and laundry (although much of this work was still to be done by servants). The prescient planner Ebenezer Howard suggested similarly innovative schemes. The reality, however, fell short of the ideal.

In Britain, communal dining was only taken up in a large way during the Second World War, when the stolidly patriotic 'British

Restaurants' were established to provide wholesome food for war workers. In spite of some resistance, these were closed down after the war because they were seen as a threat to domesticity. Private dining was a mainstay of traditional family values and roles.

Many urban designers and architects have understood the centrality of kitchens for family life, however this notion of family is conceived. The authors of one visionary design manual, *A Pattern Language*,[1] boldly suggest that 'without communal eating, no human group can hold together'. They go on to say that 'there are almost no important human events or institutions which are not given their power to bind, their sacral character, by food and drink'. They summarise the meaning of communal eating as follows:

> A feast is of such a nature that it draws people to itself, and makes them leave everything else in order to participate in its joys. The mere act of eating together, quite apart from a banquet or some other festival occasion, is by its very nature a sign of friendship and of 'communion' ... The table is in a certain sense the centre of family life, the expression of family life.

It follows that kitchens must allow physical space for this sharing to occur.

> The isolated kitchen, separate from the family and considered as an efficient but unpleasant factory for food, is a hangover from the days of servants; and from more recent days where women willingly took over the servants' role.

As long as we maintain the hidden supposition that cooking is a chore and eating a pleasure, every woman is a kind of servant.

Most modern house plans still partly separate the kitchen from social areas. What is needed—and if it seems to be stating the obvious, think of all those house plans!—is to make the kitchen

---

1. Christopher Alexander et al., *A Pattern Language* (Oxford University Press, New York, 1977).

bigger. To paraphrase *A Pattern Language*, the kitchen should be big enough to include the family-room space; it should be near the centre of the house, with a big table in the middle, lots of chairs (soft and hard), and the stove, counters and sink around the edge.

The eating atmosphere is also important. It's obvious that some rooms invite people to eat slowly and pleasantly, while others make them feel like bolting their food so they can go somewhere else to relax. This is partly to do with comfort, and also to do with light. If there is the same level of light over the whole space, the intensity of feeling is dissolved and the sense of gathering is dissipated. A sociable kitchen needs a heavy table in the centre of the eating space with a light that creates a pool over the people, leaving the surrounding walls enclosed in semi-darkness.

This concept of enclosure of space is also related to the dualist conceptions of the city where dining is privatised. We have understood inside/outside, private/public, somewhat inflexibly, using solid walls to demarcate the private and public worlds. In some other cultures space isn't so clearly defined by walls but is a scene of 'fluid change and constant transformation, like that of the human relationship to nature'. This fluidity or transformation is expressed, for example, in the Japanese practice of building temporary restaurants on wooden platforms over a river in summer. Here physical design relates to the seasons and the natural world closely and flexibly.

Our restaurants, by contrast, tend to replicate the conditions of private houses—to be enclosed from the surrounding natural or urban world or provide some alienated fantasy that denies the real conditions of the city. And when we do sit outside to eat we tend to do so in our own back yards and gardens, which we have developed into lavishly detailed private worlds. This outside dining can be curiously discomfiting. Often there is no central table but a collection of disparate chairs without a focus—plates on laps, plastic cups all over the grass—all inducing a kind of conversational inertia and dislocation that is utterly at odds with the atmosphere of a good eating place.

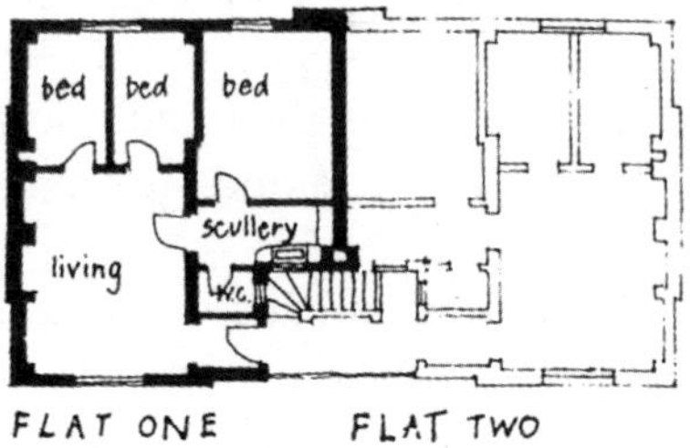

This 'model dwelling' was designed by Henry Roberts for the 1851 Great Exhibition as an example of good housing for the working class.

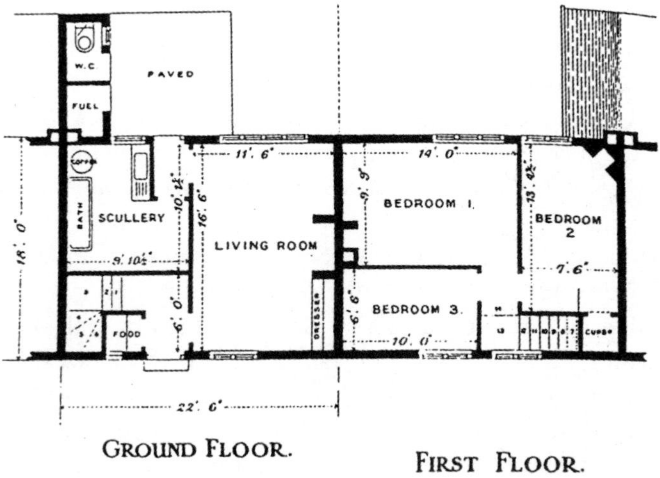

A standard design for British council housing, 1917.

A contemporary house design has the kitchen partly integrated into dining and family areas, but the working space is still very limited.

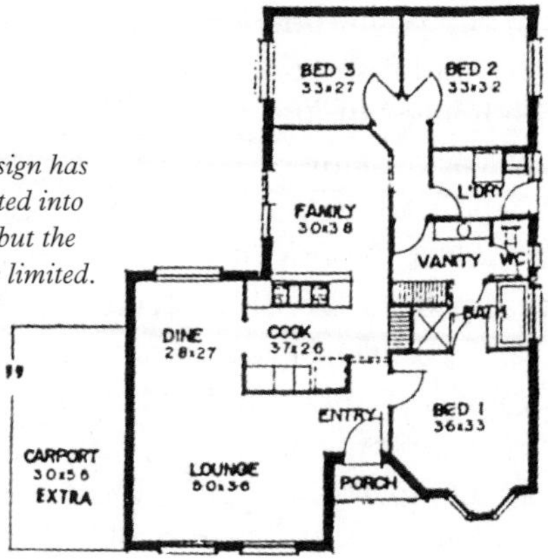

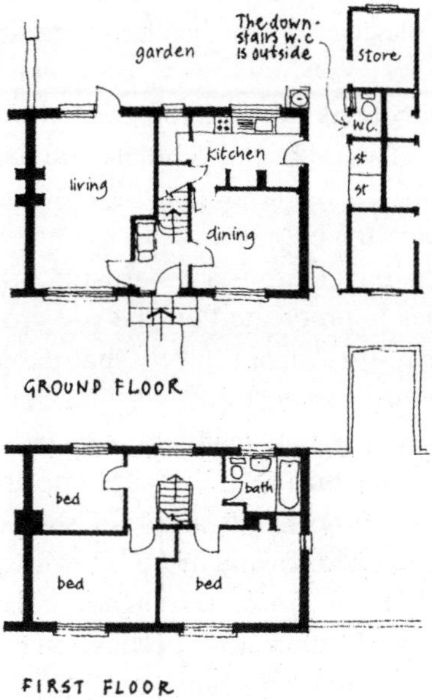

In this 1949 design, the kitchen has been squeezed into a corner to make space for a separate dining room.

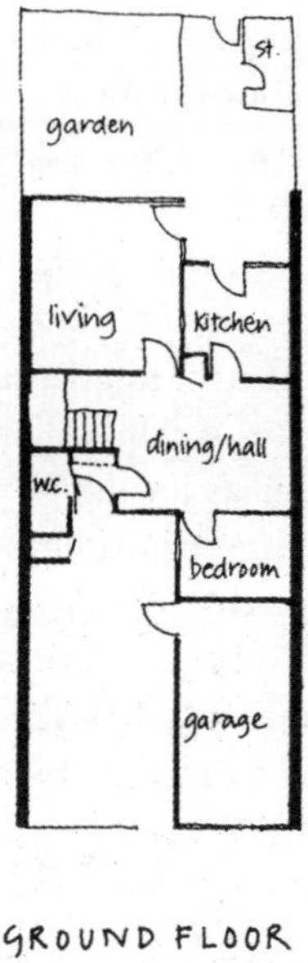

The ground floor of a 1960s house, designed for a family of five.

One of the main reasons for this privatisation of open space—and this has a lot to do with why we don't dine in the street—is the physical design and purpose of modern roads. An Italian designer called Camillo Sitte wrote a lot in the late nineteenth century about positive outdoor space, which is also sometimes described as the outdoor room. In this conception the road is the floor and the trees and buildings are the walls. Sitte worked out a mathematical relationship between the two, a ratio of height to width that defines the space. Within a certain ratio the space feels good to be in; outside this ratio the space feels either too closed or too open. Getting the ratio right is absolutely fundamental to good street and square design. In Australia, roads and squares tend to be much too big and too wide. They don't work as comfortable, usable, positive space for pedestrians. This has large implications for outdoor dining.

Cars are a key problem. Streets became too wide when their basic use changed from pedestrian space to vehicular carriageway. When vehicles became motorised and grew in power and numbers, the street as a place for people was on the way out. It has been suggested that cars have a god-like status in Australia. The form of Australian cities is predicated on the pre-eminence of the car as a transport form. It is most unlikely that people will stop using cars unless they are forced to do so. The density of people and houses is so low that people really do need cars to get around. The suburbs were built on the (false) assumption that everyone would have cars—so who needs a corner shop? Most people don't grow their own vegetables any more. They buy them at a shopping centre where things come packaged, stored and shipped regardless of season or distance, for purchase on a weekly basis and separate consumption in private houses. Meanwhile, the low-density suburbs move ever outwards, encroaching on land once used for agricultural production of fresh, local, seasonally available produce—or so the romantic would have it.

Not only do the streets suffer from their primary role as paths for cars and trucks, but they offer little pleasure and comfort to pedestrians. Urban designers suggest that in one sense 'the edge of the space is the space'; detailed attention to the edges is crucial to good pedestrian space. You have to treat the edge of a building 'as a thing, a place, a zone with volume to it, not a line which has no thickness'. There should be places that have depth and a covering, places to sit, lean and walk, particularly at points along the perimeter where people can look onto interesting outdoor life. The argument is that people prefer being at the edges of open spaces; people will usually place themselves *near* something—a façade, pillar or furniture if these are provided. This is why arcades, galleries, porches and terraces are good structures for the edges of street space. The example of Bologna springs to mind, with its miles of porticoed streets, but there are many other cities where canopied space has helped support street life. It seems an obvious idea for our climate as well. This kind of environmental and psychological protection for the pedestrian provides a space within which outdoor cafés can develop. Why does Australia have so few good alfresco cafés? Is it because we are indifferent to the mixture of sociability, contemplativeness and introspection that is associated with café society? Or is it because our city design sends people scurrying back into private space? A fairly high density or concentration of people is necessary to provide a café with clientele. It's imperative that there be a lot of customers. People like the physical closeness to others the café allows—the chance to listen to interesting conversations as well as the dangerous and exciting opportunity to meet someone unknown.

A good café has to be within easy walking distance of home and open to the street. It will usually serve simple food and drink (some of it alcoholic). With these in place, talk, lectures, debate and controversy are all possible. Yet the opportunity to sit at a table, eat, drink and converse is very limited in our cities. For one thing, public space, where cafés are situated, has been very much a male domain. Australia has traditionally lacked a well-developed culture of local cafés. Some men and a few women may have a local pub, but practically no-one else has a local place to meet, eat, drink and talk to people. Almost the only place where we get a high enough density of people to make cafés work is in and around the centre of the city. In Adelaide, for example, the city plan and its urban-design guidelines stress the need for lots of cafés with outdoor sitting places, but with too few people and unsympathetic building and road design it just will not happen.

I was intrigued to read that in various places—the examples I saw were Italian, Spanish and Greek—local restaurants and communities just rope off the road and set up tables for their patrons or themselves in front of the premises, maybe under a canopy of trees, or in a miniature park across the street, or sometimes on a traffic island. One picture showed a group of working-class families who had taken over the space in front of a cathedral in Trastevere for a feast of mussels and suckling pig. They looked as if they were having a really good time.

At the recent Adelaide Festival of Arts a grand public dining event was held in Gouger Street, home of many and varied restaurants and the city's central food market. It was difficult to stage this event; it met skepticism and doubt from the bureaucracy, and from local retailers. In the event, it succeeded, thanks to the organisers and to the charisma of the festival. But it is clear that this was a special case, not a precursor to spontaneous outbursts of public dining.

What the Gouger Street experience showed was that people really do like eating together in the street. On the other hand, the space itself illustrated many of our typical design problems. Gouger Street's ratio of building height to road width was too big to get a sense of enclosure. There was no shelter from the heat and glare of the sun. And, perhaps most importantly, the impetus for the project came from without.

I would like to see this repeated on a smaller scale, much more often, with more spontaneity and local impetus. What I have tried to show is how the arrangement of private space and of street space in terms of scale, treatment of edges, density of people, presence or absence of cars, affects the chances of increasing the number and diversity of dining experiences—and how this is linked to our ideas about the public and private domain.

It is clear that cities need to change. We need human-scale streets for pedestrians, a higher density of people and houses, public outdoor rooms and private indoor rooms that are good to eat and drink and converse in. Communal eating is absolutely basic to human life. It seems we really are fundamentally convivial. We know how to adapt our cities to our needs and fit them with nature, and we have seen how life can be impoverished when we get city design wrong on such a grand scale. But if we are to enhance the richness of our urban experience, good gastronomers will have to become good urban designers too.

Susan Parham's career-long interest in food and cities began with this 1990 piece. Today Associate Professor Parham heads Urbanism and Planning at the University of Hertfordshire's School of Life and Medical Sciences. Her research interests include food and spatial design, nature-based solutions to place issues, sprawl retrofitting and transport-oriented, compact and sustainable cities, and planning, urban design and urbanism. In 2022 and 2023 Parham ran the food and urbanism stream of an international Summer School on health and urbanism in Venice as part of the Biennale, and co-coordinated an international Garden Cities of Tomorrow Congress, which she offers again in 2024.

The Cultural Cringe

Arthur Phillips

Meanjin 9.4 Summer 1950

THE AUSTRALIAN BROADCASTING COMMISSION has a Sunday programme, designed to cajole a mild Sabbatarian bestirment of the wits, called 'Incognito'. Paired musical performances are broadcast, one by an Australian, one by an overseas executant, but with the names and nationalities withheld until the end of the programme. The listener is supposed to guess which is the Australian and which the alien performer. The idea is that quite often he guesses wrong or gives it up because, strange to say, the local lad proves to be no worse than the foreigner. This unexpected discovery is intended to inspire a nice glow of patriotic satisfaction.

I am not jeering at the ABC for its quaint idea. The programme's designer has rightly diagnosed a disease of the Australian mind and is applying a sensible curative treatment. The dismaying circumstance is that such a treatment should be necessary, or even possible; that in any nation, there should be an assumption that the domestic cultural product will be worse than the imported article.

The devil of it is that the assumption will often be correct. The numbers are against us, and an inevitable quantitative inferiority easily looks like a qualitative weakness, under the most favourable circumstances—and our circumstances are not favourable. We cannot shelter from invidious comparisons behind the barrier of a separate language; we have no long-established or interestingly different cultural tradition to give security and distinction to its interpreters; and the centrifugal pull of the great cultural metropolises works against us. Above our writers—and other artists—looms the intimidating mass of Anglo-Saxon culture. Such a situation almost inevitably produces the characteristic Australian Cultural Cringe—appearing either as the Cringe Direct, or as the Cringe Inverted, in the attitude of the Blatant Blatherskite, the God's-Own-Country and I'm-a-better-man-than-you-are Australian Bore.

The Cringe mainly appears in an inability to escape needless comparisons. The Australian reader, more or less consciously, hedges and hesitates, asking himself 'Yes, but what would a cultivated Englishman think of this?' No writer can communicate confidently to a reader with the 'Yes, but' habit; and this particular demand is curiously crippling to critical judgment. Confronted by Furphy, we grow uncertain. We fail to recognise the extraordinarily original structure of his novel because we are wondering whether perhaps an Englishman might not find it too complex and self-conscious. No one worries about the structural deficiencies of *Moby Dick*. We do not fully savour the meaty individualism of Furphy's style because we are wondering whether perhaps his egotistic verbosity is not too Australianly crude; but we accept the egotistic verbosity of Borrow as part of his quality.

But the dangers of the comparative approach go deeper than this. The Australian writer normally frames his communication for the Australian reader. He assumes certain mutual preknowledge, a responsiveness to certain symbols, even the ability to hear the cadence of a phrase in the right way. Once the reader's mind begins to be nagged by the thought of how an Englishman might feel about this, he loses the fine edge of his Australian responsiveness. It is absurd to feel apologetic towards *Such Is Life*, or *Coonardoo* or *Melbourne Odes* because they would not seem quite right to an English reader; it is part of their distinctive virtue that no Englishman can fully understand them.

I once read a criticism which began from the question 'What would a French classicist think of *Macbeth*?' The analysis was discerningly conducted and had a certain paradoxical interest; but it could not escape an effect of comic irrelevance.

A second effect of the Cringe has been the estrangement of the Australian Intellectual. Australian life, let us agree, has an atmosphere of often dismaying crudity. I do not know if our cultural crust is proportionately any thinner than that of other Anglo-Saxon communities; but to the intellectual it seems thinner because, in a small community, there is not enough of it to provide for the individual a protective insulation. Hence, even more than most intellectuals, he feels a sense of exposure. This is made much worse by the intrusion of that deadly habit of English comparisons. There is a certain type of Australian intellectual who is forever sidling up to the cultivated Englishman, insinuating: '*I*, of course, am not like these other crude Australians; *I* understand how you must feel about them; *I* should be spiritually more at home in Oxford or Bloomsbury.'

It is not the critical attitude of the intellectual that is harmful; that could be a healthy, even creative, influence, if the criticism were felt to come from within, if the critic had a sense of identification with his subject, if his irritation came from a sense of shared shame rather than a disdainful separation. It is his refusal to participate, the arch of his indifferent eye-brows, which exerts the chilling and stultifying influence.

Thinking of this type of Australian Intellectual, I am a little uneasy about my phrase 'Cultural Cringe'; it is so much the kind of missile which he delights to toss at the Australian mob. I hope I have made it clear that my use of the phrase is not essentially unsympathetic, and that I regard the denaturalised Intellectual as the Cringe's unhappiest victim. If any of the breed use my phrase for his own contemptuous purposes, my curse be upon him. May crudely-Dinkum Aussies spit in his beer, and gremlins split his ever to be preciously agglutinated infinitives.

The Australian writer is affected by the Cringe because it mists the responsiveness of his audience, and because its influence on the intellectual deprives the writer of a sympathetically critical atmosphere. Nor can he entirely escape its direct impact. There is a significant phrase in Henry Handel Richardson's *Myself*

When Young. When she found herself stuck in a passage of *Richard Mahony* which would not come right, she remarked to her husband, 'How did I ever dare to write *Maurice Guest*—a poor little colonial like me?' Our sympathies go out to her—pathetic victim of the Cringe. For observe that the Henry Handel Richardson who had written *Maurice Guest* was not the raw girl encompassed by the limitations of the Kilmore Post Office and a Philistine mother. She had already behind her the years in Munich and a day-to-day communion with a husband steeped in the European literary tradition. Her cultural experience was probably richer than that of such contemporary novelists as Wells or Bennett. It was primarily the simple damnation of being an Australian which made her feel limited. Justified, you may think, by the tone of Australian life, with its isolation and excessively material emphasis? Examine the evidence fairly and closely, and I think you will agree that Henry Handel Richardson's Australian background was a shade richer in cultural influence than the dingy shop-cum stuffy Housekeeper's Room-cum-sordid Grammar School which incubated Wells, or than the Five Towns of the eighteen-eighties.

By both temperament and circumstance, Henry Handel Richardson was peculiarly susceptible to the influence of the Cringe; but no Australian writer, unless he is dangerously insensitive, can wholly escape it; he may fight it down or disguise it with a veneer of truculence, but it must weaken his confidence and nag at his integrity.

It is not so much our limitations of size, youth and isolation which create the problem as the derivativeness of our culture; and it takes more difficult forms than the Cringe. The writer is particularly affected by our colonial situation because of the nature of his medium. The painter is in some measure bound by the traditional evolution of his art, the musician must consider the particular combinations of sound which the contemporary civilised ear can accept; but ultimately paint is always paint, a piano everywhere a piano. Language has no such ultimate physical existence; it is in its essence merely what generations of usage have made it. The three symbols m-a-n create the image of a male human being only because venerable English tradition has so decreed. The Australian writer cannot cease to be English even if he wants to. The nightingale does not sing under Australian skies; but he still sings in the literate Australian mind. It may thus become the symbol which runs naturally to the tip of the writer's pen; but he dare not use it because it has no organic relation with the Australian life he is interpreting.

The Jindyworobaks are entirely reasonable when they protest against the alien symbolisms used by O'Dowd, Brennan or McCrae; but the difficulty is not simply solved. A Jindyworobak writer uses the image 'galah-breasted dawn'. The picture is both fresh and accurate, and has a sense of immediacy because it comes direct from the writer's environment; and yet somehow it doesn't quite come off. The trouble is that we—unhappy Cringers—are too aware of the processes in its creation. We can feel the writer thinking: 'No, I mustn't use one of the images which English language tradition is insinuating into my mind; I must have something Australian: ah, yes—' What the phrase has gained in immediacy, it has lost in spontaneity. You have some measure of the complexity of the problem of a colonial culture when you reflect that the last sentence I have written is not so nonsensical as it sounds.

I should not, of course, suggest that the Australian image can never be spontaneously achieved; one need not go beyond Stewart's *Ned Kelly* to disprove such an assumption. On the other hand, the distracting influence of the English tradition is not restricted to merely linguistic difficulties. It confronts the least cringing Australian writer at half-a-dozen points.

What is the cure for our disease? There is no short-cut to the gradual processes of national growth—which are already beginning to have their effect. The most important development of the last twenty years in Australian writing has been the progress made in the art of being unselfconsciously ourselves. If I have thought this article worth writing, it is because I believe that progress will quicken when we articulately recognise two facts:

that the Cringe is a worse enemy to our cultural development than our isolation, and that the opposite of the Cringe is not the Strut, but a relaxed erectness of carriage.

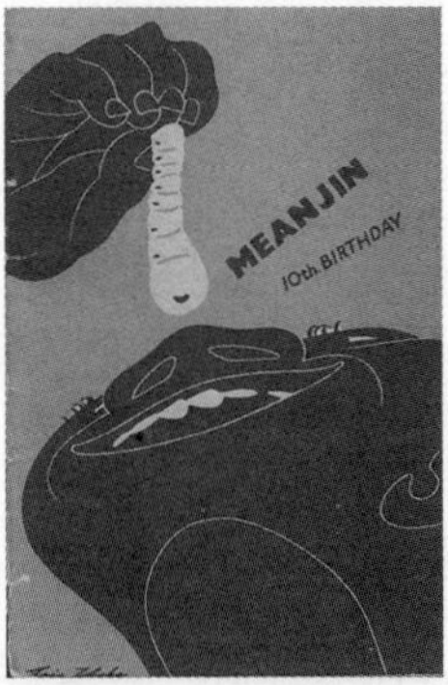

Arthur Angell Phillips (1900–1985)—widely known as AA Phillips, but who wrote this piece as **Arthur Phillips**—was a highly influential writer, critic and teacher, and an early exponent of post-colonial theory in Australia. He was educated at the University of Melbourne and at Oxford, and was a schoolmaster at Melbourne's Wesley College. He published several books of criticism including his 1958 *The Australian Tradition: Essays in Colonial Culture*, which built on the ideas first presented in this essay.

A quarterly of literature

Clem Christesen

Meanjin 4.3 Spring 1945

> Move then with new desires;
> For where we used to build and love
> Is no man's land, and only ghosts can live
> Between two fires.
>
> —C Day Lewis

THIS IS THE first peace-time issue of *Meanjin*. A series of world-events of great significance occurred between the Winter number and this Spring number. The war in Europe ended with the complete collapse of Germany; the San Francisco conference was held; John Curtin, Australia's wartime Labour leader, died; Mr. Churchill was decisively defeated and a Labour Government elected in Britain; the Potsdam conference was held (Australia again not being consulted); the atrocities of Belsen, Buchenwald and Auschwitz were revealed; atomic bombs were used against Japan (the further spiritual shock of that mass horror!); the Pacific war ended; surviving members of the 8th Division were rescued from Japanese prison camps ... What are the implications to us of events during those crowded few months?

The world has been convulsed by six years of war: it is now a vastly different world from that of 1939. The atomic bomb, if nothing else, has seen to that: it severed the old world from the new with guillotine-like decisiveness. 'The atomic bomb,' said Professor WJ Dakin in a recent broadcast, 'means something very different from the discovery of a new explosive. It means something entirely new in man's relationship to the world about him. It is a crossroad signpost in the history of human existence.'

These wartime experiences have surely made the creative artist realise (if he lacked that realisation before) that his responsibilities in world-society have increased in weight and in urgency. For a century Western writers have known the temptation of social irresponsibility: this has been almost the proprium of a literary career. The writer can no longer succumb to that temptation without alienating himself from the most progressive elements in present-day society. In the light of events leading up to and during the second world war the man of letters must be held responsible for the decision he makes. Jean-Paul Sartre, one of the leading writers of the new generation in France, claimed recently that there were writers in Europe who, when reviled or punished for having hired out their talents to the Germans, registered grieved astonishment: 'Why,' they asked, 'is one responsible for what one writes?' This miserable heritage of irresponsibility must not be allowed to continue.

Since by their very existence writers influence their time, they must decide, deliberately, how this influence is to be used. What will be the pattern of life in postwar Australia? What reforms must be effected? What will be our relationship with other countries, particularly East Asia and in the Pacific Basin? The writer today must be informed on external as well as domestic affairs, and must use his powers deliberately to influence public opinion. No longer can he sneak off to some frangipani-scented gazebo, remaining aloof from the mounting postwar problems. He must identify himself with the aspirations of the people towards community and national reform.

Let us not be misunderstood. The chief responsibility of the man of letters—a responsibility he shares with other creative artists—is towards his art. While concerning himself with present-day social and political problems he must retain his artistic integrity. As a responsible member of society he cannot dissociate himself from the problems which face modern society; as a writer he must interpret these with the greatest artistic skill and imagination of which he is capable. He can no longer seek to escape his responsibilities as a man by pleading 'art for art's sake'; nor can he jeopardise artistic standards by claiming the urgency of his social responsibilities.

At all times literature has revealed man to himself, in his unchanging essence; but we turn to the writer of our own time to make us aware not only of the changeless nature of the human heart but of the changing nature of the present. We ask him to reveal and clarify our life by showing it to us through a vision different from ours and deeper. We ask him to organise the conflicting welter of impressions, which is the actual process of living, into the ordered integrations of experience, which are works of art. By becoming part of the uniqueness of our time we finally merge with the eternal; and it is the task of the writer to cast light on the eternal values which are involved in present political and social issues. If evasion now becomes more difficult, decision becomes easier and its implications more apparent. The writer is situated in his time: each word has its reverberations; each silence, too. *He is responsible.*

And there is also the writer's responsibility to the reader: responsibility in terms of communication. The tide is beginning to set against the esoteric and obscure. As J Donald Adams says in *The Shape of Books to Come*, we are emerging from a period of intense experimentalism in all the arts. When the experimenters have accomplished their work of cutting away the dry rot of decayed attitudes and forms, art is ready to turn outward again and to re-establish the connection between life and the social order, in which, completely to fulfil its functions, it must play its part.

In 1945, Clement Byrne Christesen—often styled CB or simply **Clem Christesen** (1911–2003)—had just relocated *Meanjin* from Brisbane to Melbourne. Christesen went on to edit *Meanjin* until 1974. He wrote and edited several books including *On Native Grounds: Australian writing from Meanjin Quarterly, Selected with a preface by C.B. Christesen*, published by Angus and Robertson in 1968. He was made an Officer of the Order of British Empire in 1962 in recognition of service to Australian literature, and was presented with the Medal of the Order of Australia in 2000 for service to the development of Australian creative and critical writing as founder and editor of *Meanjin Quarterly*. In 2001 Christesen was awarded the Centenary Medal for service to Australian society and the humanities in writing and literature.

Makunschan, Meeanjan, Miganchan, Meanjan, Magandjin

Gaja Kerry Charlton

Meanjin 82.2 Winter 2023

> *Every tribe … has its own dialect, if not language … stamps their locality much, know every acre of land belonging to their 'home' … each plant, flower, tree, shrub, grass, bird, beast, insect … every mile of a river or watercourse its own appellation, from the highest source to the mouth or junction always had a name of its own.*[1]
>
> —Henry Stuart Russell

THE INVITATION TO write for the *Meanjin* magazine is welcomed in the spirit of Reconciliation and Truth-telling. I share from my *Goori doogal* (Aboriginal heart) about my family and tribes, culture and history with colonisation; our *Wularanguru* historical language mapping project; and of matters still to be resolved, including the original language placenames. 'Brisbane, port, the capital of Queensland, Australia and the country's third largest city. It lies astride the Brisbane River on the southern slopes of the Taylor Range, 12 miles (19 kilometres) above the river's mouth at Moreton Bay.'[2]

1. Henry Stuart Russell, *Genesis of Queensland*, 1888, p. 315.
2. 'Brisbane', Britannica Online: www.britannica.com/place/Brisbane

Our 500-year strategic plans

Our Elders' words echo always—language is culture, culture is language—but what does this mean with a history of being forcibly removed, shredded by disconnection? Goori-ness hinges on connection to Country. Unpacking original placenames and their meaning is paramount for Truth-telling, and healing People and Country in the light of *Story of Place*. Self-determined language repatriation is a fundamental right of First Nations peoples.[3] Several acts of government implemented in Queensland exerted increasing levels of control over the lives of its First Peoples.[4] *The Protection of Aboriginals and Restriction of the Sale of Opium Act 1897* (The Act) increased institutionalised racism and assimilation through forced removals of First Nations peoples, firstly the vulnerable and sick, then all, from family, tribe, Country.

3. UN Declaration on the Rights of Indigenous Peoples.
4. *Industrial and Reformatory Schools Act 1865*; *Native Labourers' Protection Act of 1884*; *Protection of Aboriginals and Restriction of the Sale of Opium Act 1897.*

Our Moreton Tribe was impacted for six generations by 'the Act'—a time of attempted assimilation, destruction and terrible losses. Siblings *Mookin* and *Winyuba* secured exemptions after decades under its rule. Back on Country they were concerned to find their languages being inaccurately published, including placenames.[5] The mandate from our Elders was to 'get it right, do it our way'—'protocols proper way' to repair and protect our culture and lingo.[6] Now we are Elders. *Our Yagara—Magandjin* Aboriginal Corporation continues their Vision. We talk in terms of 500-year strategic plans; of cultural custodianship, and sustainability, for our grandchildren's grandchildren.[7]

Ancient Cultural Connections

The above coastal map shows *Yagara* country and bordering language neighbours in this section of Moreton Bay.[8] Their names *Gabi (Kabi)*, *Wakka*, *Yugam* and *Jinibara's Gurai* are derived from the negator word in each of their languages for no, not, nothing, never, nowhere, etc.[9] Suffixes *-bul*, *-wal*, *-bir* denote 'is, is of'; –bara: people or group; –uba: uses first word as a name.

Who am I? Firstly, I am *Yagarabul* and *Gabi Gabi* with ties to *Walangama* in North Queensland. *Goori way*, I am a senior cultural custodian. *Dugai way* I hold formal teacher, trainer and counsellor qualifications. I'm also a researcher and writer.

We have tribal ties across the southeast and are recognised as traditional owners in three registered native title claims: 1. *Quandamooka*, 2. *Yuggera Ugarapul* Peoples (YUP), and 3. *Kabi Kabi* (*Gabi Gabi*).

---

5. K Charlton and B Brown, 'Languages of Moreton Bay' transcription by K Charlton from taped interview of *Winyuba* (Mary Jane Sunflower Morton) by Elwyn Flint, c. 1960. 2019, p. 1.
6. Commonly used term that refers to our languages.
7. Uncle Steven Coghill and Moreton family Elders.
8. *Yagara Djarra* and its nearest neighbours with approximate boundaries. Wularanguru map of languages of Moreton Bay, 2019–2023.
9. Kate Ballard, *Brisbane, the Beginning: Being a story of 18th Century Miganchan and the environs*, 2007, p. 5.

Quandamooka, the name chosen for the first native title claim, means 'Spirit of the Dolphin'[10] or 'the Spirit of Moreton Bay'[11] based on a creation story about the culturally significant relationship between Goori and dolphins in Moreton Bay. The *Yagara* name for Moreton Bay is *Boroogar*.

Our Moreton family's completed connection report shows our intangible cultural heritage—family oral history—confirmed in records. Tangible connection to *Djerrangerri*, our original name for Stradbroke Islands, verifies these old ties through *Mookin*'s father. It states:

> The Moreton descent group is said to have descended from Charlie Moreton, *Dandruba*. The documentary records are consistent with the oral history regarding the existence of *Dandruba* at North Stradbroke Island at or around the time of settlement.[12]

Mookin, son of *Dandruba*, was our great grandfather and grandson of *Kerwalli*, King Sandy of Brisbane. Born in 1871 at Amity Point on *Djerrangerri*, his remarkable athletic and linguistic abilities earmarked him to be a message-stick bearer, and holder of knowledges across Queensland. Naturally, *Mookin* received training and knowledge from his renowned grandfather. *Kerwalli* provided names and story of place including Mt. Kut-ha. In 1905, a journalist interviewed his daughter *Dinaba*, *Mookin*'s mother, on the meaning of the name Wynnum (*winnam*).

When *Ngugi* author Paul Tripcony asked *Mookin* about any known letters on any 'Aboriginal Letter Sticks', he replied, 'What we classed as letters were signs that the sender of the letter stick, and the person who received the same, and their close associates, understood the symbols engraved on the letter sticks as containing news of past events, or heralded the prediction of future important

10. Donna Ruska, personal communications, 2000–17.
11. Christine Peacock, *History, Life and Times of Robert Anderson, Gheebelum, Ngugi, Mulgumpin*, 2001, p. 64.
12. *Quandamooka* native title claim, summary of Moreton family connection report, 2007.

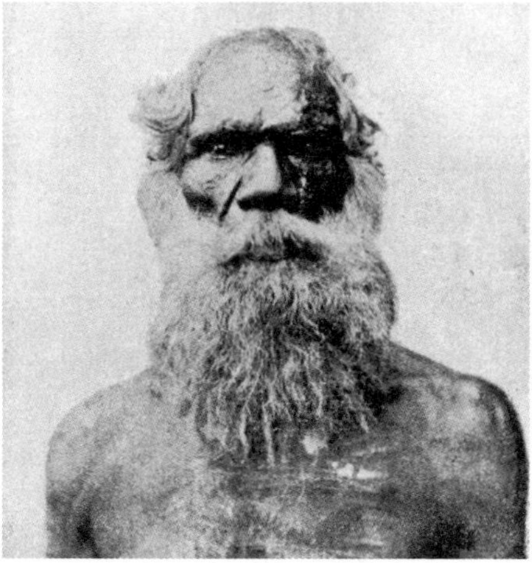

Kerwalli, grandfather of Mookin, told naturalist James Craig that he was 'King of the tribe' of the land where Brisbane now stands. In James W Craig, Australian Joint Copying Project, National Library of Australia, and State Library of New South Wales: Papers of James Whitelaw Craig [microform]: [M978] 1873–1877; entries 5 and 23 December 1875.

tribal ceremonies, and also the sealing and ratification of a previous sacred ceremonial agreement on the subject of peace and friendship. The person delivering a Message Stick was given safe conduct throughout the territory of his travels.'[13]

Mookin was a renowned *Malara*[14] remembered by others as a visitor to their Country, who travelled long distances and spoke many languages. Most Goori spoke more than one language. Such cultural roles brought resistance to taking 'exemption', a key tool of assimilation, with the condition requiring applicants agree they were no longer an Aborigine; didn't associate with Aborigines which limited culture and speaking ones' lingo. *Mookin* and *Winyuba* were among a group of old knowledge holders on the reserves working to preserve Goori knowledges, language and culture to protect it from 'extinction', an intention of the Act! Both were recorded by academics. The tapes and written materials are vital to resourcing our language repatriation and maintenance for future generations.

---

13. Paul Tripcony (1901–1975), manuscript: 'Moongalba: Birthplace of a Great Chief, Stradbroke Island', Paul Tripcony Papers, Fryer Library, University of Queensland.
14. 'A completed warrior' who had achieved all feats of initiation and ceremony.

Healing the past brings a healed future

Table 1. The below *Goori Nharul-Milen* (family/kin group) table illustrates the Moreton Tribe's ancestral affiliations, languages and territories based on Country, flora and fauna. Read across the table to learn about the names of Moreton family members, their clans/tribes, and where they were based. *NB This work is my Indigenous Cultural Intellectual Property. It is not to be used without my written permission. This is our Goori Milpulbul (living Goori).*[15] © *Kerry Charlton*

Family Members		**Clans / Tribes**		**Place or Area**	
Names	**Translation**	**Clan / Tribe Names**	**Translation**	**Place Names**	**Translation**
Mookin / Mugin Yagara (son of Dinaba and Dander-uba) 1871–1949	Big, strong Uses Country as a name -uba: suffix	Koenpal / Goenpul Janderwal / Jandai Kirkham / Gergum Ngunda (Ngoonda) Joondabari/ Undanbi	Pearl oyster shellfish Narrow leaf Ironbark tree Brisbane – Yagara tribe He / she is, very coastal -bari: group; -gal: 'is of'	ɗerraŋgeri Goompi, ɗerraŋeri Magan-djin Gabi Gabi	Stradbroke Island Dunwich, Strad.Is. Tulipwood trees Negator word
Winyuba, Janie (1883–1964)	Dugong bird -yuba (same as -uba suffix)	Janderwal / Jandai Kirkham / Gergum Ngunda (Ngoonda)	Narrow leaf Ironbark tree Brisbane – Yagara tribe He / she is, very coastal	Goompi, ɗerraŋeri Magan-djin Gabi Gabi	Dunwich, Strad.Is. Tulipwood trees Negator word
Di:naba / Sarah (mother of Mookin and Winyuba, 1845–1907)	Clan name	Gergum/ Kercoom Gorbenpan Ngunda (Ngoonda)	Brisbane – Yagara tribe Brisbane – Yagara tribe He / she is, very coastal	Magan-djin Benarrawa Gabi Gabi	Tulipwood tree Oxley, Oxley Ck. Negator word
Danderuba Charlie Moreton (c. 1840–1873)	Ironbark tree -uba: suffix	Danderr / Tanderoo Koenpul / Goenpal	Ironbark tree, thin leaf Pearl oyster shellfish	Goompi ɗerraŋeri	Dunwich area Stradbroke Is.
Nawin / Sarah (c. 1825–1880)	Dugong bird	Ngunda (Ngoonda) Darabul / Turrbal	She / he is, very coastal Oyster, clan / tribe name	Nambor – Pine River Ngooyeera	Ti (tea) tree Toorbal Point
Kaerwalli / Gairballie King Sandy (c. 1820–1900)	Split, spilt Yandee	Gergum / Kercoom Gorbenpan Ninge Ninge	Brisbane – Yagara tribe Brisbane – Yagara tribe Oyster, Redcliffe group	Magan-djin Benarrawa Gabi Gabi	Brisbane district Oxley Creek Negator word

15. Moreton Family Cultural Oral History, Indigenous Cultural Intellectual Property.

The *Wulara-Nguru* historical language mapping project

Wulara-Nguru is a historical language mapping and repatriation project mandated by the Moreton Elders. The term 'repatriation' points to our history of colonial conflicts, resistance and dispossession.[16] The definition 'to return one to their Country' accurately describes our situation. We didn't 'just stop' using our languages. It was forcibly removed from daily use under the Act instituted to 'smooth the dying pillow' for survivors of colonial terrorism.[17] Begun in 2007, after a decade or so of initial community-based language revival efforts, it consists of myself and *Dugai* colleague Barry Brown and a Language Support Group. *Wulara* means speak, talk, language, while *Nguru* is shadow, spirit or breath. We're a work in progress. As a Language Fellow at the University of Queensland in the School of Languages and Cultures, I'm involved in transcribing the tapes for reconstruction of our language and community-based programs. We have achieved a substantial database of the languages of *Yagara* country and south-east Queensland. The years of data compilation, evolving methodology and cautious surveying led to our 2019 lexical handbook, *An Introduction to the Languages of Moreton Bay*: *Yagarabul and its dialect Djandewal and Moreton Island's Gowar.* It's a major step towards our vision of 'healed' language; community-based language programs and growing language fluency. This field periodically emerges waves of vicarious trauma from what eminent *Yagara* Elder Dr Aileen Moreton-Robinson describes as 'ontological disturbances from encounters with the white western paradigm, racial blindness and cultural bias.'[18] We work to heal *Budjang dja*, Mother earth, too.

---

16. Rod Fisher (ed.), *Brisbane: The Aboriginal Presence 1824–1860*, Brisbane History Group, 1992.
17. Rural Health Training Unit, *Cairns: Introduction to Recent Aboriginal and Torres Strait Islander History in Queensland*, 1997, p. 8.
18. Aileen Moreton-Robinson, *Talkin' Up to the White Woman: Indigenous Women and Feminism*, 20th anniversary edition, preface, 2020, p. xi.

It's important to highlight that many language words were historically recorded with multiple spelling demonstrating the challenges for early writers with foreign ears attempting to phoneticise an ancient language. Versions of *Yagara* include *Yuggera*, *Yuggara*, *Yugara*, *Jagera*, *Jagara*, *Ugara* and *Ugarapul*. Margaret Sharpe, a linguist of Australian Aboriginal languages who specialised in *Yugambeh—Bundjalung*, with special regard to *Yugambir*, explained this comes from linguists trained in Europe, using the International Phonetic Alphabet (IPA), which writes the small 'j' for the 'y' sound in 'yes'. 'In German, "j" is used for the "y" sound, but some Germans who kindly wrote down Australian languages did use "y" because they were writing for an English reading audience. "Y"s should always be read as "Y"s.'[19] In his consonant sounds list, Nils Holmer wrote: '"j" is a palatal semivowel, like "y" in English "yes"'.[20] We knew the *Yagara* word early as a name for great grandfather *Mookin*. His sister *Winyuba* (Janie Sunflower) confirms its pronunciation on tape recordings by academics from the University of Queensland.[21] *Yagara* is said correctly with a 'y' sound.

In our research *Wulara-Nguru* works to a four-level ratings scale with sources of language, which include original Goori speakers of south-east Queensland languages, and colonial collectors (c.1825–1900). These elderly language speakers born around and after the 1870s, whose languages and knowledges remained intact despite incarceration under the Act, were recorded on tapes between 1950–60. *Wulara-Nguru*'s four-level scale starts at 0: the native speaker; 1: you're at the source, speaking with, listening to and learning from a native speaker; 2: you're reading records of primary source who spoke with, learnt from the source, a native speaker; 3: you're hearing from or reading a secondary source who was informed by primary sources. Therefore, the higher

---

19. Margaret Sharpe, Report to FAIRA on the Linguistic Literature of the Brisbane Region, July 2000, p. 6.
20. Nils Holmer, 1983, *Linguistic Survey of South Eastern Queensland*, p. 390.
21. Janie Sunflower (Moreton) to Lindsay Winterbotham, 1940s to 1963.

the score, the further away from the original Goori speaker the material is. In the early days of colonial presence, First Nations language speakers taught their few *Dugai* friends and allies their languages. These became fluent speakers, primary sources and some recognised 'experts'. Prevailing racial attitudes or ignorant assumptions led to excluding original speakers from providing correct information. Watson wrote: 'For many years, there have been no full-blooded *Yugarabul* who could speak the language.'[22] At the same time native speakers like *Mookin*, *Winyuba* and others were locked away on reserves continuing to speak their languages with each other. The incomplete or mixed-up vocabulary continued be regurgitated.

Magandjin the district; Darabul (Turrabul) Tribe; Yagara the Country

> Several natives were seen on the side of river opposite to the settlement [Edenglassie] ... Natives upwards of 30 men, women and children; seemed desirous to cross the river had swam across higher up ... couldn't be persuaded into the settlement nearer than 2 or 3 hundred yards; where they remained looking at (for about an hour) the buildings and the cattle for about an hour, then went off and weren't seen again ...[23]

This group witnessed incomprehensible changes: destruction of the village, renamed river and site. Some original names have persisted since, albeit with distortions, *Meanjan* being one. Popular use, however, does not make it accurate. It is the right of First Nations peoples to address historical errors. The desire to support some reinstatement of the right language on Country is influenced by Reconciliation, Truth-telling and Healing; the UN's

22. FJ Watson, 'Vocabularies of Four Representative Tribes of Southeastern Queensland'. Supplement to *Journal of the Royal Geographical Society of Australasia* (Queensland), p. 9.
23. Edmund Lockyer, Esquire, 'Journal of an Excursion up the River Brisbane in the Year 1825', *Australian Quarterly Journal*, vol. 1 (1828), p. 590.

Declaration on the Rights of Indigenous Peoples of 2007 and International Decade of the World's Indigenous Languages, as well as Queensland's *Human Rights Act*; Many Voices Indigenous Languages Policy and Tracks to Treaty.

Reports show early collections of vocabularies recorded between 1836 and 1878. These informed each other and later collectors, some of whom appear in this article. Thomas (Tom) Petrie was six years old when he and his family arrived in Brisbane in 1837 and began learning the languages of his Goori playmates. Eventually he excelled in what he called the '*Turrubul*' language and tribe.[24] Tom's understanding of and friendships with Goori people proved providential during an era of colonial influx. He became a primary source who provided vocabularies to many, including Reverend Ridley and Archibald Meston, who became secondary sources. Each generated substantial public interest and greatly influenced all the following writers, shaping knowledge, and errors, about Goori language, clan, tribe and Country.

In 1841 Reverend Eipper wrote: 'The Aborigines of the district were subdivided into small tribes, each of which has a certain territory allotted to it, from which they generally derive their names; may number from 50 to 60. Tribal areas could span up to 60 miles, each with a recognised leader.'[25] Reverend Schmidt related about a trip to *Toorbul* and Wide Bay, Moreton Bay District in 1842–43, that Aboriginal guides refused to go beyond *Durundur*, then the limit of settlement.[26] In fact they were observing Goori lore-law protocols with territorial boundaries.

---

24. Thomas Petrie, 'Letter to Editor: Native Name of the Brisbane River' in *Science of Man*, 22 Jan, 1902, p. 203.
25. Niel Gunson, 'A Missionary Expedition from Zion Hill (Nundah) to Toorbul, Moreton Bay District', in 1842–43: The Journal of the Reverend KWE Schmidt, from *Aboriginal History*, vol. 2, 1–2, 1978, p. 120.
26. Rev. Niel Gunson, 'Journal of KWE Schmidt to Toorbul, Moreton Bay District, in 1842–43'. p. 115.

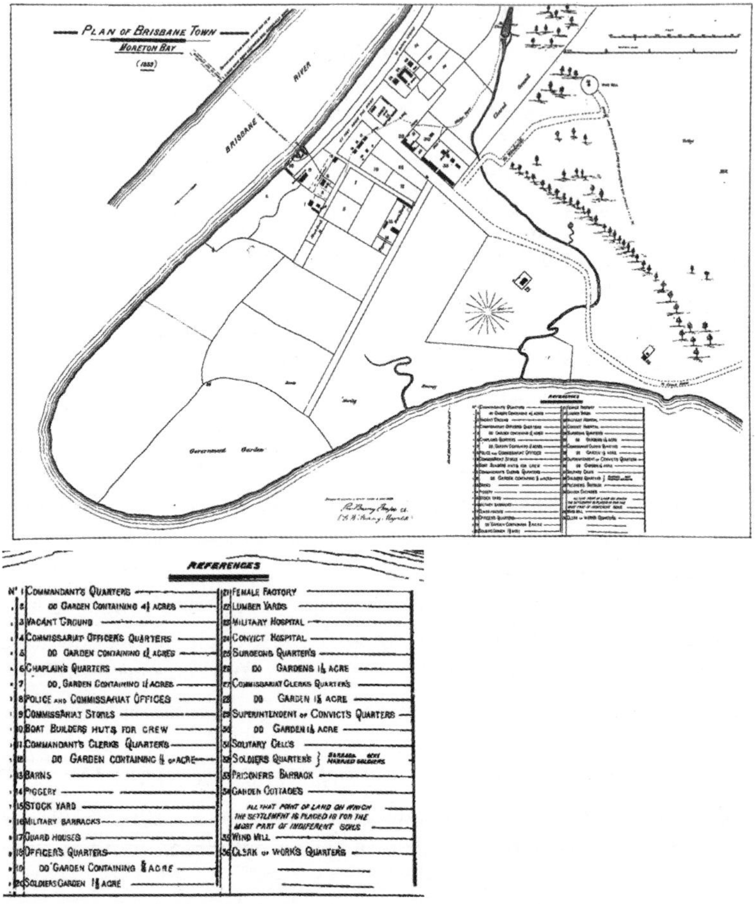

Map of Brisbane Town in 1839 from *Tom Petrie's Reminiscences of Queensland*.[27]

In 1851, Tom Petrie supplied Ridley with *Turrubul* vocabulary for his collection projects.[28] The Melbourne Exhibition 1868 procured a survey of vocabulary in 1866 from Petrie and his

27. Constance Campbell-Petrie, *Tom Petrie's Reminiscences of Queensland* (Brisbane: Watson, Ferguson & Co., 1904).
28. Rev. Ridley, *Moreton Bay Courier*, Saturday 1 December 1855, p. 2.

co-author *Nununga*, a *Kabi* man.[29] Two newspapers reported on the two 'dialects' used around Murrumba and the Pine Rivers catchment, describing '*Thurwell*' as additional to the better-known Brisbane 'dialect'. Ridley wrote 'we see *Turrbul, Durubul* and *Turrbal* as the same dialect name pronounced with a softened "b" and an aspirated (breathy) initial consonant, 1866's *Thurwell* for *Turr-bal* … the native Brisbane dialect and the Thurwell dialect …'[30] Ludwig Leichhardt described his visit with the *Nynga-Nynga* (*Ningy Ningy*) tribe, at *Turrabool* Point, in September 1843, describing the *Turrabool* and *Bribie* tribes as 'a fine race of men, tall and well made'. Archibald Meston in 1923 called them and their language *Churrabool*'[31] the '*Darabul*' mentioned by *Yagara* speakers to Holmer in 1970.[32] *Turbal* / *Durbal* is a *Kabi* word for oyster.[33] *Turrubal* is the name of a clan or tribe, not the Country.

Reverend Eipper wrote about the Brisbane language, describing it as 'very meagre as their words go no farther than their wants or employments'; an unsupported view. In contrast, in 1875, Ridley wrote of the grammatical structure that 'the inflections of verbs and nouns, the derivation and composition of words, the arrangement of sentences, and the methods of imparting emphasis, indicate an accuracy of thought, and a force of expression, surpassing all that is commonly supposed to be attainable by a savage race'.

Ned Harper, well-known timber-getter and intimate friend of Aborigines, and therefore a primary source, stated: 'the whole of the blacks on the southside of Moreton Bay and all along its shores to Amity Point use the word *Yug-ger-a-bool* to signify their respective dialects. The Lytton and South Brisbane blacks

---

29. *Sydney Mail* (*Guardian*), 14 July 1866, p. 6.
30. *Sydney Morning Herald*, 10 July 1866, p. 2; RH Mathews, 'L.S. Aborigines of the Northern Ter., W. Aus and Q'Land', p. 11.
31. Marcel Aurousseau, ed. *The Letters of F.W. Ludwig Leichhardt*, (Farnham: Ashgate Publishing, 2010).
32. Nils Holmer, *Other Languages of South-Eastern Queensland*, p. 402.
33. Dennis Bannister, MS2171, IAIAS Folder 7, Njula The Aboriginal Language of Bribie Island. p. 4.

used the same word.'[34] Meston correctly identified distinct languages existed in southeast Queensland. His public attention to the '*Turrubul*' vocabulary, given by Petrie to Ridley in 1851 and consisting of four languages ignited debates between them. Meston's access to native speakers at *Deebing* Creek mission,[35] where *Mookin* was also, generated new information; Meston was remiss in naming the speakers. He too caused confusion, writing both that *Wakka* was the language and tribute of Brisbane and *Wakka* one of the negator words spoken on Fraser Island.[36]

Confusion would later reign when colonial reporters mixed ethnonyms (tribal names) with glottonyms (the names of languages). The whole of Moreton Bay between Deception Bay and the *Jumpinpin* area is in the eastern part of the *Yagara* language group. This includes the river mouth regions of the Pine, Brisbane and Logan. Hay's Inlet (Redcliffe) forms the coastal boundary that runs northwest. This is *Yagara*-speaking country to the southwest and *Kabi*-speaking country to the northeast.[37]

In 1901 Meston and Petrie again debated *Yagara* or *Turrubul*, despite the *Yagara* speakers now at Purga mission outside Ipswich. Meston's son Leo, like Watson, later helped explain how decades of analysis were needed before the confusion could be properly dealt with, writing: 'Ridley and my father acquired their first knowledge of the Brisbane River and Moreton Bay dialects from Tom Petrie, and verified and extended it through their own observations among the aborigines.'[38]

---

34. Edward Harper. *The Queenslander*: 'The Early Days on the Tweed. Some Errors about the Blacks'. Saturday 1 September 1894, p. 410. National Library of Australia http://nla.gov.au/nla.news-article20719678
35. 'The Old Brisbane Blacks', *Brisbane Courier*, Saturday 31 August 1901, p. 15. National Library of Australia.
36. *Brisbane Courier*, Saturday 31 August 1901, p. 15.
37. *Gaiarbau* cited in John Gladstone Steele, *Aboriginal Pathways: in Southeast Queensland and the Richmond River*, University of Queensland Press, 1984, figure 81, p. 161.
38. *Brisbane Courier*, 10 September 1901, p. 7.

Reverend John Mathew, Kabi specialist and author, considered that apart from native speakers, Tom Petrie was most knowledgeable with *Kabi Kabi* languages,[39] Archibald Meston foremost with *Yagara* language.[40] *Jinibara* Elder *Gaiarbau* related that he knew and talked with both men; that both mixed up words of one tribe with those of another; Petrie, who chiefly spoke the *Undumbi* tongue very fluently, but did not know the *Jinibara* tribe and its dialect, had affirmed both as one tribe. *Gaiarbau*—also fluent in *Undumbi*—gave him the correct details.[41]

Leo Meston commented on the confusion of dialects on the Brisbane River in Petrie's time and the influx of native speakers from other areas.[42] Watson identified that learning a local language often involved becoming familiar with any neighbouring dialects, and that 'Tom Petrie was most familiar with the blacks who lived near his father's property on the north of the Pine River, and near to the boundary of the territories of the *Toorbal* and *Kabi* tribes, and he could speak their languages, the local one fluently.'[43] Norman Tindale's interview in 1938 with original *Yagara* speakers at Cherbourg and inclusion of *Dugai* writers brought both clarity and confusion when he wrote of the *Jagara* (*Jagarabal*), 'their language was *Turubul*, also *Ninghe*.'[44]

Watson analyses the linguistic diversity in southeast Queensland, in particular the border country where he worked for many years. He specifies 'lingual division' in the title of his 1940 pamphlet, *A vocabulary of the language of the Yuggerabul lingual division of Australian aborigines and, incidentally, of the*

---

39. Malcolm D Prentis, 'Research and friendship: John Mathew and his Aboriginal Informants', *Aboriginal History*, vol. 22, 1998, p. 64.
40. Dennis Bannister (1986) Manuscript #2171, *Archibald Meston's words and placenames collected 1870s–1900s*, AIATSIS.
41. *Gaiarbau*, in LP Winterbotham, *Gaiarbau's Story of the Jinibara Tribe of South East Queensland, 1950–1957* Manuscript. University of Queensland.
42. LA Meston, 'Letter to the Editor: Wooloowin and Wonga', *Brisbane Courier*, Fri 5 Jun 1931. p. 15.
43. *Brisbane Courier*, 9 June 1931, p. 5.
44. Norman B Tindale, *Aboriginal Tribes of Australia*, Australian National University Press, Canberra. 1974, p. 169.

Turrbul sub-tribe at Brisbane. Watson rightly distinguished the non-linguistic term and the broader, overarching 'lingual' name *Yugarabul.* He wrongly used a *Yugam* word, speculating on the *Turrbul* name meaning of the word as 'People of the Stones'.[45] Perhaps he was inspired by an article about the Toara (To'-a-ra) Ceremony.[46] Leo Meston rightly corrected a suggested meaning behind '*tar'au-bul*': '*Darra* does not mean "stones", as stated by Mr Watson.'[47] It's 'stone' or 'stoney' in *Yugam*.[48] The next major linguistic survey was Holmer in 1970–72 but his key material was based on Watson, who based his work on Ridley and Petrie. Anyone using Holmer will continue this cycle of sourcing incomplete and inaccurate material.

This demonstrates why early wordlists and languages spoken must be carefully cross-referenced before inferences are made about tribes, their district and territorial boundaries.

Original names of Brisbane: Magandjin, Miganchan, Meeanjan

> Where Brisbane stands today, was covered mostly by scrub, very thick on the site of the Botanic Gardens, where the tulip trees, *Maginnchin*, gave the 'aboriginal' name to the Brisbane River.[49]

The original name of Brisbane can be traced back to just two phonetic versions of the one name. The table below shows the history associated with them. An examination of the Original Speakers who passed their information to primary sources is crucial in determining which is the likely name. Also critical is correct cultural information based on ancient oral history,

---

45. FJ Watson, *Turrubul or Turrbul: a sub-division of the lingual division of Yugarabul aborigines which occupied the territory about what is now the City of Brisbane,* 1940.
46. RH Mathews, 'The Toara Ceremony of the Dippil Tribes of Queensland', *American Anthropologist (N.S.),* vol. 2, January 1900.
47. *Courier-Mail,* 2 September 1933, p. 7.
48. FJ Watson, F. R. G. S. A. *Vocabularies of Four Representative Tribes of South Eastern Queensland.* University of Queensland. p. 62.
49. *Daily Mail,* 1 December 1923, p. 9; Trove at NLA, <https://trove.nla.gov.au/newspaper/article/218970350>.

some of which appears in the *Goori Nharul-Milen* table. There are possibly three explanations of the same word for spike (*migan*): the shape of the point, ground being dug up, and weaponry.

Table 2. Table shows historical distortions of Yagara name for Brisbane

Name	Meaning	Sources
Magoo'jan Magan Magandjin / Maganchin	Tulipwood Tree Tulipwood district	Yagara speakers to Meston
Makandschin Megandsin	Region from the mission to Breakfast Creek	Yagara speaker Kabi Kabi speaker to Leichhardt
Magenchen Magenjie / Meeanchin Mi-an-jin (Me-an-jin) Meeannjin / Meegannchin	Brisbane, Brisbane River Name of the Garden Point from the bridge round to Creek Street, taking in the settlement	Petrie
Miantjun, Mientjin	Town	Ridley
Magandjin Meeanchin Meeanjin / Meeannjin Meegannchin	Brisbane River Brisbane Brisbane River Brisbane River	 Meston
Migan Dhagun (chargun) Djarra / char / dja' etc. Migan Chagum / Migan Chagun Miganchan / Mianchan Meginchin, Meginchen Miguntyun Megendjen (-djin) Megenden /Migindjin Megendjin)	Spike (Yagara word) Yugam word for earth, ground, soil Yagara for ground, soil, country Name for early Brisbane from Migan chagun 'place or land shaped like a spike' for land where Botanical Gardens and Domain form the point Brisbane Tribe Name of a tribe on lower Brisbane River (Toorbal tribe), later the native name of Brisbane	Petrie Watson Charlton and Brown Watson and versions Ballard collected from newspapers Bunjoey in Bell Holmer via Tripcony via Watson

Leichhardt offers the earliest written source of the name for Brisbane, which includes the Gardens Point area as shown in Petrie's map. In 1843, he was given two names: *Makandschin* from an original Brisbane man and *Megandsin* from an original speaker from a different country.[50] Ridley via Petrie wrote *Miantjun* and *Mientjin*. Meston listed *Magoo-jin* then *Magandjin*, based on *Magan*, the name of the Tulipwood tree, from elderly Goori speakers who asserted they were 'Brisbane natives'. Their knowledge is based on *Goori Nharul-Milen*.

From a Goori knowledge base the names based on the Tulipwood tree fits best for the original Goori name. The suffix -djin indicates plural, e.g. people, district, river. The *Migan-dar-gu-n* (*Mi'andjan*) version describes the use of a sharp tool, possibly ground being dug up, likely the first convict garden, which the Petrie map shows multiplied across the whole of the promontory. Another explanation of this name is 'land shaped like a spike'. Both these are based on *Dugai* activity and *Dugai* lens. Dredging of the river for navigation purposes further defined the shape. The secondary names are the result of the arrival of newcomers, not from Goori customs.

Spike is a foreign word. Goori technology of agriculture based on cultural beliefs and spirituality differed greatly to the European practice of rendering all the ground bare due to our spiritual connections to ground, flora and fauna. For example, my family history connects my totem *Cabool*, carpet snake, to the grasstree as brothers, which determined our practice. Our Creation Stories give us specific spiritual connections to sites and aspects of language regarded sacred; sign language; gendered language—words that belonged to the women which men could not use and vice versa. *Mookin*'s custodial role prevented him being recorded on tapes although he guided the stories and

50. Darragh and Fensham, 'Memoirs of the Queensland Museum', *Culture* vol. 7 pt. 1, 2013; 'The Leichhardt diaries: Early travels in Australia during 1842–1844' Edited by Thomas A Darragh and Roderick J Fensham, Queensland Museum 30 June 2013.

language that could be shared. He gave permission for *Winyuba* and *Gaiabau* to be recorded, specifying content that could be discussed. This is based on our traditions and customs. It can't be freely shared. Therefore, harming or eradicating trees on a massive scale breaks Goori lore/law. These traditions and customs live on through family oral history, intangible and tangible cultural heritage. *Magandjin* fits as the original word for an area of what is now called Brisbane. *Migandjan* refers to digging the ground—either gardens or buildings. However, the term *Migandjan* spread.

As demonstrated, language repatriation is a work in progress. Because of the extremely close connections between languages, wider First Nations cultures and ways of relating to and belonging on Country, it is of the utmost importance that First Nations languages be recorded and transmitted accurately. It's also imperative that historical mistakes be acknowledged and rectified. Goori wisdom guides us to the future. As Pat Dodson said, 'Nothing about us without us.'

Wirrepi: Return to us.

Gaja Kerry Charlton is a Yagarabul person, an Elder and traditional owner from south-east Queensland, with ties to the Gulf. Her Tribes are recognised in three native title claims: *Quandamooka*, *Yuggera Ugarapul* (YUP), and *Kabi Kabi* Peoples, and she was taught by elderly speakers while growing up. Gaja Kerry is a trained teacher, counsellor, community worker, cultural educator and consultant, and an experienced member of boards, committees and working groups.

With colleague Barry Brown, Gaja Kerry co-founded the Wulara-Nguru historical language mapping project, publishing a lexical handbook titled 'An Introduction to the Languages of Moreton Bay, Yagarabul, and its dialect Djandewal, and Moreton Island's Gowar' to celebrate the 2019 United Nations Year of Languages of the World's Indigenous Peoples. The Wulara-Nguru lexical handbook contains comprehensively researched and compiled wordlists, surveyed words and cultural insights to assist language revitalisation across Moreton Bay and south-east Queensland. Twelve years of inquiry produced this exceptional resource for language custodians and their partners in reclaiming languages. Gaja Kerry is Indigenous Industry Fellow at the School of Languages and Cultures at the University of Queensland.

This piece was edited by Melissa Lucashenko, an award-winning novelist, essayist, short story writer and editor of Goorie and European heritage.

Acknowledgements

Firstly, my warmest thanks to every one of *Meanjin*'s writers from 1940 to today. Poetry is how *Meanjin* began; fiction, critique, memoir, experimentation and the essay articulate this Australian cultural moment equally powerfully. The impact of this work continues to resonate in ways our writers couldn't possibly have imagined.

This book has emerged from rigorous conversations with some of Australia's indefatigable literary champions—

> Wholehearted thanks for the valuable guidance of the inaugural *Meanjin* Cultural & Literary Advisory: Dan Bourchier (First Nations coastal Victorian), Sophie Cunningham AM, Winnie Dunn, Grace Lucas-Pennington (Bunjalung), Samantha Faulkner (Wuthuthi/Yadhaigana and Badu and Moa Islands, Torres Strait), Jinghua Qian and Christos Tsiolkas.
>
> The advice of *Meanjin*'s past editors has also enriched this collection. I am grateful for the ongoing collegiality of Jim Davidson, Judith Brett, Jenny Lee, Christina Thompson, Stephanie Holt, Ian Britain, Sophie Cunningham AM, Sally Heath, Zora Sanders and Jonathan Green; former deputy editor Tess Smurthwaite; and of course, *Meanjin*'s founding editor, the late Clem Christesen OAM OBE—in writing, at least!—whose provocations constantly stimulate new thinking.
>
> Melbourne University Publishing's venturous publisher, Foong Ling Kong, and superb senior editor Catherine McInnis, have both previously worked on *Meanjin*, making it

even more joyful to work on this book together. Big thanks to Foong Ling and Cat, as well as MUP's Pilar Aguilera, Jaclyn Booton, Daniel Chelchowski, Dominika Greinert, Duncan Fardon, Holly Hendry-Saunders, Kate Mahoney, Jackie Money, Owen Ouyang, Remy Ren, Cathy Smith, Dillon South and Louise Stirling for every one of our impromptu meetings. Thank you, so very much, to designer Stephen Banham and typesetter Patrick Cannon: as well as the handsome book you're holding, they make each edition of *Meanjin* a pleasure to read.

Meanjin's production editor, Eli McLean, has a special talent for making just the right observation at just the right time. Great big thanks, Eli. Thank you so much to poetry editor Jeanine Leane and reviews editor Cher Tan for their pivotal advice on this book.

I delight in highlighting Emma Sutherland, *Meanjin*'s archives editor, for special thanks: her wisdom has contributed invaluably to this anthology. Every weekday at 7:00am, we all get to enjoy the *Meanjin* Daily Reading: an archival piece in our inboxes, curated by Emma for timely impact. A gift to the nation.

The University of Melbourne has been a grounding and vital supporter of *Meanjin* since 1945, and I thank them for their ongoing investment and support. The work behind several essays in this collection has only been possible with thanks to the Australia Council for the Arts—today's Creative Australia—and the Copyright Agency, both proud investors in artists' labour and writers' fees. I thank Creative Australia and the Copyright Agency for all of their important work.

For permissions to reproduce literary excerpts, it's many thanks to Bruce Dawe's literary executor Liz Dawe for the quotations in David Yencken's essay, and the Abner Stein Literary Agency for the Audre Lorde quotation in Amy McQuire's essay.

Finally, to all *Meanjin* readers, subscribers and collectors: Australia's finest writers pursue their ambitious practice because you embrace Australia's finest writing. Thank you.